READY, AIM, HIRED

Charleston, SC
www.PalmettoPublishing.com

Ready Aim Hired

Fourth Edition

Paperback ISBN: 978-1-63837-700-9
Publishers Cataloging-In-Publication
Coon, Fred.
        Ready Aim Hired: Job Search Tactics That Really Work! / Fred Coon and Conne Reece
p.cm.
        1. Job Hunting I. Title.

READY, AIM, HIRED:

JOB SEARCH TACTICS THAT REALLY WORK!

4TH EDITION

Fred E. Coon, LEA, JCTC, CRW and
Conne Reece, Ph.D.
Edited by Conne Reece, Ph.D.

CONTENTS

FOREWORD

DON ORLANDO—_ONE OF FRED COON'S MENTORS IN THE CAREER FIELD._

Dear Reader: Congratulations! What you hold in your hands is a uniquely powerful tool to help you win the career you have always deserved.

You've probably been assaulted by the sea of "pernicious" folklore surrounding career development. Collections of "tips & tricks" seem to be everywhere. Some are misleading, some are out of date, some can destroy your career.

This book is the equivalent of hours and hours of careful, tailored guidance from some of America's leading career coaching experts: Fred Coon and his team. Dr. Conne Reece's contributions and superlative editing make this not only highly impactful, but easy reading.

I was tempted to use the word "interactive" to describe "Ready, Aim, Hired." But that falls far short of its real value. A much better word is "mentoring."

Perhaps for the first time, you'll be able to see far beyond **what** you should do and understand fully **why** and **how** it all comes together. More importantly, you will appreciate _your_ true value, perhaps for the very first time.

What you'll master in these pages goes far beyond just helping you get your next job. This book will guide you to optimize your career for the rest of your work life. Keep it close by from now on.

As you use this book, you will acquire more than wisdom. It should give you the confidence you need for a sustained and rewarding career from now on.

And so, I won't wish you good luck.

With "Ready, Aim, Hired" you'll make your own.

DON ORLANDO, MBA, CPRW, JCTC, CCM, CCMC, CJSS, MCD, CVCS

THE MCLEAN GROUP—ONE OF AMERICA'S FIRST PERSONAL, EXECUTIVE CAREER COACHES -BOARD OF DIRECTORS, PROFESSIONAL ASSOCIATION OF RÉSUMÉ WRITERS AND CAREER COACHES - DIRECTOR, CERTIFIED VETERAN CAREER STRATEGIST PROGRAM

ROBERT C. HAZLETT—*A PLACED SC&C CLIENT*

Ready Aim Hired, by Fred Coon and Dr. Conne Reece, has been a go-to resource as I found myself unemployed at 60 years old and unemployed due to the pandemic for the first time in nearly 40 years. I was not aware of the changes in hiring practices, terrified that I might never work again and filled with anxiety, wondering what to do next.

I had the great fortune to meet Fred Coon. He shared *Ready Aim Hired*, what I consider to be the definitive resource guide for preparing you for the next step in your professional career. Fred lays out a comprehensive blueprint for success in the hiring process. *Ready Aim Hired* provides all the information one needs to conduct an effective, successful, and rewarding job search. Fred's insight and experience helped me to focus on what really matters in today's hiring process and changed many misperceptions I had about what it takes to secure my career objectives and land a position that is both challenging and rewarding. Dr. Reece's authoritative editing makes it easy for any level to read, comprehend, and act upon.

I cannot overstate the impact *Ready Aim Hired* had in preparing me for my next step in my professional career. *Ready Aim Hired* was the fuel I needed to take my career search to the next level, and it will be a tremendous benefit to those who take advantage of the pearls of wisdom contained in this invaluable resource.

CRAIG "BLUTO" BAKER—*USAF BRIG. GEN. (RET)*

I had a blast reading your book Fred...the tactics and strategies it contains worked for me because I am now happily moving forward with my career in the private sector. I followed your processes you laid out in the book during my transition and landed my first set of jobs. It is a proven testament to your methods. They work! Your book was THE reference I used for my transition from the military into the civilian job market.

Actually, I couldn't imagine going through the transition without it. It's easy to use and brilliantly laid out in such a way that parallels the real job search process. The content is extremely understandable, and the book is very practical and not theoretical. The detailed information, sound processes, and proven, techniques in your book apply to anyone who is transitioning from the military.

It's a must read and should be the #1 reference, the top of anyone's transitioning list, military or civilian. This book is certainly a reference that I will read again and go back to when I change jobs and go through the process again, as we all eventually do. I wouldn't have been so successful in gaining the job that now challenges and fits me with the highest "happy factor" if it wasn't for your book.

Thanks for the opportunity to review your latest edition of *Ready Aim Hired*. What a great read...absolutely an honor and privilege for me that you would consider me as a reference source.

ACKNOWLEDGEMENTS

I would like to thank the following contributors who graciously helped us or provided materials included in this book.

Conne Reece, Ph.D. I wish to thank Conne Reece for her dedication and the perspective she provided on the millennial and post-college job seeker point of view, and for sharing the hand's-on information she gathered as a professor at Lock Haven University. Also, Conne gets high kudos for her excellent job organizing and editing this manuscript.

Rob Pignatello, former Lock Haven University of Pennsylvania president. I wish to express my gratitude to former Lock Haven University President, Rob Pignatello, whose education and learning approach is visionary. His personal impact is felt far beyond the classroom. Rob granted Dr. Reece a full sabbatical to co-author and edit this book.

The Stewart, Cooper & Coon Team. What you read in this book would not be possible were it not for the Stewart, Cooper & Coon coaches and team subject matter experts. For over 20 years, they have tested, refined and implemented my ideas, and work each day to guide our clients to great success as they seek their next best career move. Each SC&C team member is an expert in their respective specialty area. Their praises are sung by our clients in multiple videos housed on our website. While there are too many team members to list here, they all play a critical role in making sure our clients are successful in their job and career transition efforts. Having the privilege of working with these experts is one of the things I have been most proud of throughout my entire business career.

The Stewart, Cooper & Coon Client Branding Team. Our branding team have received rave reviews from clients, companies, and recruiters worldwide. What a great team we have!

Michelle Settle. I specifically wish to single out and acknowledge Michelle Settle, Chief Operating Officer (COO) of Stewart, Cooper & Coon. Without Michelle, our company and the ability of the Stewart, Cooper & Coon team to share all of their collected knowledge with you would simply not be possible. Without her, SC&C would not be the company it is today. Thanks Michelle!

Helen E. Prien, Ph.D. Assistant Professor of Communication and author, Lock Haven University, who proofed this 4th Edition. Thanks, Helen, for a fine job.

Robin Schlinger. Master Career Director, Certified Master Resume Writer, Certified Federal Resume Writer, and Certified Electronic Career Coach, Certified Professional Resume Writer, 360 Reach Branding Analyst, and Job and Career Transition Coach. Robin, owner of Robin's Resumes, contributed several resume examples. When I want additional information about a resume subject, I personally call Robin.

Laura Slawson. Certified Professional Resume Writer and Credentialed Career Manager, owner of The Creative Edge. Laura, who specializes in resume, LinkedIn profile and career document writing, contributed four resume examples to this edition.

A JOB SEEKER'S ADVICE

This narrative is extracted from an email from an SC&C client to his SC&C Campaign Director. We share this so that you can gain an understanding from a job seeker's point of view as to what his experience was during his job search. This has been edited to remove too much of the praise heaped upon Stewart, Cooper & Coon.

"NEVER GIVE UP!" – Eric S.

"...today I start a new journey. Not only in a new industry but also as only the 2nd Brand in my professional career after college, some almost 22 years ago! THANK YOU, to all of you, family & friends, who gave me support, advice, perspectives, leads, feedback, practiced interviewing and unconditional love. During a worldwide pandemic (and getting COVID!)....Sometimes it does take a village to get through some stormy times!

I could not have done it without all of you. I thank my SC&C coach for the professional rebranding and continual confidence building, AND most of all, a special thank you to my wonderful wife who is my number #1 supporter and kept our balance with our faith. The path was not exactly easy...and a bit more than we anticipated...

Out of *76 applications*, dozens with no response, dozens of callous template rejections, **10+ HR screenings**, only **5 hiring manager interviews**, **hundreds of emails/texts/networking**, and every minute tirelessly scouring through Linked In/Glassdoor/Indeed/Company Career Pages.... ***this is what I learned it really takes to land a leadership role as an external candidate***:

the right role | at the right company | at the right time | through the right connection | to the right hiring manager | who really wants you | when you have all your stuff in order | and you beat out all the competition.

"I now contend that *luck* happens when opportunity meets being prepared."

My wife and I imagined God's comforting voice saying..."relax, it will happen." What we saw as setbacks and change were really the only path we are supposed to take. Our unwavering faith reminded us to focus on HOPE.

We prayed for future stability/growth (amazing company with so many opportunities). We prayed for financial comfort ($ similar to old job). Many tears were shed, through the struggles, frustrations, disappointments, uncertainties, and *steady creep of a potential defeat*...which will NOT EVER happen as long as you have hope and NEVER give up!

One often doesn't see the entire iceberg, but mostly just a portion of the iceberg that is visible above surface of the water. Here are the final numbers...

76 points of interest over 49 companies | 9 general resume submissions | 67 specific job applications | 32 rejections | 41 no response | 10 HR screenings | 5 full interview processes varying from 1 week to 6 weeks each | 2 consulting opportunities since April | 1 final permanent role

If that isn't divine intervention, I don't know what is! Things don't just happen. God makes it all possible.

NEVER, EVER GIVE UP.

Thank you again, I could not have done it without all of you. Let's do our best to continue to make this world a better place."

Eric

EXAMPLE CLIENTS USING PRINCIPLES OF *READY, AIM, HIRED*

- Bruce M. – $200K + 2K shares + $25K bonus + $10K signing bonus
- Mack G. – Military to private sector – $160,000 base + great package
- Dan R. – Mid-50's – no relocation – ideal job – $165K base – search time 2.5 months
- Curt R. – Moving up In career path – $250,000 + 100% commission
- Rod N. – Age 60 – no relocation required
- Mike S. – Search time 17 days – $240,000 annual income – 45% salary increase
- Al P. – Age 60 – no relocation – ideal job – industry change + 15% annual bonus
- Neil B. – Industry change – 4.5 month search – $15K signing bonus
- Glenn I. – Age 59 – HR—$186,000 – industry change – 60-day search
- Steve C. – Contract to perm – $200K first year – 2-month search time
- Rich G. – No experience in new industry – $150K base – 3-month search
- Beth T. – Recruiter got in the way – went to the top – tough negotiator – $300K+ base
- Harry F. – From consultant to Sr. Program Manager at Fortune 500 company
- Bonnie G. – 90-day job search -20% bonus – car—came out of retirement
- ZB – International client – 2-month search – multiple interviews
- Kelly K. – $200K base – multiple offers – $43K bonus – home purchase
- Michael K. – Expat relocation – $20K relocation – $150K base salary
- Bill F. – 43-day search – industry change – took 10% less for better fit
- Michael S. – Marine officer – 8-week search—20% bonus—20% annual stock
- Patrick V. – Dream job – new career – non-profit
- Kevin F. – Offered $5K more than top company ceiling
- Jon M. – Age 64 – no relocation – health care company

- Dawn G. – 125 applicants, 2-week interview process – $170K base + options
- Rick K – Gov't to private sector transition – $65K more than original offer
- David F. – 6 companies offers – whirlwind interview – $155K base
- John C.—Retired military – $180K salary – sign on bonus $25K+—relocation—$4k rent
- Bob D. – 6-month search – $450K base+ $250K sign bonus – $1.8M with desired family time
- Mary K. – $250K base—$100K signing bonus—$200K exit bonus from former company
- Sarah B. – $300K base – 3 bonus plans – $300K stock—work from home
- Dan A – $80,000 base – 5-week vacation – 200% less commute time—90-day promotion review
- Rick K – Government to private sector transition – $65K more than original offer

and 5,000+ more...

The contents of this book are now also being taught as a course at Lock Haven University under COMM370, Job Search Tactics.

For more information contact Conne Reece at CReece@lockhaven.edu.

PREFACE

Imagine yourself in an empty hotel restaurant late in the evening after a long day of travel and getting ready for a conference the next day. You think your day will end uneventfully when a man who is also attending the conference enters the restaurant, sees your conference nametag, and strikes up a conversation with you. He reveals that he is an author and presenter, and it turns out you have a lot in common. This is how I met Fred Coon, entrepreneur, best-selling author, CEO, pod- and video-cast producer, executive coach, executive recruiter, and nationally known job and career transition expert.

I am a professor of communication at a Lock Haven University in Pennsylvania, and I focus on teaching my students how to use the education they just paid thousands of dollars for to get a job. My conversation with Fred piqued my interest so much that I bought his book, *Ready, Aim, Hired: Survival Tactics for Job and Career Transitions* (3rd ed.), and began using it as a textbook in a senior-level class. Students loved it and I loved it, too.

Fred was generous in Skyping with students and visiting campus to give workshops to career center staff. He also addressed the student body in an unusually well-attended evening session. As years went by, however, we both knew that the third edition of *Ready, Aim, Hired,* required an update and I was delighted when Fred agreed to let me co-author this version.

Lock Haven University understood the importance of the project and granted me a year-long sabbatical to work on it. They know that it isn't enough for students to have the knowledge to *do* a job; they must know how to *get* a job.

This book is a toolbox that includes every gadget, widget, or instrument you will need to craft the materials you need to find a job or change your career. You will learn to market yourself as the true professional you are and maximize your skills to the fullest potential whether you are just entering your career or looking for your last job before retirement.

Ready, Aim, Hired is a manual, a workbook and a resource guide. Every chapter is important. Every chapter will get you closer to your goal: finding the job of your dreams.

Conne Reece, Ph.D.
Professor of Communication, Author, Certified Professional Resume Writer
Lock Haven University of Pennsylvania

INTRODUCTION

Ready, Aim, Hired: Job Search Tactics that Really Work is a highly directive book designed to enable you to develop an action plan for making your next career move. My co-author Conne Reece and I will walk you through each step to market yourself as the best candidate for the job you want. We will focus on what to do, how do it right and when to do it.

No one is too good, makes too much money, or is too exalted to gain valuable insight from this book. If some of my advice seems silly, or beneath you, don't be fooled. All my clients, including those with annual incomes exceeding $1,000,000, have benefitted from it.

This book is also appropriate for those of you at the beginning of your career whether you are on the corporate ladder or not. You don't have to be an executive to use the principles in Ready, Aim, Hired. The principles of creating a brand, developing job search materials, and effectively marketing yourself, are applicable to almost anyone. The interview techniques and salary negotiation advice are universal.

This purpose of this book is threefold. First, it will help you understand your job search from the employer's perspective. Second, it will provide you with tools you need to speed your search. Third, it will illustrate interview techniques and negotiation strategies that will result in your getting a better hiring package. Specifically, we will cover the following:

- Understanding hiring process
- Getting ready for your search
- Knowing why an employer would want to hire you
- Developing your brand

- Writing an accomplishment-focused resume
- Creating attention-getting cover letters
- Establishing an online presence
- Securing an interview through targeted research and networking
- Acing your interview by knowing how to answer questions and control your nonverbal communication
- Evaluating, negotiating, and accepting job offers
- Managing your job search if you are over 45 or at entry level
- Keeping a job once you have it

A job search can be a difficult and grueling task. To be successful, you must make a commitment to yourself that, for the duration of this effort, most of your time will be spent working toward this end. You must act deliberately, steadily, ceaselessly and, at times, swiftly. You must be tough and persistent. Nothing less will achieve the desired result. However, if you follow our instructions and complete all exercises, you will cut your search time dramatically, increase your income package significantly, develop a more rewarding career path and construct a better financial future.

I hope this book encourages you to develop the required discipline to create a career search plan, manage and execute it successfully, and meet your goals. Please share your success stories and let me know what worked best in your situation. I heartily welcome your comments.

Fred Coon
Founder, Chairman, and Chief Executive Officer
Stewart, Cooper & Coon, Inc.
Licensed Employment Agent, Nationally Certified Job and Career Transition Coach, Behavioral Consultant and a Certified Disc Administrator

CHAPTER 1
THE HIRING PROCESS

The hiring process can be intimidating whether you are at the beginning of your career or at the top of the corporate ladder. If you have never hired anyone before, you may not know much of the critical information you need to manage your search. This chapter will help you appreciate the hiring process both from your point of view and an employer's. The exercises and supporting narrative in Chapter 1 will help you understand:

- Why people leave jobs
- Why you need to understand the newest trends in job searching
- How dramatic changes in searching for a job will affect you
- How a cultural crisis, like Covid-19, can change job searching and employment forever
- How employers see the hiring process
- What the differences are between working with recruiters, hiring managers, and human resources professionals
- How long your job search should take

Additionally, exercises found at the end of each chapter will bring focus to your job search.

Focus Facilitates Action—
Meaningful Action Reduces Search Time

WHY PEOPLE LEAVE JOBS

Whether you are a Baby Boomer, Gen Xer, Gen Z, Millennial, or Digital, you are searching for a job because you fall into one or more of the following categories:

- Unemployed or about to be
- Underemployed
- Underpaid
- Been with same company too long
- Facing an acquisition or merger
- Bored and need a change
- Under recognized
- Intellectually curious
- Career path blocked
- Under appreciated
- Wanting to change your life
- Life changes due to personal event

You are undoubtedly frustrated, scared or, at the very least, in need of change. You may feel like you have a monumental set of tasks ahead of you, but you don't know where to begin.

If your needs for promotion, growth, recognition, life balance and the like are not being met, chances are you will consider a shift in job or career. Millennials and Digitals in particular change jobs often, entering growing fields such as healthcare, technology and energy. As predicted by the Work Institute in 2016[1], over 30% of Millennials left their jobs voluntarily in 2020.

There is also a chance you are reading this book because you have been terminated, either for poor performance, economic reasons or a change in corporate culture or goals. Life Coach Lorraine Beaman asserts that the right mindset and an understanding that termination is not usually all your fault is essential before moving on. Often managers hire you because of your personality, then realize that you don't have the necessary skills to meet their needs or were not well matched with their team. Regardless of why you were let go, you have taken an important first step in reading this book and gaining control of your career, so take heart. You will have a job much more quickly if you follow my advice. Don't panic. Just read on.

---

1   Work Institute (2016). 2018 retention report. Retrieved June 12, 2019 from https://workinstitute.com/retention-report/

YOU ONLY THINK YOU KNOW WHAT YOU'RE DOING

Ask 100 people if they need help in a job search and the answer will usually be "No." They are wrong. They haven't looked for a job for a long time or have never been properly educated in the process and think the methods they used the last time they sought employment will still work. They are very confident about this. Why? Because they run companies, make decisions, and achieve results because of their dynamic performance every day.

You only THINK you know what you're doing, though. The job search process has changed a great deal in recent years. Perceptions, processes and techniques are much different than they were just a few years ago.

The truth of the matter is that few people really know how to get a great job. They were either never taught how to look for a job or they are stuck thinking methods they learned years ago will work today. Searching for a job is complicated, time-consuming, and exhausting. It is also necessary, exciting, and rewarding.

As a job seeker, you are also no different from 100 comparable job seekers out there whether you are an executive or at entry-level. You need help to stand out.

Unless you are tuned in to the recent changes in the job search process, you are probably not aware that there are also tactics you should avoid as you conduct your search. **Some long-held beliefs about job searching simply don't work anymore.** Distinguishing the correct strategy and in what sequence you need to perform search tasks will give you the edge over your competition.

Proper marketing begins with proper packaging. On paper, on the web, on social media, you will want to be perceived as the one perfect candidate.

Once you are properly packaged, you must conduct excellent research and select your target companies carefully. Your marketing efforts will be multi-faceted and carefully designed to reduce the time you spend in your job search. You must position yourself outside the box, beyond narrow vision, away from outdated and traditional implementation tactics to conduct a successful campaign. If you understand this, you are ready to embrace the latest trends and information available. You are ready to align your talents with an organization that will appreciate everything you have to offer—and pay you well for it. Let's begin by learning about looking for a job in the 21st Century.

DRAMATIC CHANGES IN THE JOB SEARCH PROCESS

Finding yourself actively in the job market, whether it's your first time or after a long period of uninterrupted employment, can be intimidating. In fact, it's possible that the landscape has changed quite a bit since you last searched for a job, especially if it's been more than ten years. Applicant tracking software (ATS) and pre-employment testing are used by most organizations. Virtual interviews are commonplace. Your online presence is critical, and resumes must be thought of as accomplishment-focused marketing and branding tools, not just lists of responsibilities. At least six factors have had a dramatic impact on the job search process in recent years. These include: the pandemic of 2020, changes in the application process, the use of pre-employment testing, virtual interviews, digital networking, and changes in resume content.

THE COVID-19 PANDEMIC

Unless you were living in a cave in 2020, you already know that COVID-19 changed the world...and the process of finding a job. Most notably much business is now conducted virtually, and interviews are no exception. It is now possible that you may be hired to do all your work virtually and never meet your coworkers before moving on to another position.

The usual concerns surrounding networking, composing a quality resume, creating an impressive LinkedIn profile and elevator pitch are consistently present, but now companies are typically not seeking face-to-face interviews. In fact, many companies are putting their hiring needs on hold, as certain industries are seeing a downturn in profits, not to mention voluntary pauses in the name of safety. COVID changed the world of work forever.

The recent economic and stock market changes coupled with the fear of further outbreaks of viruses related to COVID-19 will certainly have an impact on the speed of your job search. This may not be easy, and it's perfectly logical to experience a sense of disappointment after devoting the time, effort, and money necessary for a chance at your dream job, only to face difficulty in the job market. You will need to maintain a sense of patience as well as mental and emotional resilience. Don't give up! Your dream job is right around the corner.

This book is designed with an eye to the future. I will address the technology currently utilized in job searches, as well as tried and true, unchanging guidelines to creating effective materials that will gain the attention of potential employers. Eventually, I predict that a new normal in job searching will emerge, but face-to-face interviewing will resume to some extent.

THE APPLICATION PROCESS

Perhaps one of the most significant transformations is the way technology has revolutionized the job search and application process. These practices are now typically completed online and applicant tracking software **(ATS) is used by almost all organizations to rank applicants according to key word matches**. The days of printing out and mailing copies of your resume and cover letter are all but obsolete. Now, job candidates must learn how to properly digitally format their resumes before sending them electronically to prospective employers and, most importantly, match words in their search materials to words used in job descriptions. ATS will be further explained in the chapter entitled Accomplishment-focused Resumes.

PRE-EMPLOYMENT TESTS

Applying to dozens of jobs from the comfort of your own home is simply the groundwork for the technological evolutions that continue to take place. Many companies require that candidates take pre-employment tests as part of the application process, gauging their skills, aptitude, and personality traits. In fact, according to a Glassdoor report, personality test usage has increased from 12 percent in 2010 to 18 percent, with skills test usage increasing from 16 percent to 23 percent.[2] Pre-employment tests are convenient and useful for employers.

Software companies such as TestUp are now offering mid-size employers comprehensive packages that allow them to upload tests, track results, and compare and manage candidates from one convenient location. The lesson for job seekers: do everything you can to become comfortable with pre-employment tests, as they are—and will continue to be—a vital part of the modern job search and interview process.

---

2   Chamberlain, A. (2015). Why is hiring taking longer? New insights from Glassdoor Data. Retrieved January 14, 2021 from https://www.glassdoor.com/research/app/uploads/sites/2/2015/06/GD_Report_3.pdf/

VIRTUAL INTERVIEWS

Another factor that has been noticeably affected by technology is the job interview process itself as remote and even traditional job candidates are now interviewing for jobs via video conferencing applications such as Skype and Zoom. Additionally, an increasingly popular concept called Gamification, has recently been integrated into certain interview environments. Gamification allows employers to create virtual game-like scenarios in order to learn more about the personalities, tendencies, and skills of potential employees.

DIGITAL NETWORKING

While word of mouth will always be a viable networking method, in today's job market there is no substitute for a thorough online professional network. LinkedIn, the internet's most popular professional networking website, is the best place to start if you have let your networking skills fall by the wayside while you were employed. LinkedIn is also one of the first online stops for employers seeking talented job candidates. I will address this topic more in a later chapter, but you should be thinking of digital content as you build your materials. I also highly recommend obtaining a copy of my book, *Leveraging LinkedIn for Job Search Success*.

RESUME CONTENT

Your resume is still the most important document you will need to get hired, but the expected content and delivery method may have changed a great deal since your last search. Today's resume is designed to provide the **proof of success** organizations expect. *Quantifying* your accomplishments is critical in attracting the attention of an employer. In addition, your resume will have to be formatted and delivered with applicant tracking software in mind.

Denise Hemphill, President of Confident Career Moves, also suggests that changes in industry trends make necessary the need to list transferrable skills—broader abilities that can be used across industries—on your resume. [3] A walk-around management style, for example, might be useful no matter where you work. More on this later.

---

3   Coon, F. & Hemphill, D. (Hosts). (2018, October 9). Challenges facing job seekers today [Audio podcast episode]. In *The US at Work*. Fred Coon Studio. https://theusatwork.com/2 15-challenges-facing-job-seekers-today/

HOW EMPLOYERS SEE THE HIRING PROCESS

One of the most common mistakes job seekers make is to not look at the hiring process from an employer's point of view. Especially if you are seeking entry-level employment or if you are stressed about losing your job, you may be tempted to focus too much on your needs and not embrace the fact that employers are not hiring you because you need a job. **They are hiring you for one reason only: you can make them money or benefit them in some way.** What can you do that will contribute to an increase in sales, profit, customers or productivity? If you want to work for a non-profit, how will you contribute to their mission?

Conne Reece, my co-author, has a friend who is talented at saving organizations money by streamlining procedures. When interviewed for a hospital accounting job, she said, "I saved the hospital I'm working for $10,000 a year by reviewing and changing a few of their processes." They offered her the job because she focused on *their* needs and demonstrated her ability to benefit them.

The contents of this book, including the exercises, are designed to help you align your needs with the needs of potential employers. Learning about yourself will help you figure out which organizations need your particular skill set, but you must keep in mind that there is a vast difference between how employers typically hire and how most job seekers go about the search process.

Richard Bolles, author of *What Color is Your Parachute?*[4] indicated that most job seekers look at the process upside down. They don't realize that organizations want to keep the process as easy, safe and cheap as possible and, therefore, prefer to hire known commodities—those already working for them. If not possible, the next best thing is to hire someone with a proven track record of success doing what they need. Also, companies will often hire business associates and friends of people who are trusted in the organization. Still others prefer to hire entry-level applicants who will typically work for less.

If you are looking for a job, however, you are likely to overlook their point of view and begin a shotgun approach to submitting online applications. You may even apply for a few

---

4   Bolles, Ro. (2019). *What color is your parachute? A practical manual for job-hunters and career-changers* (2nd ed.). Ten Speed Press.

jobs for which you are not qualified. This is a huge waste of time. Through careful strategy and targeting you can reduce the length of your search considerably.

The search process may go something like this, depending on the level at which you are applying (entry, middle or executive) and type of organization:

- **Phone/video interview**—They are screening you against other candidates.
- **In person/video interview**—The pool has narrowed. You have their attention.
- **Second in person/video interview**—The pool is even more narrow, possibly 2 or 3 candidates.
- **Third interview**—Most likely you are the one and they just want to be sure before offering you the job.

I have had clients who went through 14+ interviews before they received a written job offer. The record to date is 20 interviews before receiving an offer. Don't get discouraged if you don't hear from the organization right away. Scheduling and many other factors can delay the process on their end.

WORKING WITH RECRUITERS

Recruiters specialize in matching potential employees to jobs offered by organizations that retain their services. They are always focused on the needs of the company, not your needs. None the less, contacting recruiters will benefit you because you may be the perfect fit for one of their clients. Recruiters charge their client companies fees to find the best person for the job. They don't charge you.

Let's say you have given your resume to a recruiter. To your good fortune, they have a job order for which your skills are a match. Now, they will be your advocate until either you are hired or until someone else has been determined to be the better candidate. When this occurs, they move on to another bright and shining money-making star who fits the next job posting they must work on. Conversely, if they don't have a job order for which your skills match, they generally won't give you the time of day. They may interview you, but when you finish your conversation with them, your name is put in their database and, at some point in the future (generally 60-90 days), your resume is purged from their system. You feel good, but nothing has really transpired. Timing is everything with recruiters.

Don't think for a minute that submitting your resume to a few recruiters will do the job. It won't. It is best to circulate your resume to as many appropriate recruiters as possible. The best rule is to target recruiters specializing in your specific job skills or targeted industries. Doing so ensures you of a higher probability of success. When recruiters get job orders from companies, their own database is the first place they look for viable candidates. If they do not find a candidate in their database, recruiters go into sourcing mode by first calling people who might fit the job profile. They call you and try to convince you to switch companies.

Retained recruiters are contracted by companies to recruit people as positions open. The retained recruiter is often called a "headhunter" and usually works with higher-salaried positions. Most people never hear from a retained recruiter. Most likely, you will hear from a contingency recruiter. The contingency recruiter is not on contract with any particular company. These recruiters usually work with lower-salaried or positioned employees. They are trying to pick as many qualified candidates as possible, to send them to their client company, and hope one fits. That is when, and only when, they get paid. The job or company may not be right for you but, many times, it appears this is not their main concern. Placing someone and getting paid is the name of the game. Beware.

You should seriously consider selecting both contingency and retained recruiters no matter how high your income level. Small emerging companies have neither the finances nor the status needed to utilize big name recruiters. They almost always start out using contingency recruiters. Among these small emerging companies might just be the next Microsoft. If you are in the higher income bracket, select both kinds of recruiters but let the contingency ones know that you are looking for emerging companies.

Once you have a list of recruiters, you will need to email them a cover letter and a copy of your resume. Not only are recruiters an excellent source of job leads, but they can also provide valuable feedback on the market and how your skills might fit into that market. One of three things will result from this mailing to recruiters:

1. They will call you with questions about your credentials or with possible positions of employment.

2. You will get a letter telling you that there is nothing currently available but that your resume will be kept on file.

3. You will hear nothing.

The recruiter's first question usually involves your current employment status. If you are working, say so. The next question will probably be about the reason you are looking for a job. You should have an answer prepared. A good response might be that you are looking for more growth potential than your current company can offer.

If you are unemployed, let the recruiter know. Present yourself as a victim of downsizing. Don't conceal having been fired. Remember that the recruiter is not the potential employer, but merely a channel to that employer. The employer who will be making the decision regarding your hiring, not the recruiter. Save your explanations for the employer.

The recruiter's next question might be about relocation. Even though you might have no desire to move, keep the door open. Tell the recruiter that you would consider relocation for the right compensation package. Many people work remotely these days and that perk may be negotiable.

Another question will focus on your salary expectations. Bill Temple, Senior Vice President, Stewart, Cooper & Coon, says, "Whenever possible, ask the recruiter what the position pays before they ask you your expectations. So long as their range is not ridiculously out of line, say, 'Thank you for sharing. That sounds like a good place to start.' If the range is too low for you, say so. Your honesty will be appreciated!"[5] If you are employed, tell the recruiter what you are currently making and give him/her a brief description of your benefits package. Tell him/her that you anticipate increasing this package by more salary, responsibilities, benefits, equity or stock options.

A good rule of thumb is a total compensation increase of 15% or more. Don't forget to specify that this 15% excludes any cost-of-living adjustments that may have to be made for relocation.

Don't be fooled into thinking that the recruiter will naturally want to place you at as high a salary as possible because he/she will then make more in commission. Employers make quicker hiring decisions for lower positions. Take a look at your budgetary needs and your cash reserves and give an educated answer to the "How low will you go?" question.

---

5   Coon, F., & Temple, B. (Hosts). (2019, March 12). National career experts discuss value propositions—jobs, money, negotiations and more. In *The US at Work*. Fred Coon Studio. https://theusatwork.com/221-special-podcast-national-career-experts-discuss-value-proposition-jobs-money-negotiations-more/

While the recruiter is picking your brain, you should be doing likewise. Ask him/her what he/she found appealing about your credentials. Ask him/her about market conditions for someone with your skills and background.

Ask about the recruiter's firm and his/her length of tenure in the industry. You can really waste time with inexperienced recruiters. If things look good, arrange to meet online or in person. Make a responsive recruiter a valuable ally.

Be realistic—not every recruiter will have a position that matches your credentials. That, in a nutshell, is what the recruiting game involves. Matching! If there is a possible match, you'll get called. If not, you'll get a rejection card or letter, or silence. Do not take these rejections personally. Avoid attributing rejection to inadequate qualifications.

Some recruiters will not call or send a rejection letter. Don't let them get off that easily. Call them! This is your first opportunity to promote yourself. The purpose is to try to generate some interest in your skills. Pat yourself on the back if you can generate genuine interest, get an interview with a potential employer or merely get an audience with the recruiter. Being able to generate interest in your skills, when none existed before, is a very valuable skill to learn.

To do this most effectively, you'll need to have an **interest-generating opening statement prepared** for the recruiter. The recruiter will probably respond that he has nothing that fits your credentials. You must then ask the recruiter questions about the general marketability of someone with your skills. Leave the conversation, if not with an actual job lead, at least with a referral to another recruiter who might be looking for someone with your skills.

Just remember, if you are dealing with an inexperienced recruiter, finding the position you desire is unlikely. However, it can serve as good practice in honing your skills. One or two practice sessions are all you need to arm yourself with excellent techniques. If you haven't learned to separate the less experienced from the more tenured recruiting professionals, you will spin your wheels uselessly, so ask questions.

Executive career strategist and nationally known career expert Louise Kursmark, provides us with the following additional tips for working with recruiters. "Use a reverse chronological (not functional) resume, and make sure you are clear about the kind and level of position you're seeking. This does not mean you need to write an objective statement, but do be sure that your introduction (summary, profile, core competencies statement) clearly positions you, so the recruiter can tell quickly just what you're qualified to do. For e-mail submissions, use the subject line and a brief cover letter to describe yourself and your primary qualifications. Then paste a text-only version of your resume below the cover letter and attach an MS Word version to the e-mail."

If you have contacted only a handful of recruiters, follow up with a phone call, and be prepared to state your key qualifications and briefly summarize your background. If you are mass-mailing (or e-mailing), don't bother to follow up; the recruiters will contact you if interested.

Don't put all your eggs in one basket. Remember, relying on one recruiter to "find you a job" is a futile strategy. Instead, distribute your resume to as many recruiters as you can find who place people with your qualifications. Recruiters DO specialize, so take the time to find the right ones.

"Working with recruiters should be just ONE of your job search strategies," says Kursmark, "Use multiple approaches to increase your chances of finding a position that meets your personal and professional goals."[6]

THE LENGTH OF YOUR SEARCH

How long should your overall search take? The U.S. Department of Labor states that, in normal economic and market conditions, one should allow about 1 month for each $10,000 in expected annual income. At that rate, if you expected to make $75,000, the search should take you about 8 months. My personal experience is that in the best of times, for Stewart, Cooper & Coon's clients that are in the $150,000—$$350,000 base salary level, search times range between five and seven months after expert branding, packaging, and coaching. However, at the time of this 4th Edition update, there are no statistics reflecting the impact of the Covid-19 pandemic on these numbers.

---

[6] Coon, F. & Kursmark, L. (Hosts). (2019, March 12). Working with recruiters: The inside story. In *The US at Work*. Fred Coon Studio. https://theusatwork.com/working-with-recruiters-the-inside-story/

> **I highly recommend reading the *Job and Career Transition Guide*, which is a free download at StewartCooperCoon.com.**

SUCCESS STORY, CHAPTER 1: HIRING PROCESS PATIENCE

CONTRIBUTED BY BILL TEMPLE, EXECUTIVE COACH, STEWART, COOPER & COON

Andrew pursued an executive position with a private equity firm that invests in energy projects but he could not at first come to an agreement regarding compensation. However, the opportunity to work for the organization surfaced again and Andrew had meetings with the CEO and other managers, including the fund manager. For Andrew, the hiring process was complicated.

The interview with the fund manager was grueling, but Andrew rose to the challenge and presented SHARE stories (to be covered in another chapter), which resulted in the following offer:

- $250,000 base salary
- 40% bonus plus equity. As the sixth highest-ranking employee, he was eligible for equity once a plan was developed.
- Additional week of PTO
- Title. Andrew bargained for a title change from Manager to Vice President of Supply Chain and Contracts. He felt the change was important since his responsibilities expanded as conversations with the company progressed.

Andrew is now involved in a $500 million capital-funded program in Louisiana, though he will be doing the work from his home in Texas.

ADDITIONAL RESOURCES

- Bolles, R. & Brooks, K. (2020). *What color is your parachute? Your guide to a lifetime of meaningful work and career success.* Ten Speed Press.
- Criteria (n.d.). *What are pre-employment tests?* CriteriaCorp.com. https://www.criteriacorp.com/resources/definitive-guide-validity-of-preemployment-tests/what-are-pre-employment-tests
- Hawkes, B., Cek, I., & Handler, C. (2018). *The gamification of employee selection tools: An exploration of viability, utility, and future directions.* In J. C. Scott, D. Bartram, & D. H.

"SWEAT OF YOUR BROW"

CHAPTER 2
GETTING READY

Remember that you are in a competition and preparation is the key to winning. You may be tempted to jump ahead in the book, but don't. Your next career move will take more than great job search materials. You'll need to be organized and focused to succeed. In this chapter, I'll discuss six directives for starting your job search. These include:

- Prepare your workspace
- Manage negative emotions
- Find a search partner
- Gather job search materials
- Update job search education
- Avoid common job search mistakes

PREPARE YOUR WORKSPACE

Before you perform any job, you need the right tools and a place to work. For the duration of your job search, set aside a place to work where no one else will bother your materials. The actual place is not important, but it should include a professional-looking area with proper lighting for conducting video conference interviews. Select a place where you can easily start and re-start projects and follow up tasks with a minimal amount of set-up time. Keep the area neat and do your filing and posting daily.

Your work environment must be well-lit, have a comfortable chair, and be free of distractions. There should be one hard and fast rule: NO electronic devices, such as cell phones or TVs that can rob you of the precious time you need to focus. Develop discipline in checking texts, etc.

Second, make sure you have reliable voicemail with a short, businesslike outgoing message. Save the cute, funny stuff. Your 5-year-old daughter may be wonderful, but the busy president of a company calling from an airport to schedule an interview with you might not think so. Don't do anything to eliminate yourself in advance. Something simple like, "Hi! You've reached Dan Killick. Please leave a message" is fine. Keep your tone of voice upbeat. DO NOT use an automatic greeting. Employers need to know they have reached the right person.

Third, purchase two notebooks or portfolios. One will be used during face-to-face interviews. In it, you will not only carry additional resumes and reference sheets, but you will also have your core skills summaries and other items that play a critical role in your job search. The other notebook or binder can be used to keep track of your contacts, outcomes, job search expenses, etc. They are tax deductible.

Next, you will need an appropriate, coordinated wardrobe when you interview (even if you are interviewed via video conferencing). Keep in mind that most positions require more than one interview. Therefore, make sure you have a different outfit for the second and third interviews. What I am about to say may be perceived as old fashioned, but it is the truth. If you have any questions about what to wear, do some research on interview attire. In today's work at home environment the rules have changed, and casual is the standard. When you attend online meetings, however, you are still presenting yourself to others and you should dress to present the image you want to project.

Finally, make sure you have business cards. They must be simple. Put your name, address, phone, email and any other essential contact information on them. The most important thing to put on them is the list of your key skills. Carry them with you at all times. See Chapter 4 for business card formatting.

MANAGE YOUR EMOTIONS

A friend of Conne's lost his job as a college advancement officer due to layoffs. An expert networker, he enthusiastically began searching for another job but, after 6 months with no luck, was overcome with depression and anger and all but gave up.

Career transitions are an inevitable factor in the lives of most professionals. The Bureau of Labor Statistics reports that the typical worker averages around 10 jobs before the age of

40.[7] In fact, due to growing career options in today's ever-changing employment landscape, this number will continue to increase over the next decade. Whether you have been asked to leave your job or chosen to change your career path, you are likely to experience some negative emotions.

No matter how focused, determined, positive or jovial you are, if you have lost your job there might come a time when depression will raise its ugly head. Everyone experiences it. Depression is often associated with the "dead" time between getting ready for your search and the first interview. It can also arise between interviews and certainly at the time you are told that you didn't get a position for which you felt you were a perfect fit. Rejection hurts, but don't give up! Acknowledge the feeling but take the steps to move on.

Any number of things can work against a positive outcome over the course of your job search and knock you out of the running for that "ideal" job. Perhaps the funding for the position was eliminated, or personnel changes necessitated a change in the organization. Even though you may have been highly qualified for the job, there could have been one other applicant—it only takes *one*—who had a little more experience than you.

What makes the difference between winners and losers in this situation isn't *who* got the job. It's how you handle the setback. Will you take it personally and spend hours ruminating, or will you keep a positive attitude about the future? An old boss of mine, Howard Tullman, always said, "Good enough never is." There is always something you can do or re-do to improve your situation. Don't get mad, get busy!

Purposeful changes in your professional life can also warrant a significant set of stressors and emotional hurdles. This is not to say that a career shift should be considered a negative experience. Such a crossroad is most typically accompanied by a greater sense of fulfillment—both professionally and personally—provided the change results in more satisfactory working conditions.

Learning to identify feelings and manage your emotional health during this process is vital to the overall success of your search. Outlined below are four **typical emotional responses to career transition and solutions** for each.

---

7   Bureau of Labor Statistics (2017). *Number of jobs, labor marketplace experience, and earnings growth: Results from a national longitudinal survey summary.* Retrieved January 14, 2021 from https://www.bls.gov/news.release/nlsoy.nr0.htm

RESPONSE #1: THE GUILT FACTOR

Even though you've made the practical decision to change jobs, it's still possible that your last position provided you with at least some sense of value or enrichment. Perhaps your superiors awarded you for a job well-done. Maybe you developed a close bond with coworkers. While your new career move is a step in the right direction, it's not unusual to look back nostalgically on the positive times you've spent with a company, possibly even developing a sense of unsubstantiated guilt that you've somehow left your employer high and dry.

REMEDY: LOOK TO THE FUTURE

Remember that any feelings of remorse, while not unusual, are likely unfounded. If your career transition was based on a series of well-informed decisions and assessments, resist the temptation to second-guess yourself. Review your original list of pros and cons and remind yourself that there were identifiable reasons that led to your decision. As long as you provided ample notice of your departure, any residual feelings of guilt for leaving your previous employer should be replaced with a sense of hope, optimism and aspiration. Remember that old friendships can be maintained separately from the workplace, and new achievements can always be realized. This is your time to plan your future and remember that you are making a change for better.

RESPONSE #2: ADAPTATION CONCERNS

If you spent a considerable amount of time at your previous job, you probably became used to a certain work lifestyle. Whether you realize it or not, everything from your daily tasks and attire to your hourly schedule—even your commute and how you spent your lunch breaks—have played an inherent part in shaping your way of life. Suddenly, you find yourself struggling to acclimate to a schedule that seems foreign. This can be a daunting experience, especially for those encountering their first career transition.

REMEDY: STEP BACK AND PREPARE

When transitioning from one career to another, take some time off to regroup and prepare for your new position. If timing or financial concerns prevent you from taking off a signifi-cant amount of time, try a long weekend to mentally step back from your previous position as well as to prepare for your search. This will offer you not only a sense of closure, but also a clean slate from which to start anew.

RESPONSE #3: IDENTITY CRISIS

Your career is not only central to sustaining your lifestyle and financial stability, but also to promoting your credibility, identity, and value in society. Even a change for the better can leave you in a temporary state of psychological flux. A business director who decides to launch a new company may mourn his or her former status. While a new endeavor such as leaving behind the 9-5 world may be dream-fulfilling, there may also be a certain amount of identity adjustment involved, if only on a subconscious level.

REMEDY: SEEK GUIDANCE

When redefining yourself both personally and professionally, the proper guidance can be crucial and, fortunately, it can be sought in a myriad of ways. You may first try searching for books on the topic. Reading can be a great way to not only relax your mind, but also immerse yourself in knowledge specific to your circumstance.

Next, you might consider reaching out to your network for advice. Have any of your connections gone through similar experiences? How did they cope with reinventing themselves? Seek a mentor. Joining groups and forums will allow you to connect with those in your field who can help you in your new journey.

> # To be successful you need to eliminate the biggest stumbling block: FEAR.

RESPONSE #4: FEAR

Many years ago, I had the painful, but extremely beneficial experience of attending Dr. James Farr's leadership development institute in North Carolina. Why painful? My first exercise was to sit in a bathtub and play with a rubber duck and then report my feelings the next day to those attending the "stop being crazy" (my name for it) group. Dr. Farr forced me to look at perception and reality and understand the filters I was using to approach the world. These filters were being used to interpret the behavior of others towards me. Then, I reacted according to my emotional survival programming.

Because I was wrongly filtering and, therefore, misinterpreting most behaviors, I was reacting according to *my* understanding and approaching life in a way that was having a negative impact on me and those close to me. As I was going through the sessions, I was angry and frustrated, and hated facing the reality of my fears. I worked through them and now assert that it was the most powerful and beneficial experience of my entire working career.

There are two reasons for failure. The first is grounded in the concept of fear. The second is lack of determination and discipline. Think about this for a moment. Do you like rejection? Do you get up every morning saying to all who listen, "Please reject me?" Of course you don't! No sane person seeks rejection. However, Jim Farr taught me an important behavior modification rule that I would like to share with you.

REMEDY: UNDERSTAND AND CONQUER

Fear really means—**F**alse **E**vidence **A**ppearing **R**eal. Those of you who feel that you need no assistance can skip this exercise. However, for 99.9% of you, the exercise on fear at the end of the chapter will be of value in helping you come to grips with barriers that might stand in your way as you attempt to manage and execute a meaningful job search.

When you were a child and put your hand on a hot stove, you soon discovered that you would be hurt. You didn't do it again, intentionally. These learned behaviors apply equally to the mechanisms we employ to protect both our physical and emotional health and survival.

During our lifetimes, all of us have been subjected to a wealth of experiences, some resulting in a feeling of rejection. At first, this created intense emotional pain. Each of us reacted differently. We either blocked the pain and avoided the causes, became callous and insensitive, or grew negative and hurt. As we became adults, we eventually learned to minimize or avoid such encounters as much as possible.

The remedy for overcoming fear is not simple, but it is effective. The next time you experience fear, try to become aware of how you are reacting. Every time you face rejection, consider the situation and your feelings. When your emotions are out of control, you have a tendency to think negative, cyclical thoughts. Jim Farr used to call them **"crazy tapes."** He said the only way to modify behavior was to break the tape that is currently running and either re-record, or splice in substitute behaviors until they become your norm. Figure out what the cause of the fear is and take constructive action to change those things over which you have control.

Now, take a deep breath, lay your fears to the side and I'll walk you through the process of securing a job. If you start to feel anxious or get depressed, complete Exercise 2.2 on overcoming your fear.

FIND A SEARCH PARTNER

Searching for a job is an arduous task. It requires time, dedication, and *accountability*. You'll need a partner to encourage you and keep you on track.

Your partner should be someone who knows your skills and career well, and who will take the time to check in with you at least once a week. He or she will be receiving a telephone call from you weekly to discuss your search and to hear you repeat the 25 Rules. You should agree, in advance, on a time each week that you'll say the rules out loud while he/she follows along using a separate copy. This is one of the hardest tasks you will perform in your search because it will make you feel silly. Don't skip it. Keeping the rules in the forefront of your thoughts is essential to your success. Very few of us like accountability, especially when we may not have done enough the previous week to follow the rules. Of course, your search partner wants to support you but knowing how may be challenging. By providing a structured method of accountability you ensure the constructive support you need.

Please work with your search partner to complete Exercise 2.3, the 20-second Quiz. This exercise will get you focused on what you are really looking for in a career at this point. It will also give valuable insight to your partner.

GATHER JOB SEARCH MATERIALS

I discussed in Chapter 1 that today's hiring managers need to see *proof* that you are the right person for the job. Employers look at your past performance to make decisions about whether to hire you. In later chapters, we'll address how such proof should be presented in your resume, cover letter, e-portfolio and more but, for now, you should work on gathering a few materials that can be used to attract an employer's attention. These include testimonials, reference letters, positive performance reviews, and pictures and videos as appropriate.

TESTIMONIALS

A professional testimonial is simply someone's assertion—in writing—that you have done a good job. Look at this from the point of view of a hiring manager. He or she will want to see you as a valuable commodity and will look for verifiable statements about your contribution to past workplaces. Let's say, for example, you are a public relations specialist who lost your job because of cutbacks and I'm thinking about hiring you. Imagine I see this statement on your professional website.

> *Dan unfailingly exceeded our clients' expectations. He increased our customer base by 10% over the past year by building relationships with them and understanding their business needs.*
>
> Mark Larimer, President, Larimer Communication Strategies

Iron your shirt, Dan. It's time for an interview! Remember to ask those giving testimonials if you can use them for references because your potential next boss, will want to verify that they are true.

Don't lose heart if for some reason your last boss won't give you a testimonial. Seek out other professional contacts who can speak to the quality of your work and accomplishments. However, be sure they can verify that you really can do the job for which you are applying.

PERFORMANCE REVIEWS

Performance reviews are formal documents that reflect how well you are meeting the expectations of your organization. Usually, your performance review is done by your immediate superior, but some companies have a 360-degree approach with subordinates and others providing feedback as well.

You were probably given a copy of your performance review if you have had one but, if not, try to obtain a copy of every evaluation you have had that is relevant to your search. Statements on your performance evaluation can be used like testimonials to prove your worth to potential employers if you get the permission of the person who did the review.

LETTERS OF REFERENCE

Think of a letter of reference as a detailed testimonial. It provides the reader with a story, so to speak, of your positive attributes and successes. Letters of reference can come from former bosses, colleagues, clients and so on.

The first step in obtaining letters of reference is to let your references know of your availability in the job market and secure their help. When you finish reading this section, I want you to put together a list of 9 references. In a later chapter I will discuss the value of networking and, when you finish implementing the networking instructions, you should have accrued over 1000 contacts in this search. Just as the longest journey begins with the first step, your list of 1000+ contacts start with the development of your initial 9 reference names.

As a recruiter, I always call all references and I have a list of 12-15 questions I ask them. Ask your references to use worksheets like those at the end of this chapter. Recruiters and employers do so.

Listing your last boss as a reference is fine if you are sure he/she will say positive things about you. If you're NOT sure, don't. Your references are supposed to help you—not hurt you. If you and your last boss did not see eye-to-eye don't use him or her as a reference.

There are companies who, for a fee, will check references and previous employer opinions about you. You may wish to avail yourself of these services. My recruiting staff performs this service as a part of the search services we provide our clients. Other companies do as well, and you can find them on the internet.

However, because of lawsuits, both frivolous and valid, most companies, especially larger ones, only give out dates of employment. Consequently, should someone ask why you did not use your former boss as a reference, you can explain that the company only gives dates of employment.

Be sure the people writing your letters of recommendation are willing to serve as references as well. Securing a letter of recommendation from a business associate can sometimes signal to the writer that his/her job is done and he/she can forget about you. However, a potential employer may want to ask questions about your work.

You will need **three to five reference letters** from business peers or superiors in this search. The higher the level of position, the more letters you should have. Most of the time, references are busy. Here is a way to kill two birds with one stone. Ask your references if *you* can draft a short letter on their behalf that you will send to them for their approval, redraft and signature. Most will say yes. What an opportunity! You can incorporate aspects of your work and accomplishments into the letters, create a different perspective for each, make yourself appear more diversified and win, win, win. You can add your SHARE© stories (to be covered in a later chapter) to the letters. When you do so, you have constructed a nearly perfect scenario. The 3 Words exercise, and reference sample and reference letter at the end of this chapter will help you.

The reference letter should begin with a statement of what your working relationship was with the author of the letter. You should present a particular problem you had to overcome, stating it in terms that are general, and include your *quantifiable* results. Also, have the author insert a sentence opening the door to additional questions. For example, you could include the following sentence: "Please feel free to contact me at (put your reference's telephone number and email address there) to discuss (your name here)'s excellent qualifications." Double check for accuracy. There is nothing more frustrating than wanting to speak to someone's reference only to find that the phone number or email address is wrong.

No matter how well you think you know your references, make sure you have their permission to use their name and give out their contact information before you do so. Have the reference sign the document and, bingo, you have a great reference letter.

PICTURES AND VIDEOS

As part of the search process, you will be creating or updating a LinkedIn account and developing an electronic portfolio (to be covered in Chapter 7). You'll need a professional headshot, some action photos and some video of you in action to make your digital presence come to life.

Poke around on LinkedIn and check out the headshots people use. You'll immediately notice a difference between those who took the time to have professional photographs taken and those who took selfies with their phones. Photographers know how to make you look good and they are skilled at pulling out your character so you can best establish your brand. Most will use a variety of formal and informal poses and backgrounds that you can use to present yourself the way you want. Once you have purchased the photos, you can use them with your website, social media and so forth.

Action photos can go a long way in establishing your brand as well. Think of an action photo as a third-party view of what you do that makes you so good at your job. Let's say one of the characteristics you want potential employers to know about is that you work well on teams. You might have someone take a picture of you working with a group of coworkers. If training others has been a part of your job, include a picture of yourself in front of a group. Do you do volunteer work? Include pictures from your events and projects.

Don't have pictures like this? Stage them! As long as you aren't misrepresenting your qualifications, it's okay. Make sure the pictures you use are of high quality—good lighting, focused, etc.—because if they aren't they will work against you.

Short videos, if appropriate, can also enhance your image. If training, teaching or public speaking is an important aspect of your job, having a :30 video of yourself in action is critical. Think of it as a free sample. Be sure you are organized and above all animated. You may also want to create a video resume (more on that later). If you are applying for a high-end position, find a videographer. Often college students looking to build their portfolios can be hired inexpensively.

WORK SAMPLES

Samples of your work will vary depending on your field. Typically, work samples are tangible, like written documents or videos. Perhaps it has been part of your job to write reports or proposals, or design training. Such documents can be used as work samples and these will likely be included in your e-portfolio (to be discussed later).

Keep a few things in mind when choosing samples of your work to show to prospective employers. First, make sure the samples are **perfect**. Rework documents for style and grammar. Show them what you can do. Poorly done examples work against you. Second, choose short samples. You may have written a 40-page report, but no one is going to read it. Create a 1-page executive summary. Last, in a textbox at the top of the document or in a few frames of your video, give a *very* brief description of what you are showing. Such descriptions provide context for a hiring manager.

UPDATE YOUR JOB SEARCH EDUCATION

Reading this book is an important step to updating your information on how the job search process works in the 21st century, but it isn't enough. Savvy job seekers will make it their business to capitalize on trends in the job search industry. Changes to the way we work and look for jobs due to COVID-19 will continue to emerge, and economic and social trends will affect the way you market yourself.

Pay attention to trends in your field as well. Research areas of growth. Who in your industry is hiring?

AVOID COMMON JOB SEARCH MISTAKES

The final way you can prepare for your job search is to commit yourself to not making any mistakes that will prolong your search and cost you money.

Listed below are some major *don'ts* for your search. I have added my own thoughts to those of my colleague, Jack Chapman, author of *Negotiating Your Salary: How to Make $1000 a Minute.*[8] I have Jack's permission to lift my favorite ideas from his book. Here's a summary of our combined thoughts. Remember, these are **mistakes**.

Answering All the Want-ads. Newspaper ads generally represent entry level positions so, unless that is what you are looking for, they are mostly a waste of time. It can't hurt to look, but don't spend a lot of time on this.

Mailing Unsolicited Resumes. With so much email being received and spam beyond our control, I am rethinking the written resume submission. Just target carefully who you send it to. Think hard about why they are a good fit for your skills and why you are a good fit for theirs. Remember: wasting *other peoples'* time is a waste of *your* time.

Looking for Vacancies. Many unadvertised positions are created for particular applicants, often at the time of the interview. Promote your skills and accomplishments to targeted companies.

Inept Networking. Person-to-person networking is the most effective method of obtaining your next position. Bad networking can cause serious short- and long-term damage.

---

8   Chapman, J. (2001). *Negotiating your salary: How to make $1000 a minute.* Ten Speed Press.

Applying for Too Many Types of Jobs. As Jack puts it, "Don't confuse a job market with a singles bar." Serious jobs *don't* land in your lap if you throw enough stuff against a wall and hope something sticks. You must pick your targets and go after them.

Not Planning and Scheduling Properly. The average person spends more time planning vacations than planning their job search.

Doing It Alone. Here are some myths going around: don't pay anyone to help you; companies should pay fees to find you; you don't need any help; be self-sufficient. Society expects you to know how to get good jobs on your own, but nobody ever shows you how, do they? Hire a professional if you need to.

Letting Motivation Take Care of Itself. Jack states this one very well: "Nothing puts your self-esteem on the line faster than a job search. You face rejection and self-doubt daily." He uses an expression I think is priceless. "A single day of beggar mentality (please, somebody, give me a job) is a whole day wasted."

Not Preparing Well Enough for Interviews. How many times do you think I have heard prospective job seekers say, "Just get me in front of the decision-maker and I'll take it from there?" How self-impressed and over-confident can you be? Many people don't have a clue as to what the interview questions mean, much less how to properly answer them. Being well-prepared is the most critical factor in claiming success.

Talking About Money Too Soon. Employers always ask how much you want. If you answer too high, you are too expensive. If you answer too low, you're not worth it. What to do? Focus on value, not money, first and do your research.

Each of these myths is further addressed in the remaining chapters.

FOLLOW THE 25 JOB SEARCH RULES

Remember, the day *WILL* come when you are so consumed with your new role that you will have long forgotten the many hurdles of your career transition. Maintaining a goal-driven strategy will help you look toward the future without comparing it to the past. Through patience and dedication, your new career will soon become home to you.

You will take your first strategic job search step right now. In Exercise 2.1, I have included the *25 Rules* I ask my clients to follow during the course of their work with me. If you are smart, you will develop and maintain a positive attitude and accept responsibility for your actions as called for in these rules.

Remember, you are in charge of this search, no one else. **MAKE SIX PRINTED COPIES OF THE RULES.** Put them in the following locations:

- On the bathroom mirror
- On the refrigerator door
- Back of your front door
- In your briefcase
- One for your search partner or significant other
- In your 3-ring binder

Now, commit to your search. Many people start their campaign with excuses. The primary excuse everyone gives me is that the time they can spend on the search is limited. Don't even go there. What this really means is that they don't know how to structure their search or aren't disciplined enough to manage it. You don't have the luxury of distractions.

Set objectives for each day, record your efforts daily and quantify your results weekly. Set performance standards. For example, return all calls within 24 hours and get thank you letters in the mail the day after interviews. Above all, establish a regular job-hunting routine and stick to it!

Plan each day's activities in advance. Be resolute. Evaluate your performance daily. Don't lie to yourself and accept no excuses. Plan your work and work your plan.

SUCCESS STORY: GETTING READY

CONTRIBUTED BY CAROL D'SOUZA, EXECUTIVE COACH, STEWART, COOPER & COON

Amanda worked at a biopharma company for almost 20 years but was laid off due to an organizational restructure. She had a wealth of experience and hoped to land a job working 100% remotely and receiving a competitive total rewards package. In preparation for the search ahead of her, Amanda sought career coaching and interview prep from Stewart, Cooper & Coon, and we worked together to prioritize her preparation activities for the job search process.

We developed her brand and LinkedIn profile, which we marketed to recruiters and target companies and Amanda spent most of her time networking, chasing job leads and connecting with senior executives. She engaged in rigorous interview practice and secured four interviews that resulted in two offers. We then analyzed the organizations' cultures and potential for growth as well as a few other factors. One company stood out.

Amanda's first choice recognized her talent but initially offered her a lower base salary than expected. However, she focused on communicating her return on investment (ROI) and they increased their offer considerably. She also received a sign-on bonus and long-term incentive reward as well as a few other valuable perks as follows:

- 100% remote work
- Flexible start date
- Unlimited paid time off
- Stock options

Amanda is now happily working as Vice President of Strategic and Cross Functional Partnerships for this progressive organization.

ADDITIONAL RESOURCES

- Frost, A. (n.d.). 4 secrets to building a portfolio that'll make everyone want to hire you. The Muse. https://www.themuse.com/advice/4-secrets-to-building-a-portfolio-thatll-make-everyone-want-to-hire-you/
- Slayback, Z. (n.d.). *How to ace your job hunt by getting great testimonials.* ZakSlayback.com. https://zakslayback.com/how-to-get-testimonials/

EXERCISE 2.1 25 JOB SEARCH RULES

Life is tough and not always fair. These rules are also tough, but fair. Before you begin your job search, think about what you must start doing to make your search meaningful. I strongly recommend you secure a search partner. Select someone who will listen to you during your search, who will discuss, not necessarily agree, with your search strategy and who will hold you accountable for implementing these rules. You must place these rules in the following locations: Bathroom mirror, refrigerator door, back of front door, briefcase, and computer monitor. Give one to your search partner as well and read it out loud to him or her weekly.

- I will only see a half-full glass.
- I will not waste time and will follow my weekly search schedule.
- I will not complain.
- I will be disciplined.
- I will not accept rejection as personal, just business.
- I will exercise and maintain a balanced diet.
- I will concern myself with those things over which I have direct control, and not those things over which I have no control.
- I will develop or maintain my sense of humor.
- I will involve my family and friends and keep them involved.
- I will respect myself and be kind to my family and friends.
- I will not expect the next job to fall into my lap. I will find it!
- I will not daydream my way into my next job.
- I will take consistent and meaningful actions every day.
- I will not place blame on others, only on myself.
- I will control my job change.
- I will complete a minimum of 40-50 job-hunting activities weekly.
- I will read everything I can to improve my position in this search.
- I will complete all book exercises.
- I will always do my best work.
- I will give myself permission to fail.
- I will give myself permission to ask for help.
- I will give myself permission to make mistakes.
- I will give myself permission to succeed!
- I will do my best at whatever task I attempt.

Repeat to yourself each morning and evening, "Starting today, I am in control of my goals, schedule, job change strategy, activity level, research, effectiveness and future."

EXERCISE 2.2 F.E.A.R.

False **E**vidence **A**ppearing **R**eal:

Perception is often reality, but our perception is shaped by filters. One such filter is our own fear. When we are fearful, we don't use the right evidence to draw proper conclusions. Write your top 5 fears in the boxes below.

IDENTIFY FEARS

1.	
2.	
3.	
4.	
5.	

Using the format below, create a strategy for eliminate each of the 5 fears listed above.

FEAR

What about it makes you uncomfortable?
What three things are you going to do to eliminate FEAR?

1.

2.

3.

EXERCISE 2.3 20-SECOND QUIZ

INSTRUCTIONS FOR PARTNER:

Read each question aloud to the job seeker. Ask each question in turn allowing only 20 seconds for an answer (use a timer). When the job seeker is done say, "Is there anything else you can think of that would make your answer stronger?"

The job seeker must also answer the "Why?" portion of the question within the 20 seconds. **Indicate on the table below whether the job seeker answered the questions effectively in 20 seconds.**

INSTRUCTIONS FOR JOB SEEKER:

Answer the questions in 20 seconds with a fluid and succinct response.

No uhms, pauses, throat clearing, looking at the ceiling or hot air.

	Question	**Yes**	**No**	**Time**
1.	What type of work do you want and why?			
2.	For what kind of company do you want to work?			
3.	What type of boss do you want and why?			
4.	What type of fellow workers do you want and why?			
5.	What are your skill strengths?			
6.	In what areas do you need to improve?			
7.	What are your personal traits?			
8.	What personality traits do you dislike in fellow workers and why?			
9.	What compensation are you looking for and why?			
10.	What are your short- and long-term goals and how are you going to reach them?			
11.	What is the one behavior that you feel has contributed to your career success and describe a time or specific situation where you applied this behavior.			

EXERCISE 2.4 3-WORDS EXERCISE—WORDS THAT DESCRIBE YOU

Assignment: Ask your boss, then three peers and three subordinates what three words they would use to describe you. Write them down and look for similarities. Repeat the exercise using three people you've experienced conflicts with. Study the similarities and differences. What did you learn? Reflect on the results.

EXAMPLE:

LIKE	DISLIKE
Driven—focused on the mission	**Driven**—people don't like change or don't like risk/too competitive, I have sometimes created an "us vs. them."
Team—family, caring, fun	**Vague**—some wanted more details or be told how to do something I had asked for.
Mentor—surprising from all 7 of them	**Accountable**—this goes both ways, but people were surprised by the honest direct feedback, especially if not meeting expectations.

YOUR TOP THREE MOST MENTIONED:

LIKE	DISLIKE

EXAMPLE 2.5 REFERENCE CHECK*

REFERENCE INTERVIEWED: MR. FRED COON, PRESIDENT, RETAINED SEARCH SOLUTIONS

Relationship with Candidate at last position: Worked under Candidate in Alabama working for Allcrest Pipeline Construction Company. Consulting capacity.

Strengths: Candidate has a very broad knowledge base of construction, engineering, field procedures and all the requisite skills needed to identify and solve problems. Candidate was involved with a lot of technical and environmental issues. Candidate was the overall program manager charged with responsibility to get the company out of hot water with the Department of Energy and the US Congress. He had a lot of inexperienced people working for him and it required him to take technical staff with very little knowledge or direction and bring them up to speed quickly. He did an excellent job and when he left it was a self-running program.

Weaknesses: Very goal and task oriented and drives himself a little too hard.

Accomplishments: (example) At Allcrest, he took a company under litigation and staggering revenue losses with high pressure to stop the bleeding and when he finished they had credibility, trust of the government, state regulatory agencies and the field personnel of Allcrest Pipeline Co. At the Nordstrom Nuclear facility, he worked with a diverse number of groups, each with its own agenda, to get them to pull together on difficult tasks.

Ethical/Honest: Absolutely

Left employment because: Contract expired

I would hire (not hire) him again because: He is excellent at working with both employees and management to build a team that produces.

Overall Opinion: Candidate would be an asset to any company.

Work ethic: Exceptional. Intelligent person with excellent performance

Meet deadlines: Never knew him to miss one.

Ability to work under pressure and example: The Nordstrom Nuclear Facility was facing sanctions and fines by the NRC. Candidate developed a program the NRC recognized went above and beyond the issues and charges and caused the facility to receive a clean bill of health.

Final comments: Any company that would end up with the candidate will have a tremendous team player and a person able to get performance from all levels of personnel without adversarial nature of doing so.

*This is an actual reference survey conducted by recruiters working for Retained Search Solutions, LLC, a Stewart, Cooper & Coon owned Company.

EXAMPLE 2.6 REFERENCE LETTER SAMPLE

June 4, 2002

Re: Fred Coon

To whom it may concern:

Fred Coon has asked me to serve as a professional reference for him as he pursues career opportunities. At the time of our association, I was Senior Vice President of Sales for Direct Corporation of Minot, ND, the county's leading check printer. In June of 1996, Direct purchased Fred's firm, Acme Resources. Direct purchased the company in part because we wanted to leverage our sales organization by giving them an entirely new line of products to sell our existing clients. Since AR's sales force was calling on the same customers we were, there seemed to be a lot of synergy. However, it soon became obvious that expecting check salespeople to sell direct response products wasn't realistic. We needed to quickly develop a workable sales model.

Because of his experience in the industry and his role as National Sales Manager at American Resources, I asked Fred to head up the creation of a Field Sales Specialists group made up of people from the direct response industry with a lot of technical expertise and some sales background. These people would work as a team with our check sales reps, our folks getting the appointment, and the FSS demonstrating the product and answering technical questions. This allowed us to capitalize on long-established relationships without embarrassing our check reps in front of their customers by asking them to sell something that they didn't understand.

Fred accepted the challenge and agreed to serve as Director of Business Development for Direct's newly created Client Response Division. In this capacity he reported directly to me. Not only did he do a superior job of recruiting and training our nineteen-member FSS group, but he demonstrated a unique ability to manage and motivate his team in a very difficult situation. Although Fred's FSS group's only charge was to introduce the new direct response product line to Direct customers, he and his team members had to depend on our check reps to get appointments and close sales. Since direct response products were not the check reps' only responsibility, Fred's job also involved promoting teamwork between the two groups, a task he was unusually well suited for.

Although Fred and I ultimately both left Direct Corporation through a series of divestures, we have remained in contact. Because of my respect for Fred's abilities, I have retained him as a consultant on a number of occasions in my current capacity as Senior Vice President of Sales and Marketing for Lighter Payment Systems. I can heartily attest to Fred's qualifications as an outstanding sales, marketing and business development leader. Should you wish to discuss Fred's qualifications further you may feel free to contact me at (phone) or via email at (email).

Truly yours,

Michael Hinton

Title

CHAPTER 3
WHY SHOULD THEY HIRE YOU?

One of my favorite interview questions is, "Why should we hire you [rather than someone else]?" Most interviewers will ask this question in one way or another. Your ability to set yourself apart when you answer it is essential to your success. Remember, you're in a competition. You'd be surprised, however, how many people are stumped by this question. They seem to have no idea what makes them unique, let alone valuable.

The purpose of this chapter is to get you thinking about your personality, needs and goals, and how you can maximize them to find an organization that is the perfect fit. I'll cover:

- Why it is important to know yourself *before* searching for a new job
- How to promote your transferable skills, behavioral competencies and emotional intelligence to a potential employer

The primary value of this chapter lies in completing a series of exercises. Complete all of them because each is essential for the self-discovery that will empower you to make the right move in your career.

KNOW THYSELF

Who you are is based upon a combination of genetics, experiences, and life circumstances. Unfortunately, because most people are so busy just living, they don't take the time to find out who they are and what drives their behavior. Achieving a *life balance* is essential for initiating a good career and maintaining emotional health. You may not know exactly what you want in a job but understanding what you don't like is sometimes equally as important as knowing what you do like.

The answer to "Who am I?" partially lies in determining what turns you on. I promise not to spend a great deal of time on the areas that have been beaten to death in hundreds of books, but I can't tell you the number of people I've met who go from one seemingly "good" opportunity to another, without a clue as to how any particular job supports their career path.

Clients often say that they are "not sure what they want to be when they grow up." The changing economic forces surrounding us are forcing many to grapple with this question, often in mid-career. I have learned that life is just too short to go through it being miserable and wishing you had done something differently.

Take stock now and make some long-range plans. The exercises provided at the end of this chapter will enable you to take charge of your career path plan. You must answer each question carefully. Some of the exercises are simple and just plain fun, but they get progressively more difficult. They force you to think about what you want and don't want from your career by exploring your life balance, career health, change readiness and perception about the ideal job.

YOUR LIFE BALANCE

Life balance is becoming increasingly important in our society. The Work Institute indicates that a lack of work/life balance is the second leading reason the over 70 million Millennials in the workforce today leave their places of employment (need for professional growth is the most cited reason).[9]

Life Balance, Exercise 3.1, is a great test for assessing your current situation and need for balance. We all have family, social, cultural, health and financial problems at one point in our careers. This test will help you determine whether you want to seek personal or career counseling services.

---

[9] The Work Institute (2016). *2018 retention report.* Retrieved January 15, 2021 from http://info.workinstitute.com/2018retentionreport/

YOUR CAREER HEALTH

Exercise 3.2 provides you with a way of determining just how healthy your current career path really is. Whether you are still working or are unemployed, this test will assess decisions you have made along the way and show you whether you are doing well or need to make some changes in your decision-making.

YOUR CHANGE READINESS

Everyone handles change differently. For some, change is exciting. For others, it's terrifying. Exercise 3.3 *Your Career Health, The Change Readiness Quiz*, will tell you how ready you are to change careers or jobs.

YOUR IDEAL JOB

Most people are like a fishing bobber floating in a lake when it comes to their careers. They bounce from the shore to the dock to the boat and are carried adrift by whatever current drags them along, seemingly without purpose. Why did you take your last job? How did you secure it? Was it more happenstance than planned? Look at your career so far. Would you say that you actually calculated and planned each move? Most job seekers answer no, so you're not alone.

We go to work each day and do our jobs and try to get the most from the experience. Sometimes, though, daily pressures, pay cuts, mergers and acquisitions, bad bosses, market shifts and thousands of other reasons taint our work lives. Understanding what you can and cannot tolerate in your work environment is essential. *What's Missing in Your Job*, Exercise 3.4, will help you.

Where you choose to live is an important consideration. List the geographical locations in which you wish to reside and then describe the reasons for wanting to live there. Ask your search partner to complete the geographical selection exercise as well.

Characteristics of My Ideal Job, Exercise 3.5, brings further focus to answering the questions surrounding job characteristics. It also brings into play the "soft" issues of feelings about recognition and self-worth on the job. Don't discount these. Most of my clients tell me they used to do so and were miserable for years. This is a slightly harder exercise because you must rank your preferences. Take your time and think about why you rank each item the way you do. In each exercise in this book, the *why* is almost equal in importance to the *what* (perhaps, more).

Salary and Package Preferences, Exercise 3.6, asks you to define the difference between what you "must have," "would like to have," are "neutral" about and what you "don't need." These cover a multitude of options in considering a compensation package. If you are married or have a significant other, make two copies of the page because your partner will need to complete the exercises as well. Discuss your answers and make sure you are in agreement on the rankings. This list will become a reference during your new offer negotiations.

After completing these exercises, you should know the following: what you like and don't like about your workplace and fellow workers; what you think the ideal job is; and where you want to work. Do your homework on salary levels the area in which you want to work. You should also have a good description of what your short- and long-range career goals are. That's a lot of useful information!

WHY THEY *SHOULD* HIRE YOU

> **To become employed, you must identify and satisfy an unfulfilled company need.**

Once you have thought about your own skills and needs, you can more easily make clear to an employer why they should hire you. Each interviewer is wondering whether they are receiving the full measure of worth and talent for each dollar they may pay you. They want to know that you can meet their goals. Can they track your performance to the bottom line? Will you get along with others? If so, you are the one. If not, they will hire someone else. You must effectively communicate your talents, both verbally and in writing. When you have done this, they will hire you. All employers are looking for problem solving ability, transferable skills, behavioral competencies and emotional intelligence. These characteristics may or may not be listed in a job description, but make no mistake about their importance, so let's take a closer look at each.

YOU ARE A PROBLEM SOLVER

Let's be clear on this one point. The hiring authority employs you because you are afford-able and can harmoniously fit in, but they need to know you can solve problems they either can't or don't want to solve.

The following are the essential questions you must address in this job search: What kind of problem solver are you? How many mountains can you move? What size mountains are they? Will you fit into their company and work well with their existing team as you are meeting their objectives? Can they track your work results to the bottom line and justify their investment and faith in your abilities? All the exercises you have completed so far, and every one you will do from this point forward, will address these key issues.

YOU HAVE TRANSFERABLE SKILLS

Transferable skills are competencies that are applicable in more than one profession and across varying types of work. Some transferable skills may not have necessarily been taught outright but were rather acquired through past experiences. Others may have resulted from formal training, yet they too lend themselves to a wide range of career options.

In the professional world, typical transferable skills may include the following as well as others:

- Leadership and followership
- Planning
- Communication
- Report writing
- Negotiating
- Giving presentations
- Budgeting
- Using the telephone effectively
- Dealing with clients in person and digitally
- Problem solving
- Working in a team
- Working autonomously
- Operating office equipment
- Customer service
- Resourcefulness
- Ability to master difficult concepts quickly
- Excellent listening and feedback skills
- Sense of humor
- Ability to meet deadlines
- Operating under pressure

There are many transferable skills, but as an example let's have a look at one universally valued skill—leadership—and how you can use it to boost your worth to potential employers.

Leadership is what makes an organization and hiring managers know it. Whether you are applying for an executive or entry-level position, your leadership skills will rise to the surface in terms of your value proposition. Employers are interested in your leadership ability and style and, most of all, your track record of how you have used both to accomplish goals. They are less interested in where you developed your leadership skills than they are in your success, so you can draw examples from jobs, volunteer work and other experience to illustrate your competence with this transferrable skill.

Your leadership skills are derived from your ability to organize people, implement clear plans and manage projects. Your leadership style is a softer skill set that tells employers how you accomplished your goal in terms of communication and people management. Leadership style is a reflection of emotional intelligence and knowing how you accomplished your goals will help them determine whether you are a good fit for their culture.

When you word leadership as a transferable skill in your search materials, be sure to express your success and your style. Here's an example:

> *Raised $4,050 as coordinator of Greater Waterford Humane Society Annual Dog Walk. Used persuasive, flexible leadership style and clear communication to boost participation by 8%.*

Of course, candidates with the highest levels of expertise are going to catch the eye of potential employers. A new hire with a solid and applicable skill set requires less training, saving employers time and money. Yet, what makes transferable skills so beneficial to both employees and employers can be narrowed down to one advantage: **flexibility**. A strong set of crossover competencies makes for a well-rounded worker who can display his or her value in different roles, tasks, and settings within an organization. Holding a wider range of capabilities offers job seekers a greater competitive edge.

Transferable skills also benefit job seekers who are aiming to shift their career paths. With limited direct experience in one's field, even a few key transferable skills can assist a newcomer in obtaining an interview.

When trying to piece together your own set of transferable skills, think about the varying forms of expertise you've acquired during any of the following endeavors:

- Education or training
- Volunteering
- Hobbies or interests

- Parenting or caring for family members
- Sports participation
- Community involvement

More complex skill sets take some creative thinking to work into a new form, one that fits the vision of professional growth and business acumen you want for yourself. Exercises 3.7 on transferable skills will help you.

YOU HAVE BEHAVIORAL COMPETENCIES

Another reason an employer may want to hire you is because of your behavioral competencies. Behavioral competencies are actions you display in the workplace that lead to positive outcomes; in other words, *how* you act toward others and make decisions regarding your work. They include the abilities and characteristics that complement your technical abilities. Employers know that, depending on the nature of the job, certain behaviors will enable you to succeed. For instance, an employer might want to know:

- How you take initiative to ensure results on work assignments
- How you communicate with others—style, tactics, etc.
- How you deal with conflict or obstacles

Below are examples of competencies, behaviors and personal traits that you can use to build your search materials:

CHANGE LEADER

1. *Participates in continuous learning*—Grasps the essence of new information; masters new technical and business knowledge; recognizes own strengths and weaknesses; pursues self-development; seeks feedback from others and opportunities to master new knowledge.

2. *Creative and innovative*—Develops new insights into situations and applies innovative solutions to make organizational improvements; creates a work environment that encourages creative thinking and innovation; designs and implements new or cutting-edge programs/processes.

3. *Externally aware*—Identifies and keeps up to date on key national and international policies and economic, political, social and business trends that affect the organization. Understands short- and long- range plans and determines how best to be positioned to achieve a competitive business advantage in a global economy.

4. *Flexible*—Is open to change and new information; adapts behavior and work methods in response to new information, changing conditions, or unexpected obstacles. Adjusts promptly to new situations warranting attention and resolution.

5. *Resilient*—Deals effectively with pressure; maintains focus and intensity, and remains optimistic and persistent, even under adversity. Recovers swiftly from setbacks. Effectively balances personal life and work.

6. *Service motivated*—Creates and sustains an organizational culture which encourages others to provide the quality of service essential to high performance. Enables others to acquire the tools and support they need to perform well. Presents a commitment to public service. Influences others toward a spirit of service and meaningful contributions to mission accomplishment.

7. *Strategic thinker*—Formulates effective strategies consistent with the business and competitive strategy of the organization in a global economy. Examines policy issues and strategic planning with a long-term perspective. Determines objectives and sets priorities; anticipates potential threats or opportunities.

8. *Visionary*—Takes a long-term view and acts as a catalyst for organizational change; builds a shared vision with others. Motivates others to translate vision into action.

PEOPLE LEADER

1. *Fair-minded conflict manager*—Identifies and takes steps to prevent potential situations that could result in unpleasant confrontations. Manages and resolves conflicts and disagreements in a positive and constructive manner to minimize negative impact.

2. *Appreciative of diversity*—Recruits, develops, and retains a diverse high-quality workforce in an equitable manner. Leads and manages an inclusive workplace that maximizes the talents of each person to achieve sound business results. Respects, understands, values and seeks out individual differences to achieve the vision and

mission of the organization. Develops and uses measures and rewards to hold self and others accountable for achieving results that embody the principles of diversity.

3. *Possessing of integrity and honesty*—Instills mutual trust and confidence; creates a culture that fosters high standards of ethics; behaves in a fair and ethical manner toward others and demonstrates a sense of corporate responsibility and commitment to public service.

4. *Team builder*—Inspires, motivates, and guides others toward goal accomplishments. Consistently develops and sustains cooperative working relationships. Encourages and facilitates cooperation within the organization and with customer groups, fosters commitment, team spirit, pride, trust.

5. *Mentor*—Develops leadership in others through coaching, rewarding, and guiding employees.

RESULTS DRIVER

1. *Accountable*—Assures that effective controls are developed and maintained to ensure the integrity of the organization. Holds self and others accountable for rules and responsibilities. Can be relied upon to ensure that projects within areas of specific responsibility are completed on deadline and within budget. Monitors and evaluates plans; focuses on results and measuring attainment of outcomes.

2. *Customer service-oriented*—Balances interests of a variety of clients; readily readjusts priorities to respond to pressing and changing client demands. Anticipates and meets the need of clients; achieves quality end products; is committed to continuous improvement of services.

3. *Decisive*—Exercises good judgment by making sound and well-informed decisions; perceives impact and implications of decisions; makes effective and timely decisions, even when data is limited, or solutions produce unpleasant consequences; is proactive and achievement oriented.

4. *Enterprising*—Identifies opportunities to develop and market new products and services within or outside of the organization. Is willing to take risks; initiates actions that involve a deliberate risk to achieve a recognized benefit or advantage.

5. *Problem solver*—Identifies and analyzes problems; distinguishes between relevant and irrelevant information to make logical decisions; provides solutions to individual and organizational problems.

6. *Technically credible*—Understands and appropriately applies procedures, requirements, regulations, and policies related to specialized expertise. Capable of making sound hiring and capital resource decisions and addressing training and development needs. Comprehends links between administrative competencies and mission needs.

BUSINESS PLANNER

1. *Financially savvy*—Demonstrates broad understanding of principles of financial management and marketing expertise necessary to ensure appropriate funding levels. Prepares, justifies, and/or administers budget for program area; uses cost-benefit thinking to set priorities; monitors expenditures in support of programs and policies. Identifies cost-effective approaches. Manages procurement and contracting.

2. *Human resources strategist*—Assesses current and future staffing needs based on organizational goals and budget realities. Using merit principles, ensures staff are appropriately selected, developed, utilized, appraised, and rewarded; takes corrective action.

3. *Technologically proficient*—Uses efficient and cost-effective approaches to integrate technology into the workplace and improve program effectiveness. Develops strategies using new technology to enhance decision making. Understands the impact of technological changes on the organization.

COALITION BUILDER

1. *Influencer/negotiator*—Persuades others; builds consensus through give and take; gains cooperation from others to obtain information and accomplish goals; facilitates "win-win" situations.

2. *Interpersonally aware*—Considers and responds appropriately to the needs, feelings, and capabilities of different people in various situations; is tactful, compassionate, and sensitive, and treats others with respect; facilitates open exchange of ideas and fosters atmosphere of open communication.

3. *Organized and animated presenter and writer*—Makes clear and convincing oral presentations to individuals or groups; listens effectively and clarifies information as needed. Expresses facts and ideas in writing in a clear, convincing, and organized manner.

4. *Relationship builder*—Develops networks and builds alliances, engages in cross-functional activities; collaborates across boundaries, and finds common ground with a widening range of stakeholders. Utilizes contacts to build and strengthen internal support bases.

5. *Diplomatic and politically savvy*—Identifies the internal and external politics that impact the work of the organization. Approaches each problem with a clear perception of organizational and political reality; recognizes the impact of alternative courses of action.

Complete Exercise 3.8 on identifying your behavioral competencies.

YOU HAVE EMOTIONAL INTELLIGENCE

You know the type. They are people who may have the knowledge it takes to do the job right, but who lack the interpersonal skills to form healthy relationships. They don't work well with others and they cost organizations millions a year in turnover, productivity and profit.

Employees like this have low emotional quotients (EQ) and intelligence (EI). Your emotional quotient is your capacity to be aware of, control and express your emotions and to handle interpersonal relationships judiciously and empathetically. Your emotional intelligence is your ability to recognize your and others' emotions and use that information to guide your behavior.

Barbara Purdom, formerly the Assistant VP of Human Resources for Nationwide Insurance, told me that emotional intelligence is "...awareness and understanding that our emotions are driving behavior and impact everyone around us."[10] Emotional intelligence gives us the ability to manage our—and others'—emotions, particularly under stress and conflict.

Employers want to hire those with high EQ and EI and they are likely to ask you and your references questions designed to evaluate these competencies. They know that your

---

10   Coon, F. & Purdom, B. (Hosts). (2018, July 18). EQ eats IQ for lunch [Audio podcast episode]. In *The US at Work*. Fred Coon Studio. https://theusatwork.com/eq-eats-iq-for-lunch/

history of behavior in the workplace is the greatest predictor of your future actions. You should be keenly aware of the way you act because your reputation for being congenial will follow you throughout your career and your ability to convey to employers that you know how to act like a grown up may win you the job.

PRESENTING YOUR SKILLS TO EMPLOYERS

Properly presenting your transferable and behavioral skills to an employer is essential. Review the job description and consider which skills the employer would likely value most. Then, reference them within your resume, cover letter and during your job interview (more on this later). However, be sure not to simply list each competency. Effectively convey how each one applies to the specific job you're seeking. Your cover letter is an especially effective medium through which you can communicate the value of your transferable skills.

An important aspect of articulating who you are is found in *The Transferable Skills Ranking,* Exercise 3.9. I often hear recruiters say that a candidate isn't employable because he/she hasn't worked in a specific industry or demonstrated a specifically defined set of skills. Poppycock! The right strategy and presentation of transferable skills will show potential employers that you have what it takes to make it with them.

The transferable skills exercise will not only help you identify your transferable skills, it will help you rank them. The ranking will be important when you write your resume.

Now you have learned that the hiring process has changed considerably, readied yourself for the challenges that lie ahead and discovered your strengths. In the next few chapters, you'll develop your brand and the documents you need to position yourself as the #1 candidate of the company of your choosing.

SUCCESS STORY, CHAPTER 3: KNOW THYSELF

CONTRIBUTED BY BILL TEMPLE, EXECUTIVE COACH, STEWART, COOPER & COON

Tim was contacted by the president of a large flooring manufacturing company who wanted to hire him for an executive marketing position in Ohio. Tim was up to the challenge but had just moved his family to Florida and knew he did not want to uproot them again.

We formulated a strategy for Tim to defer negotiating about relocation until he was sure the organization really wanted him. He worked with the president to clarify how to progress with the organization of their marketing division and assured them that he could develop that direction as part of his role in the company. After several interviews, Tim was hired as Vice President of Segment Marketing and Innovation with the following benefits:

- $230,000 base salary (an increase of 30% over prior position)
- 30% bonus
- $15,000 in stock the first year
- 1-year severance pay
- *No required relocation*

Knowing what he needed and developing a strategy was critical for Tim's success in this situation.

ADDITIONAL RESOURCES

- Coon, F. & Venckus, R. (2017). *Hire the EQ, not the IQ: A 150+ question guide to help you hire the "right" fit.* Gaff Publishing.
- Stewart Cooper and Coon Administrative (n.d.). *Identify and leverage transferable skills during your job search.* StewartCooperCoon.com. https://stewartcooper-coon.com/wp-content/uploads/2019/03/Identifying-and-Leveraging-Transferable-Skills-During-Your-Job-Search_images-002.pdf/

EXERCISE 3.1 LIFE BALANCE

DIRECTIONS

If you have experienced any item on this lest in the past year, check the box to the left. Then, count the total number of boxes checked.

PROFESSIONAL

☐ Bored or stuck

☐ Unrecognized

☐ Passed over

☐ Laid off or fired

☐ Company is experiencing re-engineering

☐ Changed work hours or conditions

FAMILY

☐ Suffered death of spouse, family member or friend

☐ Family changes: adoption, birth, children moving in or out, newly married, divorced or separated

☐ Spouse's employment has changed

SOCIAL DIFFICULTIES

☐ Changed social activity, dropped or added volunteering

☐ Had a falling-out with close personal relationship

☐ Experienced loss, theft or damage to personal property

☐ Involved in an accident

EMOTIONAL AND MENTAL DIFFICULTIES

☐ Increased stress

☐ Procrastination in making decisions

☐ Losing interest in others

☐ Self-critical

☐ Underachieving

INTELLECTUAL AND CULTURAL DIFFICULTIES

☐ Started or stopped college

☐ Stopped reading or don't read books in your field

☐ Not involved in or not overly involved in outside activities

☐ Started or stopped a hobby

☐ Haven't taken a vacation this year

☐ Laughs are few and far between

FINANCIAL AND ECONOMIC DIFFICULTIES

☐ Major purchase

☐ Experienced business reversal or financial loss

☐ Change in personal finances

HEALTH

☐ Experienced illness or injury

☐ Stopped exercising

☐ Experienced weight gain or loss

☐ Experienced change in sleeping habits

5 Or Less Changes

You are having an easy year. Congratulations!

6 Through 10 Changes

This year has been challenging; you might want to reassess your priorities.

11 Or More Changes

Get help! You can't do this alone. If you're experiencing major changes in your career, slow down. Don't react immediately.

EXERCISE 3.2 YOUR CAREER HEALTH

This test is designed to give you a better understanding of your career health. First, please estimate what you think your overall career health currently is. Then, then answer questions 2 - 48. Last, compare your original estimated rating with the results of this test then act accordingly.

Circle the appropriate number Low   **High**

1. Your overall career health.   0   1   2   3   4   5   6   7   8   9   10

	Mark the Appropriate Box	**Never**	**Rarely**	**Some-times**	**Fre-quently**	**Mostly**	**Always**
2.	I like the kinds of people who are attracted to my field.						
3.	I am honest and accurate in assessing my skills.						
4.	I am honest and accurate in assessing my interests.						
5.	I am honest and accurate in assessing my values.						
6.	These assessments confirm my career or job choices.						
7.	Decisions I made at important turning points in my career were beneficial to my career.						
8.	In retrospect, these decisions seemed inevitable.						
9.	I am energetic and optimistic about my career and my life.						

	Mark the Appropriate Box	**Never**	**Rarely**	**Some-times**	**Fre-quently**	**Mostly**	**Always**
10.	Professional colleagues, mentors, advisors, and role models were important in my life.						
11.	These people have been helpful in my career.						
12.	Excellent job opportunities and offers well suited to me have come my way as if by chance or serendipity.						
13.	In my professional & social life, I present my truest and best self.						
14.	I'm honest and positive in assertions about myself and others.						
15.	I strive to lead a balanced life.						
16.	I work hard and play hard.						
17.	I don't mind (I even enjoy) necessary drudgery in my job or career.						
18.	My work and I seem uniquely suited or well matched to each other.						
19.	During career transitions, "imperfect movement is better than perfect paralysis."						
20.	I am well regarded professionally.						

	Mark the Appropriate Box	Never	Rarely	Some-times	Fre-quently	Mostly	Always
21.	I am well regarded socially.						
22.	I intuitively develop abiding relationships with my friends and colleagues.						
23.	These later on prove to be helpful in my career.						
24.	I seem to have many social and professional acquaintances and contacts who keep me up to date on what's happening.						
25.	I gain energy, pleasure, and renewal from my work or career.						
26.	I have a realistic view of trends in my field and how they fit into the larger picture.						
27.	I know what I can change, what I can't change, and the difference between them.						
28.	I can't control the wind, but I can adjust the sails.						
29.	I make things happen because I work hard.						
30.	The harder I work, the luckier I get.						
31.	When I add valuable contributions to my field, I feel personal satisfaction.						

	Mark the Appropriate Box	**Never**	**Rarely**	**Some-times**	**Fre-quently**	**Mostly**	**Always**
32.	No matter what work I do, I am fully and constantly aware of the fact that I must generate more income or value than I receive.						
33.	Logical, systematic, scientific thinking is useful in many venues.						
34.	I redirect my energies, instinct, and desires into useful pursuits.						
35.	I defer pleasures and problem solving.						
36.	I strive to be self-reliant.						
37.	When I help others, I feel satisfaction.						
38.	In order to achieve my goals and avoid pitfalls, I plan systematically.						
39.	The people I work with are people I like or admire.						
40.	I respect my colleagues at work.						
41.	I try to maximize my utility and usefulness in my work.						
42.	I am intense about my work, my family and my friends.						
43.	I try to be adaptable and to accept compromise.						

	Mark the Appropriate Box	**Never**	**Rarely**	**Some-times**	**Fre-quently**	**Mostly**	**Always**
44.	I have no career regrets.						
45.	Life is full of random events that I attempt to convert to adventures.						
46.	Humility is a great virtue.						
47.	I believe in action rather than drift.						
48.	I take things as they come, with equanimity and humor.						

Total the number of marks in each column here.

Multiply the column totals by the numbers in each column.

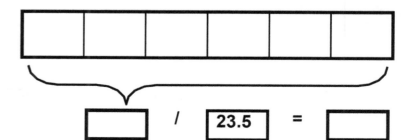

Sum the final totals and divide by 23.5.

Compare this final number with the estimate you made for question 1.

EXERCISE 3.3   JOB CHANGE READINESS QUIZ

Complete all questions then calculate your score.

1. The last time you got a promotion you were pleased with was:

    a. In your current position at your last review

    b. In your current company within the last two years

    c. In the last five years

    d. In your dreams

2. If you were asked to describe your current boss, which of the following words most closely capture him/her?

    a. Best boss ever

    b. OK

    c. Difficult, little direction

    d. Has the charisma of a wet noodle

3. How clear are your responsibilities in your current position?

    a. Very clear outline of responsibilities and expectations

    b. Some responsibilities and expectations are clear

    c. No boundaries at all; make things up along the way

    d. Are you kidding?

4. Everyone tries his/her best to be polite and civil at work. Are you the same cooperative self when you get home from work or are you tired, irritable and hard to live with?

    a. I am rarely irritable, considering we all have good and bad days.

    b. Some irritability recently

    c. Tired, irritable and hard to live with

    d. I love to be irritable and don't mind irritating my family

5. Does your contribution at work make a difference in the company?

    a.   Absolutely, my job is important

    b.   My work contributes at some level

    c.   Not really

    d.   I think my position could be eliminated

6. Do you know what you would like to be doing in your career?

    a.   I am doing exactly what I want to be doing

    b.   I have many ideas but can't seem to narrow them down

    c.   Yes, and this isn't it

    d.   I've never known what I've wanted to do

7. It's Sunday evening. How do you feel about going to work tomorrow?

    a.   I really enjoy most of what I do and like the people work with

    b.   I can take it or leave it

    c.   I have the bottle of Tylenol out already in anticipation of another week of insanity

    d.   Hate, loathe, despise and abominate

8. In the past year, have you been having thoughts of leaving the company? Have you perhaps sent out some resumes?

    a.   No

    b.   I've just started thinking of a change but haven't done anything about it yet

    c.   Yes

    d.   I should have left the company a week after I got the job

9. When you think of leaving your current position, do you get fearful because you are too old to change, don't have the right education or experience, or feel there isn't the right job for you elsewhere?

   a. No. I am confident I can make a successful career change

   b. I may experience some fear but will eventually make the move

   c. Yes. Fear has kept me from trying to leave

   d. Reality is reality. No one else will hire me. I'm a loser.

10. When I suggest a new approach to a project or a current method of operation

    a. Management is receptive to my ideas and encourages them

    b. Management listens to some of my ideas but hasn't implemented any

    c. I have learned to keep it to myself. No one pays any attention

    d. The management philosophy of this company is simple: Do it their way. Period.

YOUR SCORE

Determine your score by giving yourself 6 points for "a," 3 points for "b," 1 point for "c," and no points for "d."

Below 27 Points

You are dissatisfied. Examine your options. It might be time to move. Develop a plan to change your position within the company and for seeking a position elsewhere.

30 to 43 Points

You are coping (for now). Clarify your goals and reassess your priorities.

40 to 50 Points

High job satisfaction. Congratulations!

EXERCISE 3.4   WHAT IS MISSING FROM YOUR JOB?

	Characteristic	Always Missing	Usually Missing	Sometimes Missing	Rarely Missing
1.	social well-being				
2.	autonomy				
3.	creativity				
4.	family time				
5.	financial status				
6.	learning environment				
7.	recognition				
8.	physical well-being				
9.	stability				
10.	workplace environment				
11.	fun				
12.	teamwork				
13.	job status				
14.	intellectual challenge				
15.	promotion potential				
16.	realistic goals				

17.	performance standards				
18.	realistic expectations				
19.	defined career path				
20.	feeling good about work				
21.	dependable co-workers				
22.	diligent co-workers				
23.	smart co-workers				
24.	trustworthy co-workers				
25.	considerate co-workers				

Now, rank what was 'Always Missing' and 'Sometimes Missing' in your position.

ALWAYS MISSING

1.

2.

3.

SOMETIMES MISSING

1.

2.

3.

EXERCISE 3.5 CHARACTERISTICS OF MY IDEAL JOB

	My Ideal job should...	Agree	Agree	Disagree	Disagree
1.	have autonomy to make decisions.				
2.	be physically challenging.				
3.	have a creative work environment.				
4.	need precision work.				
5.	have a fast paced environment.				
6.	have a flexible schedule.				
7.	have customer contact.				
8.	be mentally challenging.				
9.	have an office location.				
10.	have a prestigious office location.				
11.	have recognition for my work.				
12.	be in a large company.				
13.	be in a small company.				
14.	have a structured environment.				
15.	have varied workspace.				
16.	be in a company that is a good corporate citizen				
17.	be in a profitable company.				
18.	be in a good community.				
19.	be in a stable environment.				
20.	be in a team environment.				
21.	be independent.				
22.	be indoors.				

	My Ideal job should...	Agree	Agree	Disagree	Disagree
23.	be outdoors.				
24.	be analyzing data.				
25.	be budgeting and analysis work.				
26.	have customer contact.				
27.	have detailed work.				
28.	have educational reimbursement.				
29.	have management responsibilities.				
30.	be able to manage money and budgets.				
31.	should have deadlines.				
32.	include negotiating.				
33.	require organizing and managing projects.				
34.	include people contact.				
35.	require project management.				
36.	include public speaking.				
37.	have a risk-taking environment.				
38.	have a solid benefit package.				
39.	include strategic planning.				
40.	include teaching others.				
41.	have a bonus award system.				
42.	have a good boss.				
43.	have steady paced work.				
44.	have a pressured environment.				
45.	include writing reports.				

EXERCISE 3.6   SALARY PACKAGE PREFERENCES

		Must Have	Should Have	Could Have	Don't Need
1.	Base salary stock options				
2.	Long-term disability insurance				
3.	Vacations, free travel for spouse				
4.	Continued benefits after termination				
5.	Group auto insurance				
6.	Matching investment programs				
7.	Annual physical exam				
8.	Pension plan				
9.	Deferred compensation				
10.	Financial planning assistance				
11.	Overseas travel				
12.	CPA and tax assistance				
13.	Medical Insurance				
14.	Install appliances/drapes/carpets				
15.	Short-term loans				
16.	Continuing education				
17.	Consumer product discounts				

18.	Severance pay				
19.	Athletic club membership				
20.	Country club membership				
21.	Luncheon club membership				
22.	Legal assistance				
23.	Outplacement				
24.	Shipping of boats and pets				
25.	Life Insurance				
26.	Mortgage prepayment penalty				
27.	Closing costs, bridge loan				
28.	Lodging fees while between homes				
29.	Installation				
30.	Sales Commission				
31.	Bonus				
32.	Profit sharing				
33.	Expense Accounts				
34.	Company car or car allowance				
35.	Use of vehicle in off/after hours				
36.	Company sponsored vanpool				
37.	AD&D Insurance				
38.	Real estate brokerage fee				

39.	House hunting trips				
40.	Moving expense				
41.	Mortgage rate differential				
42.	Early stock option vesting				
43.	Company purchase of your home				

Rank your "Must Have" and "Should Have" salary and package preferences in order of importance to you.

MUST HAVE

1.

2.

3.

4.

5.

6.

7.

8.

9.

10.

SHOULD HAVE

1.

2.

3.

4.

5.

6.

7.

8.

9.

10.

Let your significant other complete this exercise also. Spend the next day or two discussing the items and why you ranked them the way each of you did.

The results of this exercise and discussions with your significant other will form a foundation of healthy understanding of your common goals and make the evaluation of your next job offer easier.

EXERCISE 3.7 JOB DESCRIPTIONS: LEVERAGING TRANSFERABLE SKILLS

1. Find two job descriptions most closely fit your background, skills, behaviors. In each of the job descriptions, highlight the key words you feel best exemplify your leadership competencies, skills, and style.

2. Take an 8.5" × 11.0" piece of paper and divide it into two columns.

3. In the left column, write the keyword list you highlighted.

4. In the right-hand column, list these in order of strongest to least strong in terms of your competencies.

EXERCISE 3.8 JOB DESCRIPTIONS: IDENTIFYING BEHAVIORAL COMPETENCIES

Take another 8.5" × 11" paper and divide it vertically into two sections.

Referring to your job descriptions, circle all behavioral words you see, not just those that apply to you. Write them in the left-hand column of the paper.

Now, reorder them in priority in the right-hand column from the one you feel is your strongest to the one you feel you may have but are not certain you could explain in a story.

If you don't see any, you can turn to The Harvard Directory of Behavioral Competencies, which identifies 125 such traits. You may learn more about these in my book, *Hire The EQ, Not The IQ.*

How much do your competencies overlap the job descriptions? What do you need to adjust?

EXERCISE 3.9 TRANSFERABLE SKILLS RANKING

	I Can	Strongly Agree	Agree	Disagree	Strongly Dis-agree
1.	sort data.				
2.	use organization skills.				
3.	apply information to solve problems.				
4.	make and keep a schedule.				
5.	work with facts and figures to solve problems.				
6.	predict future trends.				
7.	use multiple sources of information.				
8.	set priorities.				
9.	keep a set schedule.				
10.	evaluate information.				
11.	gather information.				
12.	sort objects against preset instructions.				
13.	manage time effectively.				
14.	apply standard methods to analyze data.				
15.	design experimental models or plans.				
16.	identify problems.				

17.	objectively listen.				
18.	manage group activities toward a goal.				
19.	work under pressure.				
20.	take risks.				
21.	delegate tasks and responsibilities.				
22.	monitor responsibilities delegated.				
23.	be empathetic to the needs of others.				
24.	follow through on commitments.				
25.	communicate effectively with others.				
26.	place value judgments on others.				
27.	describe events with minimal errors.				
28.	identify critical decision-making issues.				
29.	analyze tasks.				
30.	maintain positive self-image under fire.				
31.	work well with peers.				
32.	work well with subordinates.				
33.	work well with superiors.				
34.	teach others willingly.				

35.	adapt to surrounding environments.				
36.	follow through with assignments.				
37.	delegate well.				
38.	organize people and tasks.				
39.	write well.				
40.	effectively communicate.				
41.	manage a course of action.				
42.	express company values to others.				
43.	foster trust in others.				
44.	accept criticism.				
45.	learn from my mistakes.				
46.	"own" my mistakes as mine alone.				
47.	persist no matter what.				
48.	effectively communicate my wants and needs.				

Rank the transferable skills you strongly agree you have on a scale of 1-10.

CHAPTER 4
DEVELOPING YOUR BRAND

What you are doing with your career is not about "job searching." It's about **product marketing** and *YOU* are the product. All products have brands, but sometimes it is hard to understand branding in terms of your own career. This chapter will cover

- Brand development
- How to communicate your brand in a variety of ways

> ## It's not about job searching.
> ## It's about product marketing.

WHAT IS A BRAND?

Your professional brand is a combination of who you are as a worker and what you can do for a potential employer. "It's how you want to be perceived in your network and beyond," states Andrew Ko, Executive Recruiter with the Lucas Group.[11] Your brand should amalgamate your best qualities and how they can be used to solve problems, make money and meet organizational goals. Think of your favorite brand of jeans, for example. Why do you buy them? Comfort? Fit? Price? How about your favorite celebrity? Sexy? Tough? Energetic?

As a job seeker, you must successfully answer eight product marketing questions. Doing so will help you develop, successfully present, and negotiate your professional brand and establish your real value in the marketplace. Failure on your part to successfully bring your product to market will cost you time and money. The questions below will make you think about your own brand. They may seem simple, but many intelligent professionals can't answer or never ask them. Over the last two decades, I have seen hundreds of executives scan this list and say, "I can answer that" or "I can do that" only to draw a blank. The following questions are IMPORTANT. DO NOT skip them.

- What is your product? Your brand?
- Why is your product better than competing products?
- Who needs your product?
- Why does your brand excite potential buyers?
- What is your plan to get your product in front of multiple buyers?
- How will you outshine your competition? (They don't hire two people for the same job.)
- What is your negotiating strategy?
- What is your strategy to position your product for increasing long-term value?

Were you able to quickly answer these questions? If you did not, or if your answers did not make sense, then you do not completely understand your own **value-added proposition**.

Your value-added proposition is what you bring to the table of a potential employer. How can you and *only* you fulfill their needs? Your value proposition(s) must include functional and behavioral competencies and a clear price-earnings ratio (how much you cost vs. how much you bring in). If you cannot define why your product is better than others, you will lose the competition.

---

11 Coon, F. & Ko, A. (Hosts). (2018, July 24). The what, the why, and the how [Audio podcast episode]. In *The US at Work*. Fred Coon Studio. https://theusatwork.com/211-personal-brand-the-what-the-why-and-the-how/

Valerie El-Jamil, Consulting Campaign Director at Stewart, Cooper and Coon, Inc., knows the value of good branding. She states, "The essential message we want our clients to deliver is 'If you hire me, I can create results that have an impact on the top and bottom lines or both. I can create harmony, collaboration, and a better culture in your company.'" El-Jamil adds that you need to have a branding message that communicates value and can be used throughout your search materials.

Branding expert William Arruda says that there are 6 requirements to build a powerful brand:[12] Your brand should be:

1. **Correct**. A successful brand reflects the personal attributes, or qualities, of its creator.

2. **Concise**. The brand is captured in one or two sentences describing the client's unique promise of value.

3. **Consistent**. The promise of value never changes.

4. **Compelling**. It's appropriate, interesting, and relevant to the client's target audience.

5. **Clever**. It's highly differentiated and unique and separates the client from others with similar skills, talents, and abilities.

6. **Current**. It is based in today, with room to evolve tomorrow.

Additionally, consider these 5 elements:

1. **Description**. One or two words that immediately identify you (e.g., business builder).

2. **Hook**. What do you do that is great? (e.g., drive double-digit growth).

3. **Measure of success**. How big? How much? For whom? (e.g., to make more than $5 million annually).

4. **Indication of uniqueness**. Distinguish yourself compared to competition.

5. **Call to action**. Give the employer a reason to hire you NOW.

---

12   Personal communication, March 30, 2009.

DEVELOPING YOUR BRAND

Now comes the hard part: finding the words that best describe you and what you have to offer. Joshua Waldman, author of *Job Searching with Social Media for Dummies*, says that your brand should reflect who you are, not a false representation designed to fool employers. "A personal brand doesn't mean you have to jump around the room pretending to be something you are not. Think about Spock from Star Trek. He certainly had a brand: meticulous, professional, and straight to the point. Spock's character was so consistent that you could almost anticipate what he was going to say next."[13] Waldman recommends a 3-step process for putting your brand into words.

STEP 1

Answer the following questions. Be sure to write your answer since putting your brand in writing will be essential.

- Why can you do your job better than anyone else? What qualities do you have that allow you to be the best? Think about what you do and how well you do it. Try to look for your *unique,* descriptive characteristics. Everyone has "exemplary communication skills."
- How would current or former employers describe your skills and qualities?
- How do you impress others? What 3 things would someone notice about you?

STEP 2

Ask yourself whether the answers to these questions reflect who you are as a person and worker. Do they show how well you can meet the needs of targeted organizations? Adjust as necessary.

---

13   Waldman, J. (2012). *How to create a personal brand without being a jerk.* Retrieved January 15, 2021 from https://careerenlightenment.com/creating-a-personal-brand-with-out-being-a-jerk/

STEP 3

Create a one-sentence brand statement using adjectives that describe your unique abilities. You can use the format below to begin, then change it as necessary. Show it to friends, family and co-workers and ask for feedback.

LET'S BEGIN WRITING

I have found that those looking to create brand statements have a great deal of trouble with wording. Here are a formula and a few examples to get you started. Don't be constrained by this language. Simply use it as a starting point. You'll have another chance to try this when you complete Exercise 4.1.

I use my _____ and _____ for _____.

I'm appreciated for my ability to _____ and _____.

Using _____ (key trait), I _____, by providing/doing _____.

Through my _____, I _____, when I _____.

Examples:

- **Manufacturing Operations Manager**: *I energize, focus, and align manufacturing organizations, resulting in sustainable acceleration of processes, reduction in waste, and growth of profits.*
- **Social Media Specialist**: *I create powerful social media presence by using cutting-edge analytics, engaging content and strong relationship building techniques.*
- **Financial Advisor**: *I use my 15 years of experience to help people find the financial freedom they deserve.*
- **Sales Representative**: *I exceed sales goals and maintain a loyal customer base with my attentiveness and low-pressure style.*

Eventually, you should expand your brand statement. Here is an example of an abbreviated brand statement followed by an improved version:

BEFORE:

I am passionate about developing diverse leaders of character and purpose-driven organizations to their fullest potential, using a lifecycle approach...from designing innovative strategies and objectives to maximize organizational strengths/ competitive advantages; to planning implementation of aligned organizational structures, processes and personnel management; to leading change and managing execution; and finally, analyzing actual performance against objectives and making adjustments in dynamic environments.

AFTER:

I use my passion for developing diverse leaders of character to help purpose-driven organizations reach their key objectives. Known for being a student of leadership and organizations, I identify and engage organizational stakeholders to accurately frame problem areas and perform root cause analyses.

Using a lifecycle approach, I assist organizations in the following:

- *Designing innovative strategies that maximize organizational strengths/ competitive advantages, conducting implementation planning to align organizational structure, processes, and personnel/talent management*
- *Applying proven execution and change management techniques to track progress and ensure accountability*
- *Analyzing actual performance against objectives to adapt to dynamic environments*

By applying my 14 years of leadership, operations management, planning experience, and executive-level accountability, I provide tailored service and high-impact solutions to my clients' needs.

We are sometimes fortunate in having opportunities that challenge us and allow us to grow and exceed our expectations. I was asked to be the course leader for the Job and Career Transition portion of the U.S. Air Force, General Officer Transition Assistance Program (GOTAP). In our course segment on branding, Major General Steve Oliver did such outstanding work on his "before" and "after" branding statements that I wanted to share them with you as follows:

BEFORE:

I am passionate about developing diverse leaders of character and purpose-driven organizations to their fullest potential, using a lifecycle approach...from designing innovative strategies and objectives to maximize organizational strengths/competitive advantages; to planning implementation of aligned organizational structures, processes and personnel management; to leading change and managing execution; and finally, analyzing actual performance against objectives and making adjustments in dynamic environments.

AFTER:

I use my passion for developing diverse leaders of character **to** help purpose-driven organizations reach their key objectives.

Known for being a student of leadership and organizations, **I** identify and engage organizational stakeholders to accurately frame problem areas and perform root cause analyses.

Using a lifecycle approach, **I** assist organizations in designing innovative strategies that maximize organizational strengths/competitive advantages, conduct implementation planning to align organizational structures, processes and personnel/talent management, apply proven execution and change management techniques to track progress and ensure accountability, and analyze actual performance against objectives in order to adapt to dynamic environments.

By applying my 31 years of leadership, operations, and planning experience in the Air Force, the last 14 years with executive level responsibility/accountability, **I am able to provide** tailored service and high-impact solutions to my clients.

Wow! This statement has impact.

Be honest with yourself and test your brand statement by asking several people you trust the questions below. Give a copy of your brand statement to your search partner. Check it against the criteria in the chart that follows.

My personal branding statement...		YES	NO
1.	is inspiring		
2.	is exciting		
3.	is clear		
4.	is engaging		
5.	speaks to my target audience		
6.	is consistent with my vision and purpose		
7.	reflects my passions and values		
8.	makes me feel proud		
9.	feels familiar and comfortable to me		
10.	evokes times when I have felt most fulfilled and engaged in my life		
Total			

If you checked "yes" for at least 7 of the statements, your brand statement is likely effective. Consider how you might revise statements for which you checked "no."

Now, and this is the most important thing to remember, **you must consistently show through your job search materials, social media and communication with potential employers that you are what you say you are.** Lace your brand through every aspect of your job search strategy. Back up your claim of having helped people find financial freedom with supporting testimonials. Indicate, using actual numbers on your resume and elsewhere the degree to which you exceeded your sales goals, or cite the engagement analytics of your average client in your cover letter. Be able to do it in writing and verbally because, to them, YOU ARE YOUR BRAND. Exercise 4.1 at the end of this chapter will further help you develop your brand.

USING YOUR BRAND TO TARGET THE RIGHT COMPANY

Why you are targeting a company is as important to know as *how* you are targeting them because you want a good fit. Are you a real match? Does your brand meet their needs? You'll use your brand to eliminate any doubt that interviewers have about you. If your personal brand is clear, your job search will be much shorter because you'll only apply to organizations that are a good fit for you.

Once you have determined that a company is a good fit for you, use your brand to target organizations as follows:

- On your resume
- In your cover letter
- Throughout your e-portfolio
- On LinkedIn
- During interviews
- On any personal web profiles
- In daily conversations
- When networking
- In your elevator speech
- In your one-minute speech
- In personal or family conversations
- To make decisions about your professional appearance

Each of these marketing channels must be laser focused and conquered simultaneously. Knowing what to do and when to do it will increase the likelihood of multiple offers. Therefore, it's critical to work your brand statement into these strategies.

THE POWER OF SHARE© STORIES

SHARE© is an acronym for **S**ituation, **H**indrance, **A**ction, **R**esults and **E**motional Quotient or, **EQ**. SHARE© stories are verbal or written examples that bring to life your accomplishments and transferable skills. They allow the interviewer to better understand your "fit" within their company and you as a person. They are absolutely essential in being able to effectively communicate your brand to any interviewer at any level within the company. A potential employer says (or thinks), "We need someone who can do/has done *this*." You say, "I *have* done that. Here's a little story that illustrates a time when I did that well." SHARE© stories provide a format for describing a problem, what you did to solve it, how well you solved it, and what it is about you that allowed the solution to take place. The format for SHARE© stories is as follows:

Situation—Briefly describe a problem you faced or a situation in which you used the competency you wish to illustrate. Focus on work-related problems but, if you just graduated, it's okay to cite a problem you faced in school. See if you can boil it down to no more than two lines or three written sentences. Begin by giving a context (where and when you dealt with the problem).

Hindrance—List a barrier(s) that stood in the way of your solving the problem. These may include lack of resources (manpower or money), product faults, seasonal timing, uncooperative vendors, suppliers or coworkers, etc. Whatever the problem, be brief and specific and don't exceed two to three sentences. Note that potential employers *want to know* what stood in the way of your solving the problem. Your articulation of the issue is the key to this exercise begins to establish your capability and benchmark your added value. This single part of your story will allow you to later confirm your value to the company in interviews and negotiations.

Action(s)—Describe the actions you took to overcome the problem. Be specific and concise (no more than four sentences). *How* did you address the people, the lack of resources, etc.? *How* did you remove the hindrances?

Results—Next, report the results that occurred because of your actions. Results (*maximum* of two) MUST BE QUANTIFIABLE/MEASURABLE and or COMPARATIVE in nature. This is the second most important aspect of this exercise. When there are anywhere from 100-1000 resumes submitted for a given position, you must be able to dramatically distinguish yourself from the others. If you can move numbers, change things for the better or make an impact, they *will* hire you. Take your time. Think, think, think! The quantifiable results stated in the "R" section of the SHARE© story can also be presented using bullet points in both your cover letters and resume.

Emotional Quotient—This part of your story is as essential as the R (result) component but, instead of revealing numerical results, it conveys how you were perceived by your customers, boss, co-workers, team or organization *after* your success. It is only through other people that one accomplishes anything. Therefore, your ability to manage people and the perception of others is the linchpin for your success or failure. The E in SHARE is only placed where it is to create an easily remembered acronym. The actual E statement – or emotional appeal—may appear anywhere in your story.

Your ability to communicate what it is about you that enables you to "play well with others" is the spice to each of your SHARE© stories. Remember, they are hiring you for ALL of your abilities, not just those that you do alone to move numbers and achieve results.

You should know that SHARE© stories will rear their ugly heads over and over again in the rest of this book. They are critical every step of the way in getting employment because you never know when you may run into a potential employer who is looking for someone just like you, with your skills. It would be a shame to strike up a conversation with someone at a gym or grocery store and not have a great success story right on the tip of your tongue. Likewise, when you finally get an interview, SHARE© stories will be worth their weight in gold in convincing your interviewer you are the best possible candidate.

The more SHARE© stories you have, the better off you will be when faced with a series of interviews at the same company. Each of your SHARE© stories must not duplicate the skills expressed in any other SHARE© story. This may sound tough but try to think of all the things you do in a given day, all the projects you manage and all of the interactions you have with other workers. Each of these represents a particular problem with measurable outcomes.

You can't have enough SHARE© stories.

Being able to define your weaknesses and address them through SHARE© stories can also work to your benefit because doing so shows maturity. SHARE© stories that focus on your weak points must conclude by turning a negative into a positive and demonstrating how you overcame another similar problem and managed the problem to a positive outcome. Be creative in your approach. You must determine what will motivate the customer (hiring authority) to buy this product (you). You must also clearly demonstrate to the buyer what benefits are to be derived from purchasing the product.

Here is an example of how a SHARE© story would be used in an interview. Your interviewer says, "One of the best ways to manage people is to teach them to manage themselves. Tell me about a time when you contributed to a team's ability to direct itself?" Your response might be as follows:

S-SITUATION/PROBLEM:

When I joined my last company, I inherited a team that was considered talented and experienced but was seen as not pulling together.

H-HINDRANCE/CHALLENGE:

A few of the group members seemed to have hidden agendas, so there was some conflict within the group. This conflict was holding the group back from meeting their objectives.

A-ACTIONS:

I know that one of the keys to bringing a team like this together is dealing with goal congruence, which is the overlap between individual goals and group objectives, so my first action was to facilitate individual meetings in which I focused on each member's interests and strengths. Then, as a group, we discussed the group's objectives and how each member's personal interests and strengths would impact the team. Also, we discussed any negative attitudes that surfaced. Last, and very importantly, I encouraged each member to challenge any of my thoughts or decisions that had an impact on the team. That really brought the team together because they learned to trust me and each other.

R-RESULTS:

Those actions resulted in the team exceeding the department's goal by 33.5%. It also led to early problem solving as the team members felt free to come to me with issues that came up along the way.

E-(EQ)(EMOTIONAL QUOTIENT):

I have learned that listening to individuals in the context of building a functioning team is essential for bringing the group together. My participative management style consistently has produced effective teams. What was really nice is that other mangers started coming to me to see what I was doing with my team. How do you see this type of style fitting into your company/organization?

This example communicates to the receiver that you have numerous competencies other than team building. These include participative management, ability to address attitudes, communication, listening, early problem solving, concern for people and task, ability to create common goals, all of which result in goal attainment and increased cohesiveness.

SHARE© STORY FOLLOW-UP QUESTIONS

You may have noticed in the example that I ended with a question. You can assess your story's effectiveness and close the deal by asking questions when you are done. There are two kinds of questions: closed-ended and open-ended.

CLOSED-ENDED QUESTIONS

Closed-ended questions are answered with "yes," "no," or some other finite response, and frequently begin with "Does" or "Is." The ones shown below are provided ONLY so you understand their nature. Try not to ask a closed-ended questions unless it is impossible not to because they limit the amount of information you may receive in response. Try rephrasing each of the questions below as open-ended. Any one or all of them can be asked after you have presented a SHARE© Story.

- Does this example illustrate the kind of X skill that you need in this position?
- Does that answer your question? When asked in an open-ended way you can immediately follow it with a question that allows you to give a SHARE© Story, e.g., "Would you please tell me about....?")
- Does this answer, and the way I managed this process, fit with the way problems are solved here?
- Is that the type of X skill that you're looking for?
- Would this experience in X be useful here at X company?
- Does this illustrate the type of results you would expect in this position?

OPEN-ENDED QUESTIONS

Open-ended questions allow for an infinite number of responses. They frequently begin with "What" or "How." You can try one of the following open-ended questions as a follow up to your SHARE© Story:

- What are the key competencies you feel are most important for a candidate to possess for this position?
- How does this process work here at X company?
- What kind of personal qualities are you looking for in a person who takes this position? (Follow up with "It sounds like you are looking for a person with XYZ personal traits. When they answer you can immediately follow with, "Do you mind if I SHARE© an example of how I ...?"). Then share your story.
- What are some of the challenges your company faces right now? (Can be used after being asked about challenges you've faced and overcome.)
- What are the most immediate objectives that need to be met? (Works well when you are asked by a key decision maker how the first 90 days might look if you are selected for the position. Follow up your response with a question such as this to ensure you are meeting the goals of that decision-maker.)
- What are some of the concerns that keep you up at night? (Ask of key decision-maker. Follow up with a SHARE© story regarding a similar situation and how you resolved that situation.)

I strongly recommend that you MOSTLY use open-ended questions because they allow you to find out more about whether the company sees you as a good fit. **Prepare your open-ended questions in advance** so you don't make the mistake of asking a closed-ended question and ruining your chance of more extended and open dialogue with the employer.

Let's try to write SHARE© Story. Leaving space between each word, write Situation, Hindrance, Action(s), Result(s) and Evaluation on a piece of paper. Next, think of a competency you would like to convey to an employer and begin writing. Don't worry about exact wording for now; just focus on the story.

When you finish each SHARE© Story, give it a number and short title such as Learning Curve, People Skills, Crisis Management, P&L Management, Terminating Personnel, New

Sales Territory, etc. Keep working with your story until it flows well and is action packed but brief. Then, practice telling it (without reading) *aloud*. **Aloud practice of your SHARE© Stories is critical because you want to be able to remember them and articulate them smoothly whenever an opportunity arises.** Limit your story to no more than 60 seconds (60-90 seconds is passable). If your story runs more than 120-seconds, rework it.

ONE-MINUTE COMMERCIAL

The barber shop, beautician, grocery store, dog park or conference center. You never know when or where you will meet someone who can help you. Having a one-minute commercial ready is essential so you don't get caught off guard. A One-minute Commercial is a brief statement that describes what you do, what your top skills are, how well you do them and why you have been successful. Your commercial will be more general than your SHARE© Story.

One-minute commercials also double as answers to the statement, "Tell me about yourself" in an interview. They allow the interviewer to get a sense of who you are. One-minute commercials include the following components:

Your product identity/professional position (what you are). Your product identity may include your actual job title or a general phrase that is descriptive of what you do (senior operations specialist, business manager, non-profit executive director). Be sure to include the industry in which you are interviewing if possible.

Top skills. Draw this from your brand statement. Include a statement about your top key qualification areas or functional strengths.

Results/successes (how well you do what you do). Add a sentence providing some relevant quantified results you have achieved (a hard number like a percentage) and state a reason (behavioral competency) for your success as sort of a "teaser" for a SHARE© Story. You need to have the hard skills an employer seeks as well as the "likability" factor.

A question. Transition back to the acquaintance or interviewer by asking a question so he/she will know you are finished. Stay other-focused (not self-focused).

The length of your commercial should *not* exceed 60 seconds because if you are doing all the talking, then the focus is on you and it should always be primarily on the needs of an employer. Practice so your commercial flows naturally without sounding rehearsed. You should have several one-minute commercials ready so you can work them into conversations in different situations.

Here are several examples (written in a conversational tone):

SENIOR ACCOUNTANT

I am a senior accountant working for a large healthcare facility. I'm good at things like recommending cost-saving measures based on careful analysis of organizational data and processes. In fact, the system I work for now saved over $10,000 annually as a result of my recommendation to streamline their billing and supply-ordering procedures. My initiative and drive earned me the highest raise given in the department that year. May I ask you a bit about your role as [title] at [organization]?

MARKETING AND SALES PROFESSIONAL

I am a marketing and sales professional for with over 20 years of experience primarily in cable and telecommunications. I have substantial expertise in areas including new product launches; strategic planning; customer acquisition and retention; project management; budget development and control; team and employee development, and product branding/bundling. In fact, a recent bundling and customer contract program has generated over $6 million in incremental revenue and is being embraced nationally by the company. I've been successful due to mt focus on driving results with special attention to ROI and cash flow and the ability to fill my teams with strong executives. What's your role in [organization]?

ENTRY-LEVEL SOCIAL MEDIA COORDINATOR

I recently graduated from [university] with a degree in social media strategy. While in school I had a part-time job working as the social media coordinator for the career center. In that position, I focused on driving content that was useful and visually appealing to our targeted audiences and, as a result, increased our following by 307% in one year. I also did an internship managing the Facebook and Twitter platforms for a hospital and increased their traffic considerably. Do you know anyone who is looking for someone with these skills?

ALTERNATIVE LANGUAGE FOR NETWORKING

Because following your introduction with an immediate turn-around question is so important, I have provided here some suggestions for language you can use to turn your commercial into a mutually beneficial conversation. Consider using the following statements, depending on the circumstances.

"I'm trying to learn as much as I can about different companies and industries to determine where I would have the most impact and thought you would be someone who would be willing to share your expertise."

If you were referred by a mutual connection, try this: "I'm trying to learn as much as I can about different companies and industries so I can determine where I would add the most value, and George Smith suggested we meet because he thought you would be someone who would be willing to share your expertise."

These statements can be followed by a probing line of questions designed to learn more about the person's company or industry. Use needs-, challenges-, and opportunity-based questions such as:

- What do you see as the three greatest needs of the company/industry right now?
- What are the challenges that need to be overcome to meet those needs?
- If the challenges were overcome and the needs were met, what opportunities do you think the company industry would have over the next three to five years?

BUSINESS CARDS

They may seem old-fashioned, but people in business still use business cards and you should not be without them.

The design of your business card is up to you but should reflect your brand. Your phone number must be clearly visible. If you have one, put your web page on the front of the card as well. List three but no more than four competencies you have on the front at the left side of the card. Don't forget to use the back of the card to state your most import-ant accomplishments.

JAMES K. LONG

999-999-9999   Jklong9999@mail.org

CFO

www.careerwebfolio.com/JLong

- Cross-functional Leadership
- Performance/ROI   631 Charles Ct.
- Process Imp./Project Mgmt.   Somewhere, IN 46999
- International Management   999-999-9999

On the back of your card, put four of your outstanding accomplishments on the back of the card. There is absolutely no sense in wasting valuable real estate. Here are four from my client that he put on his card.

- 20% Reduction in compensation costs from productivity studies
- $6.0 million improvement from employee think-tank
- 89% improvement in manufacturing discrepancies

REBRANDING WHEN CHANGING CAREERS

Employees seeking a career shift must remember that the process requires patience. Switching to a new, more demanding career not only requires tenacity, finely tuned skills, and expertise, but also attention to your own personal brand. While reinventing your professional image may seem like a tremendous feat, it's important to remember that it's actually quite common in the corporate world and beyond.

According to Kandia Johnson, Communication Strategist, Corporate Motivator, and Business Writer/Entrepreneur,[14] it's important to seek out and remember many of the success stories of personal reinvention as a reminder and inspiration to stay motivated. Luckily, Johnson has shared some valuable guidelines for those ready to adjust their personal brand for the better. They are as follows:

CREATE A CLEAR MENTAL PICTURE OF YOUR PLANS

Ask yourself what is your chosen legacy? What are your strongest skills, interests, and values? Will the job you are seeking fit properly with your lifestyle?

Take the time to recognize your weaknesses and strengths and bridge any pre-existing gaps in experience before transitioning into your desired role. Create a clear strategy that includes your existing expertise, as well as a plan for obtaining any skills you may be lacking. This may include furthering your education or even pursuing lateral professional moves to build upon the experience you already have. Be patient as you execute your strategy.

Conne, my co-author, began her career selling radio advertising. Eventually, she was hired by a client to sell management development training and became interested in becoming a trainer herself. "I knew I needed a graduate degree. At 28, I quit my job, moved in with my mother and earned a master's, then a doctorate. It took a long-range plan and a lot of hard work, but it paid off."

---

14   Johnson, K. (2017). *Seeking an executive role? 5 tips for personal rebranding.* Retrieved January 15, 2021 from https://careerenlightenment.com/creating-a-personal-brand-wit h-out-being-a-jerk

IDENTIFY AND RECOGNIZE YOUR PRESENT PERSONAL BRAND

This process may require a certain sense of honesty and objectivity. Kandia Johnson suggests beginning by asking colleagues, mentors, or trusted managers about how you are perceived. Ascertain whether certain skills and strengths were mentioned repetitively or if there are any incongruencies between your own perceptions and the responses you received. Being candid about your own shortcomings, without being self-denigrating, is one of the most important steps toward self-improvement. Johnson further states, "Your brand is much more than your job description or title. It is defined by your relationships, and the value that you've delivered over time. Let your previous experience shine to help you stand out." One option is to create a couple of sentences that narrate what makes you a great match for the position you're seeking. Use your past experience description as a "selling point" toward your career objectives and focus on what makes you stand out among your competition.

ESTABLISH YOUR PRESENCE

For your efforts to be noticed, the public should have a general idea of your plans and skills. Create an e-portfolio, or professional website. Of course, be sure that you are active on LinkedIn, Facebook, and other applicable social media platforms, and ensure your resume is up to date. More on this in a later chapter.

SUCCESS STORY: BRANDING BENEFITS

CONTRIBUTED BY BILL TEMPLE, EXECUTIVE COACH, STEWART, COOPER & COON

Bob had relocated seven times and was on the road 40 weeks per year. He felt it was time to take control and build a life that was more balanced. Working in the constricted market of executive-level human resources, he had to develop a brand that made him really stand out.

I took Bob through the process of product branding to help him understand how he could differentiate himself. We focused on his intellectual (IQ), emotional (EQ) and historical (HQ) quotients to develop a product definition that was clear, succinct, and easily communicated in writing, orally and online. Then, we made sure he was targeting the right types and sizes of companies and using multiple channels simultaneously to communicate his value proposition to the right people.

The result of our effort was that Bob accepted an offer for a senior vice president of human resources role with a first-year total compensation package that exceeded $1,800,000.

ADDITIONAL RESOURCES

- Block, R. (n.d.). The value proposition. StewartCooperCoon.com. https://theusat-work.com/the-value-proposition/
- Coon, F. (n.d.). Revisiting the basics when creating your personal brand. StewartCooperCoon.com. https://theusatwork.com/revisiting-the-basics-when-creating-your-personal-brand/
- Tombrakos, J. (2020, July 22). A digital-first approach to personal branding is no longer optional. LinkedIn. https://www.linkedin.com/pulse/digital-first-approach-personal-branding-longer-joanne-tombrakos/

EXERCISE 4.1 PERSONAL BRAND STATEMENT

The goal of a carefully crafted and transparent personal brand statement is to be an opportunity magnet. It is not a promotional tagline. Don't feel compelled to stick exactly to this formula. Be creative in your approach to the format!

I use my _____ and _____ for _____.

Known for _____, I _____.

Using _____ (key trait), I _____, by providing _____.

Through my _____, I _____, when I serve _____.

EXAMPLE:

I energize, focus, and align manufacturing organizations to create sustainable acceleration of processes, reduction in waste, and growth of profits.

Write your personal brand statement here:

YOUR PERSONAL BRAND STATEMENT CHECKLIST:

My personal branding statement...	YES	NO
Is inspiring		
Is exciting		
Is clear		
Is engaging		
Speaks to my target audience		
Reflects my passions and values		
Makes me feel proud		
Feels familiar and comfortable to me		
Evokes times when I have felt most fulfilled and engaged in my life		
Total		

If you checked "yes" for at least 7 of the statements, your PBS is likely very effective. Revise your brand as necessary if you checked "yes" for less than 6.

CHAPTER 5
ACCOMPLISHMENT-FOCUSED RESUMES

Many people think of resumes merely as neutral, 1-page descriptions of what they have done. This is a mistake. You should think of your resume—the premier expression of your qualifications—as a document that will show employers **your value as it relates to *them*.** You can't do that through basic descriptions of your "duties and responsibilities." You have to build your brand by focusing on your accomplishments and quantifying (proving through numbers) your successes.

In this chapter I will walk you through the basics of writing a resume. I'll tell you:

- Why perfection is so important
- How to present your transferrable skills
- What types of resumes are most commonly used
- How to format and write a resume that is compatible with applicant tracking software (ATS)

The purpose of a resume is to secure an interview. Therefore, it should include enough information to entice the reader to call *you* instead of one of the many other applicants seeking the same position. Your resume and cover letter are the first two documents potential employers see and they serve to make a first impression. **Employers need *proof* that you are what you claim to be, and they will look for that proof in your documented accomplishments.**

You must be able to demonstrate clearly and concisely what you bring to the table AND your qualifications must be deemed more valuable than those of your competitors. You need a strong **value proposition**. Otherwise, you are just another piece of paper with lots of words and no compelling reason for them to call. You should not, however, falsify your capabilities or misrepresent yourself in any way. Andrew Ko, author, executive recruiter and career coach, indicates that recruiters and hiring managers get frustrated when you misrepresent your qualifications.[15] If you don't have the necessary degree or skills, move on with your job search. If you don't read the job description, how good an employee would you be?

THE MESSAGE UNDER THE MESSAGE

Before beginning the resume writing process, you should consider one very important concept that will increase your value proposition: **the message you send *under* the message**. Each of your job search materials conveys several messages about you as a worker. Employers want more than just your technical job skills. They want you to have high standards for yourself because they know your standards will be reflected in the quality of your work. They want to know you are articulate and detail oriented, and you can relate these personal qualities by making sure your materials are perfect. Their first impression of you will likely come through your resume, cover letter and webfolio/e-portfolio – *written* documents. You must consider the message you are sending about *yourself* that is related through how well you craft your documents. **In other words, the message *under* the message.**

Your resume is a living document in that it will evolve over the course of your career, but one thing must stay constant. Hiring managers, human resources professionals and recruiters are looking for, in addition to your hard and soft skills, your attention to detail, intelligence and judgement. Therefore, your resume must be perfect. **Perfect means *absolutely free* of spelling, wording and punctuation error, aesthetically pleasing, uncluttered, consistent and correct.** Tall order? Yup.

---

15   Coon, F. & Ko, A (hosts). (2018, September 14). Resumes: The good, the bad and the ugly (as told by an executive recruiter) [Audio podcast episode]. In *The US at Work*. Fred Coon Studio. https://theusatwork.com/208-resumes-the-good-the-bad-the-ugly/

The message a potential employer will receive is that not only do you have the right degree, experience and skills, you can also present your ideas professionally and correctly.

Conne told me this story. "I was at a bed and breakfast in Gettysburg, PA once. As is the custom, I had breakfast with other guests. After discovering my interest in resume writing one woman, who was the national human resources officer of a major non-profit organization said, 'If I open a resume and see even one thing out of place, it goes in the trash and I move to the next one.' The man sitting beside her, a vice president of his company, nodded his head and said, 'Absolutely.'"

Imagine receiving a resume on which someone had written they have excellent "intention to detail" or "exemplary communicational and writhing skills." You'd get a good laugh out of it, show it to a few colleagues and pitch it. Clearly, the applicant who does not take the time to proof his or her work is not the one for you. Worse, he or she may have proofed the resume and not have known the difference between "intention" and "attention" or "writhing" and "writing." Message sent: "I am lazy and won't make a good impression on clients or co-workers. I will also make you look bad because you hired someone who isn't up to par."

These are not the characteristics they have identified when they say they want a problem solver and good communicator who can get the job done. You may very well be able to get the job done, but at what level of performance and what level of quality? Enough said. Find at least three other people to critique and proof your resume and cover letter before they are sent.

Furthermore, you may need several versions of your resume. Perhaps you have just graduated with a degree in Communication. You may have taken classes and completed field work in production, public relations and social media and you'd be happy to begin your career in any of these fields. You should consider designing two or three customizable resumes for your targeted search and they should all be exemplary. Also, **every resume should be tailored to the job description because applicant tracking software will look for word matches**.

RESUME PREPARATION EXERCISE

Most people make the mistake of rushing the resume writing process. I urge you not to hurry. Instead, complete the *Resume Questionnaire and Work History,* Exercise 5.1. This exercise, found at the end of the chapter, includes steps for outlining your work history and identifying competencies. Completing it will take hours of thinking and preparation on your part. It is used to identify terms specific to your field of work, summarize your strengths and quantify your performance results for each position you have held. These are the building blocks of your resume.

I use this exercise with my clients. It helps them identify job skills and is used by my staff recruiters to code each candidate for placement on one or more national recruiter consortiums to which we belong. As you prepare answers to the questions, review all the exercises you have completed so far. You will find that certain ideas and words will jump out at you and you can use them to complete your history. Make sure you have each section filled out. Think about connecting your SHARE© stories to your job experience.

When you get to the Job History section, write a paragraph for every position you had in each company. You may want to show your journey of promotions at an organization. Establish unique and distinguishing items for each position that will set you apart from all the other candidates.

Once you have effectively described your talents and your problem-solving abilities, and can tell them how many mountains you can move, how far you can move them, and what resources you will use, you should be able to answer the most important question they will ask: "Why should we hire *you* [rather than someone else]?" The answers to this question should be documented on your resume worksheet and in your SHARE© stories.

TYPES OF RESUMES

My friends who are professional resume writers use many different formats and rules. This book will provide you with the basics of an effective resume. Choose whatever format makes you comfortable. However, **you must not try to shovel 10-lbs of dirt into a 5-lb bag**! Preparing two resumes is more effective than writing one resume that is confusing and cluttered. Also, don't get lazy and just change the title on your resume from one job application to the next. Think "tailoring" and match your resume language to the words used in each job description.

There are, however, several broad types of resumes to be used depending on your career field. These are the combination resume, the functional resume, the curriculum vita, the key word resume and the creative resume. It is okay to combine types to achieve your goals.

TRADITIONAL COMBINATION RESUMES

My personal preference is reverse chronologically ordered resumes. Combination resumes use the strengths of both the chronological and functional resume types. They feature key words that can be used for applicant tracking software (ATS) matching.

FUNCTIONAL RESUMES

Functional resumes are structured such that your accomplishments are grouped according to specific skill sets. Generally, employment information is listed separately from skills. The functional format is good to use for those over age 50, but recruiters hate this format (many employers as well) because it doesn't show whether you have the experiences they might be seeking.

CURRICULUM VITAE

CVs are detailed and lengthy documents listing all aspects of your education, publications, awards, service to institution, and work history. Nobody outside the academic systems of this country would even consider reading such a document because they are extremely long and most often don't tell the hiring authority how well you do your work, only what you did. You may want to combine your CV with elements of the traditional.

KEYWORD RESUMES

These documents are the least used and probably the least effective types of resumes. They do show specific skills but don't elaborate on them and, therefore, do not provide a basis for answering the question "Why should we hire you?"

CREATIVE RESUMES

Creative resumes are sometimes useful for those in graphic arts, desktop publishing or other industries in which being creative counts. They can be highly effective in fields demanding creativity and visual style, but don't use this type of resume otherwise. Consider combining this resume with a combination format and you might have a winner. Conne once told me, "I had a student who wanted to go into graphic design. She designed her resume as a trifold color brochure. It was well done and very creative. She got a lot of offers with it."

I've listed recommended books and provided several examples of professionally written resumes at the end of the chapter. Begin your strategy by choosing the right type of resume for you.

WRITING YOUR RESUME

This section may be why you purchased *Ready, Aim, Hired*. There are enough books on writing resumes to fill a small, town library. You can find sites with page after page devoted to resume writing on the internet. There is no one-size-fits-all type. However, certain elements covered here will increase your chance of attracting a potential employer and send the message that you are serious about working for them. These elements include the following:

- Effective word matching that works well with applicant tracking software (ATS)
- Proper formatting
- Accomplishment focus with numbers that support your claims
- Correct, non-neutral, sophisticated (but not fancy) word choices

EFFECTIVE WORD MATCHING THAT WORKS WITH APPLICANT TRACKING SOFTWARE

First, you *really* want to send your resume to the decision maker if possible but, since you may be told to submit your materials through a corporate website, you need to think about how to do both.

Try to secure the email address of the decision maker or, at least, the HR director, and you will be more likely to receive a call or an audience. Don't know who that is? Find out by phone or internet and send it to him/her. When you send your resume via email, put the job title or position number and your name in the subject line. Only send your cover letter and resume if you are truly qualified.

Put a short 3- or 4-line note in the email, nothing longer. A busy boss does not have time to read a long email. At some point in your campaign, a "gatekeeper" might screen you out, so apply online as well.

As I indicated in Chapter 1, one of the most dramatic changes in job searching over the past 10 years is that most organizations now use **applicant tracking software (ATS)**. You will use this software to upload your application materials.

Applicant tracking software, which from this point on will be referred to as ATS, is used to prescreen materials and rank applicants according to how well their materials match the job requirements and description. Many organizations get hundreds of applicants for a single position. ATS saves hiring authorities a great deal of time because many may simply look at the top 10 applicants. The downside is that a human being may never look at your application. You may be the best person for the job but, if you haven't tailored your materials such that they match the ad, you may be overlooked.

Robin Schlinger, Certified Resume Writer and Career Coach and owner of Robin's Resumes, is an expert on ATS. She says that there are hundreds of ATS systems but the one used most often is called Taleo and, if your materials pass Taleo's muster, they will get through most other systems.[16]

According to Jon Shields, Taleo, now owned by Oracle, is used by many heavy-hitting companies such as AT&T, Walgreens, Nike, Hewlett Packard and Starbucks.[17] Taleo will filter and rank your materials in several ways, depending on how the user sets it up.

First, Taleo incorporates "knockout questions" into the program. Knockout questions are often yes/no questions that may eliminate you from consideration. For example, for a warehouse job you may be asked whether you can lift 50 lbs. If you can't, you're eliminated. Knockout questions may also be set up with ranged answers that will be given fewer or more points. For instance, 3-5 years of experience will score lower than 6-10 years.

Second, you can earn bonus points on your score for having certain key word matches that the employer thinks are most important. Pay attention, therefore, to the "extras" section of the job description. If experience with Excel is mentioned and you have it, work it into your application.

---

16   Coon, F. & Schlinger, R. (Hosts). (2018, July 25). Beating the system: What job seekers should know about ATS scanning. In *The US at Work*. Fred Coon Studio. https://theusat-work.com/job-seekers-identifying-and-leveraging-transferrable-skills/

17   Shields, J. (2018). *Taleo: 4 ways the most popular ATS ranks your job application.* Retrieved January 15, 2021 from https://www.jobscan.co/blog/taleo-popular-ats-ranks-job-applications/

Third, Taleo will do a simple key word match. The more you have, the higher you'll rank. Users of this software can conduct Boolean searches for skills they particularly want to see, so closely examine the job description for repeated words and phrases and work these into your materials. Remember, though, not to be misleading.

When you are done writing your resume, run it through a program such as **jobscan. com**. These programs are designed to score your resume against the job description and give you a score. Aim for 80% or higher.

Schlinger also recommends NOT submitting your resume or cover letter as a PDF since many ATS will not read a PDF correctly. Send a Word file, but do not use tables, headers, footers or text boxes as they are also not ATS friendly.

Do not insert pictures, graphs, decorative lines, special characters like "é" or extra spaces into the document as these will sometimes cause ATS systems to reject your application. Use of italics and bold is okay.

RESUME FORMATTING AND CONTENT RULES

There are many types of aesthetically pleasing, effective formats to use when writing your resume. Personally, I avoid templates because I find them limiting. Most documents can be set up easily in Word or a similar program. Several factors should be considered when formatting your document and creating content. These include length, mechanics, aesthetics, sectioning, accomplishment focus and word choice. However, I'll begin with a few general rules.

1. **Focused, organized and unified.** Don't try to be everything to everybody. Target and focus. Perhaps you have experience in technical writing, reporting and social media. You're willing to take a job doing each of these but, if you are applying for a social media specialist position, *that* experience becomes most important and should be the focus of your resume.

   The tight organization of your document is also important. Be sure information is grouped in the proper sections. In other words, don't mix your education into your experience section.

   The concept of unification means looking at your job search materials as a total package with everything you are saying about yourself complementing everything others have said about you. When writing your resume, think about what is going to go on your website and in your cover letter. What do your testimonials and reference letters say? What can you prove? If your website and materials all point to computer programming, don't include a section on your portrait photography.

2. **Neat and letter perfect with no abbreviations.** You may know that the PRSA is the Public Relations Society of America, but the HR rep that is reading your resume won't. Abbreviate states (like ME for Maine), but don't abbreviate street names, the word "apartment," or anything else.

3. **Written in telegraph style with no reference to your wants, needs or desires.** Full sentences take up extra space and the letter "I" is overused, so eliminate "I," "my," and so forth. Also, they only care about you to the extent that you can make them money. They don't care about your desires. Instead of "I am a public relations specialist with the desire to use my education and experience to meet an organization's goals," try "Resourceful public relations specialist with over 7 years of experience building client relationships through social media such as Facebook, Twitter and Instagram." The later sentence would be loaded with words used in the job description.

4. **Specific, not vague.** Consider this sentence: "Recent college graduate seeking employment in the field of reporting." This tells potential employers nothing about what you can do. Also, it tips them off to your age. Tell them what you ARE and what you can DO. Furthermore, tell them how successful you have been. Try this instead: "Versatile journalist with 65 published feature articles and well-researched editorials. Skilled in storytelling and multimedia distribution." Again, the later sentence would be loaded with words used in the job description.

5. **Loaded with *non-neutral* language**. Many of the resumes I see are nothing but general statements using neutral language. Don't just say you did something. Say how well you did it. Back yourself up with hard numbers such as percentages and dollar figures. I'll cover this more in another section.

6. **A reflection of your unique skills, not characteristics everyone should have.** By the time you graduate from high school, you should be organized, punctual, responsible and have good communication skills. All employers will expect you to show up on time and do the work to the best of your ability. That's the least they

expect, so there is no need to list these qualities on your resume. Focus on skills listed in the job ad.

7. **Proper length.** There is no magic formula for the number of pages you need. The rule is that one is better than two, but only if you can adequately tell your story. You have probably heard that resumes should never be more than one page but, since most resumes are submitted electronically, there is no need to limit strictly to one page. However, I'd question why your resume is longer than *two or three* pages unless you are applying for an executive position. In most cases, excess length would occur because the document has not been formatted and worded for maximum efficiency.

Erin Greenwald, content strategist for the career coaching website, TheMuse.com recommends making your resume "skimmable."[18] She adds, "HR and hiring managers are not known for spending long periods of time reading each resume that comes across their desks, so remember to format accordingly. Proper use of bold type and bullet-points, and keywords can work to your advantage when employers are scanning or skimming your resume for key facts about your skills and work history."

My best advice is to write your resume without regard to length, then look for ways to cut it down. Slight adjustments to margins, removing a few words to decrease the number of lines, creating sections with columns for lists, and a few other tricks can go a long way.

Be concise, though. Use no more than five lines for each point. You can vary this rule depending on the number of jobs you have had as long as you are not redundant. If you have more than five, combine them to create fewer lines on the page.

If you can't pack the last 15-20 years into two pages, you haven't done a good job of clarifying who you are and why they should hire you. I will tell you that I use the 15-20-year rule in most cases. You may have worked 25-30 years but the last 15-20 really tell what you can do now. The same is true if you are just beginning your career. If you are a college graduate and don't want to be perceived as a high school student, don't add high school experience. Employers will look for relevant college experiences.

---

18 Greenwald (n.d.). As cited in Coon, F. (2017). *Frequently overlooked resume advice to help you get hired.* Retrieved July 20, 2020 from https://theusatwork.com/frequently-overlooke d-resume-advice-to-help-you-get-hired/

Typically, higher level positions will require longer resumes. This makes sense because, if you are applying for a management or executive position, you have probably had a longer career. However, the young MBA, engineer, accountant, HR person looking at your application is probably thinking that you might appear too old, too expensive and probably too inflexible in your business approach with that many years behind you.

8. **Free of mechanical and technical problems with consistent margins**. Don't forget that applicant tracking software is not user friendly to every style. Call the human resources department at the organization to which you are applying and ask which system they use. Then, you can avoid incompatibility issues by researching the characteristics of the software they use.

9. **Marginated properly**. All margins are to be no less than 1 inch and a 1.25" left margin is preferred. Sometimes, you may have to go to a .5" margin but **do not** go below a .5" margin. *Readers want to see some white space*. In addition, many people will print the resumes they find most interesting and write notes in the margins. Give them a place to do that. Set your margins for flush left, NOT flush left and right, which creates odd spaces between words.

10. **Set up with standard font sizes and styles**. Some fonts are easier on the eye than others and, therefore, increase readability. Also, these fonts are more user-friendly with ATS. Arial, Calibri and Times New Roman are safe bets. Use *no less than* 10-point type size, but 12-point is preferrable. Slightly larger (14-16 point) bold can be used for your name. Italics and bold in the same font are fine. Don't use little-used or little-known fonts and **don't use more than one font style**. Readability can also be improved with line spacing increased to 13- or 14- point and paragraph spacing at 4- to 7-point. Here is what the three recommended fonts look like:

Arial

Calibri

Times New Roman

11. **Aesthetically pleasing with an F- or Z-pattern.** Many resume formats are acceptable as long as they are ATS friendly, but you should understand that *overlapping* use of bold, underline, italics, bullets, etc. will make for a very cluttered look. Think of your resume as having tight structure. You'll have major sections such as work history

and education, etc. Under each, you'll have unlabeled items such as job titles that you will distinguish using bold. Distinguishing with bold *and* italics *and* underlining is not necessary.

Overuse of bullets can add clutter as well. Think about it. If you see a list with each item appearing on a separate line, don't you instinctively know that each item is different from the others? Bullets usually create unnecessary characters for the eye to absorb. If you must use them, choose small ones and be consistent.

Employers make the decision to read resumes fully within 6 seconds. They skim the document with their eyes going in either an F-pattern or a Z-pattern.[19] **You should use one of these patterns to set up your resume but remember that ATS will look for *keyword* matches, so use keywords from the job description within whatever pattern you choose.**

MAJOR SECTIONS OF YOUR RESUME

The major sections of your resume will of course depend on you and your chosen field. For instance, medical licensing may be important in certain fields, but would not appear on every person's resume. The resume examples at the end of the chapter represent a variety of formats. However, the following sections are typical for most resumes:

- Name and contact information
- Title or position sought
- Profile, brand statement or list of key skills
- Work experience
- Educational achievement
- Technical training
- Accomplishments/honors/awards
- Professional association memberships
- References

NAME AND CONTACT INFORMATION

First, *don't set up a Word heading* as it may not be compatible with ATS. Use tabs. The key elements to be placed at the top of your resume are your name, telephone number, email address and website (LinkedIn, or another personal website). Your address is optional and

---

19   Bigman, A. (2019). *6 principles of visual hierarchy for designers.* Retrieved January 18, 2021 from https://99designs.com/blog/tips/6-principles-of-visual-hierarchy/

should be used if you think the organization may be looking to hire locally. For security purposes, think about whether you want to have your home identified on Google maps.

Type your name beginning flush left in 14-point, bold font (16-point can be used if you have room). To save lines, you can tab over a few spaces and type your phone number also in 14-point, but not bold. Use only ONE number and don't label it as "phone" or "cell." People will know it is a telephone number. Under that, type your email address. Don't label that either. Place your website on the top as well wherever you think it looks best. If you have a personal web profile, list the URL for that, as well.

TITLE OR POSITION SOUGHT

Place your current title under your contact information. Center it. If you are not working, think of using a broad title of the position you are seeking. For example, you may not currently be working as a data analyst, but you have been trained to analyze data and you want a position in that field. It's okay to list Data Analyst under your name. You can see, however, that you would not want to list Healthcare Operations Data Analyst unless 1) you were currently employed under that title or 2) you ONLY want to apply for jobs with the same title.

PROFILE, BRAND STATEMENT OR LIST OF KEY SKILLS

Profiles/brand statements have replaced goals and objectives. Profiles are **two or three sentence** descriptions of your "professional self." Think about what you have to offer an employer and, more importantly, what they are looking for in you. Keep the wording telegraphic and don't use "I." Don't distinguish yourself as a student, recent graduate or senior. The first word(s) of your profile should be what you do (data analyst, etc.). Review Chapter 4 on brand statements.

Instead of including a profile, consider listing key skills next on the document (keep the F- or Z-pattern in mind). This section is a great place to **word match with the job ad**.

WORK EXPERIENCE

Assuming you are using a combination resume format, the next section should include your work experience. If you feel your education is critical to obtaining the position, you can list it before the work section. Most employers, though, will focus on your experience—what you have done and how well you have done it.

If you have had many jobs in your career, employers may wonder whether you will quit if the going gets tough. Therefore, you should explain frequent job changes. "Job-hopping can be quite common in this day and age," states career coach Erin Greenwald, "but if you have this type of resume, don't expect hiring managers not to wonder why." Greenwald reminds job seekers to "Include a reason for leaving next to each position, with a succinct explanation like 'company closed,' 'layoff due to downsizing,' or 'relocated to new city.' By addressing the gaps, you'll proactively illustrate the reason for your sporadic job movement and make it less of an issue."

List the relevant jobs you have had over the past 15 years (fewer if you are at the beginning of your career) in reverse chronological order, by title first. See the examples at the end of the chapter. We also have provided additional before and after versions of resumes on our web site at Stewart, Cooper and Coon. They are not copy-protected, so please feel free to select one you like and use the format for your own.

EDUCATIONAL ACHIEVEMENT

List educational achievements, starting with your highest academic achievement and working backwards: Ph.D. first, M.B.A. second, etc. each on a separate line. If you are only partially through a degree, list it, followed by the phrase "expected graduation [date]."

Do NOT make it look like you have a degree when you don't. This will kill you when references are checked. Don't list high school if you've graduated from college. Be sure to list any study abroad experience you had. International study gives a very positive message under the message. It says you are willing to try new things and are experienced functioning in different cultures. Also be sure to list certificates you have earned, especially those that complement your career goals.

TECHNICAL TRAINING

Technical training is not to be confused with education, so don't mix the two. List any computer or foreign languages, courses, programs, or seminars in which you have received licenses, earned accreditation, been credentialed, or received C.E.U.s. Include certificates such as CPR, business or supervisory skills, or public relations. Even free, online webinars related to your work count as technical training.

ACCOMPLISHMENTS/HONORS/AWARDS

Whether you are entry or senior level, you don't want to omit anything that makes you seem like a winner in your field. If you won any kind of award or have been honored in some way, list it in this section. Scholarships (if you are in college) can also be listed in this section, as well as patents. If you have recently graduated from college, it's okay to list your grade point average (if it is above 3.3) or that you made dean's list. Just remember that, by doing so, you may distinguish yourself as too young for the position. Remove it after you get your first job.

Honors bestowed by your community can sometimes be listed in this section. Volunteerism is important to organizations these days because they want to be perceived as giving back to their communities. In fact, some people include a separate section on volunteer activities on their resume. I don't recommend that unless it seems germane to your career and would caution against listing anything that affiliates you with a political party or religion since those subjects may be hot buttons for someone otherwise interested in you. Use your judgement depending on the job for which you are applying.

PROFESSIONAL ASSOCIATION MEMBERSHIPS

List all relevant association memberships. If you are serving on a committee, list that as well (especially if you are chair). Sometimes people list community organizations such as Rotary here as well but do so only if the organization could in some way be perceived as related to your career or in keeping with the mission of the organization to which you are applying.

REFERENCES

DO NOT use the phrase "references available upon request" in place of listing 3-4 references. This is an outdated practice that used to be done to get an employer to contact you. Searching for the right person to fill a position is time consuming, however, and busy managers don't want to take extra time to call you for information you should have provided in the first place. **Choose references that can speak to how well you do your job and the job for which you are applying**. DO NOT list relatives or personal references. They don't care whether your uncle thinks you are good at your job. Conne once called the references for a teaching position her department was trying to fill. "When I asked, 'What are her strengths as a teacher?'" she told me, "the reference said weakly, 'Um, I don't know. I have never seen her teach.'" What? Why did this candidate list someone who has never seen her teach as a reference for a teaching position?!

Finally, ask your references for permission to list them and ask them what they might say about you. You don't want anyone to be caught off guard. Send them a copy of your resume. Think about the negative impression it would make if one of your references said, "Dan? He's looking for a job? I haven't talked to him in years." Keep in touch with your references throughout and after your job search. Be ABSOLUTELY positive that all contact information is up to date and accurate.

When you list your references, use the following format:

- First and last name with courtesy title (Mr., Ms., Dr.)
- Organizational title
- Name of organization
- Phone number
- Email address

You don't need a full mailing address since a potential employer is not likely to write to him or her.

ACCOMPLISHMENTS WITH FOCUS ON NUMBERS

Accomplishments are extremely important. In fact, they are critical. Why? Because **they establish your potential value to the company or organization**.

Reference to accomplishments in your search materials is designed to say in the barest and most simple terms *how well* you did what you did. They should always contain one or more of the following: **a number, percentage, or dollar amount**—something that quantifies how well you did your job. For example:

103.6% audience increase. Developed social media strategy and created audience centered content that grew return on investment.

Notice that I have built a bolded number into the statement. It also begins the sentence. I like to put numbers *first in the sentence* wherever possible. People read numbers first. You want them to consider why they should hire you! However, using numbers first in every sentence is boring and looks contrived so mix it up.

Also notice I used a number with a decimal point. Numbers are magical in job searching because they boost credibility. Using an odd number with a decimal point seems exact and will increase the chance that an interviewer will ask you about your success. *Don't make up numbers* but you must be able to state how well you do your job. **Use this tactic throughout your job search materials.**

Using the resume preparation worksheet, list on separate lines your quantifiable achievements for each company for which you worked. Build in past tense action verbs (implemented, managed, organized, etc.). If you are still employed, use the present tense (implement, manage, organize, etc.).

Here are some questions to get you thinking about your accomplishments. You can mentally tailor them to your job. Most jobs are related to increasing *something* like customer satisfaction, accuracy, profit, etc. What did you do that helped your organization meet goals?

1. How many customers did you serve daily/weekly/monthly?

2. How many people did you supervise?

3. How many times were you asked to do something significant?

4. For how much business were you responsible?

5. What was the highest amount of money you saved or earned your company?

6. How much inventory or stock did you move?

7. How much pressure was there? Did you work under deadline?

8. Were you "promoted in 5 [or whatever] months?"

9. What have your performance evaluations indicated about your progress?

Be as accurate as you can with the measurement of your success and DON'T add anything you can't prove. Trust me, they will either ask you or one of your references to verify your claims.

WORD CHOICES THAT ARE CORRECT, NON-NEUTRAL AND SOPHISTICATED (BUT NOT FANCY)

The phrase "sophisticated language" in terms of resume writing means using sentences that are abbreviated (also called telegraphic) and action-packed with meaning. It does not mean you will create overblown job titles like Horticulture Nutrition Specialist for Greenhouse Worker.

Here's an example (before):

I worked at Houser Aviation Museum in an internship last summer where I assisted the director of the museum with daily tasks and helped make a video. This video was for them to raise money for the museum, and it worked (41 words).

Not only is this sentence awkwardly written, but many of the words don't add *value*. An employer would likely read this and think, "What 'work' did you do? In what way did you 'assist' and 'help?' What kind of video was it? Was it successful?"

Here it is rewritten (after improvement):

$4,500 in donations attributed to impact of original promotional video created during internship at Houser Aviation Museum. Researched, scripted, photographed, and designed graphics (23 words).

Please notice that I removed the words "helped" and "assisted" because they minimize what you did. If you assisted, you *did*. However, you don't want to pull the wool over anyone's eyes so, if you think it's necessary, you can say you "collaborated with."

Also, check your resume for words that are redundant or implied, and phrases that could be replaced with single words. Is it necessary to say you did something on a day-to-day basis? Sometimes yes, but most often it isn't. "Day-to-day basis" could be replaced with "daily" if need be. Remove words and phrases like "in fact," "in the field of" and so on. If you are in *the field of* sales, you are in sales. The fact that sales is a "field" is implied.

I encourage my clients to see if they can express accomplishments in 21 words or less. Fifteen is better. One way to avoid this is to not repeat the same action verb. On your Resume Worksheets form, you used action phrases describing how you handled certain tasks. Review them and see if there are any you can use in developing the information on your resume.

NEVER repeat a verb! There are enough for you to choose from without doing this. Any good college writing instructor will tell you never to repeat a word in the same paragraph unless it is impossible not to do so. Moreover, don't repeat one in the entire document, unless there is no alternative. The reader wants to view as many facets of your work initiative as possible.

Make sure your job title is easily understandable as well and don't use obscure vocabulary. Pick words that are familiar to a variety of readers. Whenever possible, use short phrases that are easily readable and "eye scannable" by any reader.

When describing your current position, make sure that you use the current tense and in past positions, the past tense. Don't use false information or dates in your resume. They can be grounds for termination.

Check for parallel structure in lists. Parallel structure is wording that follows the same pattern, like creativity, dependability and flexibility as opposed to creative, dependable and flexibility.

If you are not getting hits on a particular style of resume, change styles. You are now ready to begin piecing your resume together. Good luck and remember you can always use the examples provided in this book.

SUCCESS STORY: THE RIGHT RESUME

CONTRIBUTED BY CONNE REECE, CO-AUTHOR AND EDITOR

Nick had been working in the hospitality field but had an interest in human resources. He had moved from his role as a banquet manager into a coordinator position in human resources and recruiting, and was ready to move up. His resume revealed a history of quick promotion, flexibility and knowledge of human resources processes but, after sending out numerous applications, he just wasn't getting any interviews.

I worked with Nick to reorganize his resume and make it more aesthetically pleasing. We moved key skills to the top, reorganized major sections, replaced unnecessary words with more descriptive, concise language and added numbers. He then customized each resume, using key words from the job ads to boost his luck with applicant tracking software programs.

Within weeks, Nick had offers for five interviews. He accepted a position as a human resources specialist with a 38% raise.

ADDITIONAL RESOURCES

- Doyle, A. (2020, September 17). *Why and how to include numbers on your resume: Tips for quantifying your achievements on your resume. TheBalanceCareers.com.*
- https://www.thebalancecareers.com/why-and-how-to-include-numbers-on-your-resume-2063136/
- The Muse Editor (n.d.). *185 powerful action verbs that will make your resume awesome.* The Muse. https://www.themuse.com/advice/185-powerful-verbs-that-will-make-your-resume-awesome/

EXERCISE 5.1 RESUME AND WORK HISTORY QUESTIONNAIRE

Please complete the information below for each position you have held. Start with your most recent job.

1. What is the purpose of your job search (new career, unemployed, etc.)?
2. What is the preferred industry for your job search?
3. What is your desired job title?

Overall, you will need a clear understanding of what types of jobs you are looking for in order to tailor your resume. **Your resume will be focused on the jobs you are looking for**, not just your past jobs. Complete the section below with your previous and possible future jobs in mind.

1. Provide 5 terms that describe you at work.
2. Provide 3-5 ways that you are a better choice than other candidates applying for the same position? If you would prefer, list 3-5 personal and/or professional characteristics that set you apart from your peers in your current position?
3. Add any additional information that is not included in your current resume that will help you develop your new branding documents.

WORK HISTORY

Current Employment:

Company:

City/State:

Brief Summary of the company:

Job title:

Start date:

End date:

Briefly describe your role, including size/scope figures in terms of dollars and people managed.

ACHIEVEMENTS

When developing a list of achievements include actions taken and results (see example).

Company:	XYZ Corporation—Texas
Position:	President
Achievement:	Increased EBITDA from $9 to $20 million, reduced working capital by $25 million or 60%, and increased ROCE from 4% to 20% by developing and implementing a new continuous improvement operating model to increase profitability, cash flow, and human & EHS performance.
Key Qualification:	Transformational Leadership

Complete the section below for each of your employers in the past 15 years:

Company:

City/state:

Brief summary of the company:

Job title:

Start date:

End date:

Briefly describe your role, including size/scope figures in terms of dollars and people managed:

Achievements at the organization (focus on **numbers** here):

1.

2.

3.

4.

5.

EDUCATION HISTORY

Name of institution:

Degree earned:

Date received (optional): If you are recently graduated, it will be okay to list your date of graduation. *However, for those that are moving from 1st or 2nd job to another position, do not list your graduation date.*

Noteworthy academic achievements/honors/GPA/study abroad/languages spoken (optional, for new graduates):

TRAINING AND OTHER SKILLS

Describe additional training, courses, workshops, seminars you have attended that are not listed on your existing resume. Include certifications.

Describe your computer/technical skills:

HONORS AND AWARDS

List awards you have received for your work or community involvement (nothing from high school):

PROFESSIONAL ASSOCIATION MEMBERSHIPS AND POSITIONS HELD

Don't forget to list accomplishments here as well.

List any other information that may be relevant:

EXERCISE 5.2 KEY QUALIFICATIONS AND CORE COMPETENCIES

Sample key qualifications/core competencies include cross-functional leadership, program/project management, operations optimization, strategic planning and implementation, business development and more.

Identify 6-9 competencies. Choose a heading for each group and list the underlying skills. See below for ideas on grouping skills under broader headings.

SALES/MARKETING:

brand management, channel marketing, new product development, new target markets, marketing plans, account management, sales forecasting

BUSINESS DEVELOPMENT:

market analysis/trending, forecasting, client presentations, partnerships/alliances

STRATEGIC PLANNING:

business plans, business re-engineering, capital expenditure planning, consolidations, outsourcing

FINANCIAL MANAGEMENT:

accounting management, auditing, cash management, debt negotiations, financial reporting, financial statement analysis, ROI analysis

LEADERSHIP:

consensus building, corporate culture and change, employee hiring / selection, performance improvement, goal setting, coaching/mentoring, motivating staff, organizational development, people management, policies and procedures, profit planning, training, team building

SAMPLE RESUMES

The following resumes, which represent entry- to executive-level examples, have been contributed by several authors. Conne Reece contributed the first and Robin Schlinger the second. Numbers 3-6 were written by Laura Slawson and the rest by my team at Stewart, Cooper & Coon. Most authors, including our team at Stewart, Cooper & Coon, use the following rules as a guideline. Use them as a review before examining the samples.

- **Brevity**—Don't bore the reader with too much unnecessary detail. Communicate value.

- **Proper Positioning**—Client positioning comes first. Use large letters in the position title, so that hiring authorities can quickly see the position or job types being targeted by the candidate. Tailor your title and supporting information for each job for which you apply.

- **Expertise Areas**—List your desired area of expertise and positioning. This is another chance to use key words that match the job description.

- **Strategic Competencies**—Examples include transforming operations, forging strategic alliances, and boosting customer satisfaction.

- **Description of Capabilities**—This section becomes the starting point for including key words that match the job description and includes behavioral competencies. ATS systems look for repeated key words matching their job description, so match as many as you can.

- **Core Competencies**—List the most important competency to head the top left column. It is the place where people begin reading. The phrase or word you use will remain in their mind as they scan the rest of the resume to see if you can do that particular thing. The second most important phrase is located at the top of the right-hand column. The rest are filled in below those and support. Competencies are important and need to match the job description key words as closely as possible. Remember this. ***Everything you list in the positioning, title, or key competency sections, MUST be supported by a quantifiable and/or measurable achievement.***

- **Company Name and Description**—Along with the company name and location, as well as the years you worked there, the next sentence should be a *brief* description (*in italics*) of what the company does and its size. For example: *A $200M widget man-ufacturing firm with 2,000 employees and production facilities in six states.*

- **Strategic Management Statements** - Under each listed position, organize your accomplishments into strategic management categories so each bullet point under that stated capability supports and reinforces your claim of competency in that area. Use different phrases and management or work styles terms to demonstrate your well-rounded problem-solving abilities.

- **Bullet Points**—Start each bullet point with a number. If the reader is in a hurry and most are, they will scan in an F or Z pattern. They **always** look at numbers before words. Odd numbers increase subliminal credibility. Numbers with decimal points are emphatic and usually will be asked about during your interviews allowing you to present your SHARE Stories.

There are many resume formats from which you can choose. Your resume doesn't need to be pretty or fancy. What *is* important is that you, the candidate, clearly communicate your value to the reader. Here's the bottom line: your objective is to have the hiring author-ity say, "We should talk to this candidate." This statement is the best one can hope for!

DANIEL T. KILLICK, JOURNALIST

(570) 555-1234
666 Vita Place
Town, State, Zip code

DanKillick@dmail.com
www.DanKillick.com

KEY SKILLS

Investigative Reporting	AP Style	News Editing
Photography/videogra-phy Research	Google Analytics Layout	QuarkXPress Layout Ethics and Journalistic Law

EXPERIENCE

Writer and Editor, Student Newspaper, XYZ University, 2020-2021

23 articles published. **42** edited. Improved clarity, accuracy and style as reviewer of all news stories. Held leadership role in brainstorming story ideas, directed staff to meet deadlines, revised drafts and wrote original features. Used QuarkXPress as layout artist of **50+** features pages.

Freelance Video Producer, ABC Aviation Museum, Summer 2020

$4,500 in donations generated from original, promotional 5-minute video during internship at ABC Aviation Museum. Researched, scripted, conducted interviews, shot, edited and created graphics.

Assistant Manager, Electronics Department, Wal-Mart, 2020-present

Quickly promoted from entry-level associate to assistant manager. Devised system of rewards for supervisees through which shift managers covered for associates during extra 10 minutes off per shift. System adopted at **5** other Wal-Mart stores.

EDUCATION

Communication Bachelor of Arts with focus in Journalism, 2021
Paderborn University, Germany, 1-year study abroad, 2019. Fluent in German.

ACCOMPLISHMENTS

Four semesters on dean's list while working full time. **GPA 3.75**

President, Lambda Pi Eta communication honors society. Provided clear information to media during crisis, managed budget of **$500**. Established and maintained Facebook, Twitter and Instagram accounts.

Treasurer of Media Club for 2 years. Coached 6 club members in 4k run for Ulman Cancer Foundation.

PROFESSIONAL MEMBERSHIPS

Student Society of Professional Journalists
    Phi Beta Delta Society for International Scholars

REFERENCES

Professor's Name (someone who knows your work)	**Manager's Name (someone who knows your work)**	**Director's Name**
Professor of Communication	General Manager	Director
XYZ University	Wal-Mart Montoursville	ABC Aviation Museum
(555) 555-5555	(555) 555-5555	(555) 555-5555
Name@XYZ.edu	Name@Walmart.com	Dir@AviationMuseum.com

CONTRIBUTED BY CONNE REECE

MIKE DOUGLAS

Atlanta, GA 30308 | info@robinresumes.com | 404.875.2688

CHIEF DIGITAL / TECHNOLOGY OFFICER

Transformational and Inspirational Leader

Proven Track Record of Leading Diverse, Vibrant Teams

Retail | Commerce | Federal Government Clients - Held Top Secret Clearance

Customer Facing | Mobile Applications | Websites

Creative and innovative thought leader and transformation agent, with direct experience as a senior executive and enterprise systems digital and technology leader for large-scale, enterprise-wide operations for retail, commercial, and government organizations. Manage and deliver IT and business strategy, roadmaps, vision, architecture, engineering, and software for complex mission-critical systems, applications, products, and services.

Provide the digital and technology vision to delight customers, meet enterprise-wide requirements, modernize and integrate operations across channels, and focus on success and growth.

Deliver exceptional results while attracting, recruiting, developing, and retaining technical talent. Quickly deliver new projects and technologies by managing a wide range of mobile applications, web operations, development, analytics, planning, and IT team efforts. Strong track record of achievement for a wide variety of organizations.

PROFESSIONAL EXPERIENCE

President | Chief Digital / Technology Officer   1994 - Present
ATLANTA Technologies Corporation | Atlanta, GA

Manage up to 190 Personnel | Contracts worth up to $300M total value | Target up to 52M customers

Provide Information Technology (IT)-based executive leadership and professional services to a wide variety of commercial and public-sector clients by running all company operations, partnering with leading organizations, hiring personnel, and directing up to 190 personnel. Obsess on delighting customers and meeting the mission requirements.

STRATEGY: Direct company's and clients' digital and technology strategic vision. Develop and deliver company operating and capital budgets to move company capabilities forward. Partner with senior executives and CEOs to provide the best customer service.

PEOPLE: Put the customer first while communicating effectively with senior leaders, clients, and team members. Demonstrate effectiveness while leading and motivating digital and IT teams. Attract, recruit, develop, and retain technical talent, making all feel a part of the business. Drive program success.

KEY HIGHLIGHTS
- **Demonstrated success with a wide variety of clients, including retail, commercial, and governmental organizations.**
- **Saved organizations millions of dollars by conceiving, developing, transforming, and implementing digital and technology solutions.**
- **Delighted customers by providing superior leadership, innovation and customer experiences.**
- **Hired and motivated digital and IT teams.**

TECHNOLOGY: Delight customers and meet program requirements. Drive new technology, product development, and management best practices by staying current with emerging trends. Partner with operations to enhance results. Evolve AGILE development methodology, achieve objectives, and ensure security.

EXCEPTIONAL RESULTS FOR RETAIL CUSTOMERS - REPRESENTATIVE PROJECTS

Rock Drug Corporation (now Major Pharmacy Chain)
- **Senior Executive:** Served as the Technology Advisor on Board of Directors (over $100 million organization).
- **Modernized company's mail order pharmacy system:** Innovatively automated fulfillment center, interaction validation, order management, and marketing and developed IT structure.
- **Led People:** Managed geographically-dispersed international 40-person senior associate/extended 70+-person teams.

Big Truck Rental
- **Analytics:** Enabled >400 users daily to project and manipulate all Big Truck Rental rates and inventory levels nationwide after automating nightly forecasting (analytics) by developing 3 Revenue Management Systems.
- **Quality | Led People:** Developed 4 systems with zero support calls by leading a geographically-dispersed team, championing the deployment of technology innovations, and developing a comprehensive error-handling system.
- **Saved Rental Firm $35M:** Developed yield management systems leveraging highly-complex demand forecasting engines, providing near real-time rates, and delivering inventory control for every retail site nationwide.

SUPERIOR LEADERSHIP FOR EMERGENCY RESPONSE CUSTOMERS - LARGE PROGRAM SUCCESS

Federal Agency Insurance Program (FAIP)

- **Managed migration and transition for $300M contract:** Migrated, transitioned, and subsequently operated and maintained business operations with over 40 distributed internal and publicly-facing web-based and mainframe systems with millions of lines of code supporting ~ 7M policyholders with above $1.50T total coverage, and the Write Your Own (WYO) Program's 49 private insurance companies with brick and mortar locations.
- **Improved policyholder customer experience | saved $12M/year support costs:** Streamlined operations, enabled modernization, enabled fact-based customer decisions, and transformed operations by migrating to the Federal Cloud
- **Led People:** Managed transition of 180-geographically-dispersed IT and business operations professionals to new operational roles and responsibilities across 7 IT groups and 5 business groups in 120 days.
- **Technical Champion:** Deployed technological innovations ensuring systems and applications scaled in the target Federal Cloud Platform as a Service (PaaS) and Infrastructure as a Service (IaaS) environment.
- **Enhanced customer engagement:** Established collaborative relationships and briefed key customers and partners.

EXCELLENCE FOR COMMERCE CUSTOMERS - SELECTED SOLUTIONS HIGHLIGHTED

Enumeration Mobile Platform for Adaptive Services and Solution (EMPASS) | Major Agency

- **Addressed $3B problem:** Informed and educated the organization how mobile technology could successfully be implemented to meet enumeration requirements (paper processing increased costs $2.5B).
- **Targeted ~1.5 M Users | ~52M Customers:** Created a strategy and architecture and directed the digital experiences' execution targeting users and customers.
- **Drove technology innovation:** Developed and delivered a solution for intelligent data collection across mobile applications and the web, which could be deployed on any platform with integrated case management, GPS location-based mapping, and routing, and questionnaire with near real-time updates of late returns, case assignments and contact strategies operating in both connected in disconnected states on Android, iOS and Web platforms

Systems Engineering Support for the Survey Design Initiative (ASDI) | Second Major Agency

- **Enterprise-wide data collection:** Collaborated and drove cost efficiencies for retiring unique, survey-specific systems and redundant capabilities via supporting architecture and engineering for the $22M Enumeration Data Collection and Processing (EDCP) program, a major initiative with the Chief Technical Officer (CTO) and stakeholders' organization-wide and delivering an integrated solution.
- **Collaborating:** Teamed with Big4 Consulting to successfully secure contract by responding to Request for Quote (RFQ), preparing and delivering oral presentations, and updating and resubmitting the proposal to the Census Bureau
- **Strategic leadership:** Developed strategy and national standards organization alignment and engagement by collaborating and championing it with the Census Chief Data Architect to form it across the organization.

Unified Tracking System (UTS)

- **Data Warehouse | Analytics:** Enabled the delivery of a data warehouse, providing Census and Survey operations leadership a view of near-real-time indicators of cost, progress, and data.

Past Survey Support

- **Operational transformation:** Led the AGILE lifecycle development of more than a dozen accuracy and coverage management, and developed proprietary systems handling extremely large datasets and implementing inline ETL from R&D through production.
- **Quality:** Ensured data quality, accuracy, coverage, and measurement by architecting, designing, developing, and implementing 14 innovative high-volume systems.
- **Innovative technology:** Enabled processing of >80M maps for the organization's Geography Division by delivering new translation technologies for its proprietary vector geographic mapping language.

CUSTOMER SUPPORT FOR THIRD MAJOR AGENCY

SUPPORT CENTER SUPPORT | Major Agency

- **Modernized operations:** Supported systems architecture and engineering across the agency's projects and programs, including a modernized vision and strategy implementation for 15 projects worth over $1.5M over 7.5 years.
- **Increased efficiency | decreased costs:** Streamlined IT and business processes by architecting and engineering solutions to unify the presentation layer of more than 57 systems supporting 25,000 support center personnel in several US locations with a single integrated presentation layer.
- **Enabled processing of millions of taxpayer accounts:** Supported implementation of the Customer Data (CD) program, a single, data-centric solution that provided daily processing of customer accounts.
- **Compliance:** Ensured compliance with the organization's Enterprise Architecture Framework (EAF) while guiding projects and programs from their early concept phases throughout the entire Enterprise Life Cycle (ELC).

ADDITIONAL SUCCESSES SUPPORTING CLIENTS

- **Major Agency Records Management System:** Enabled partner to win a $19M contract by architecting original and highly innovative solution and design for the customer-facing system.
- **Executive Decision Making for a major agency's Enterprise Information Panel:** Supported acquisition plans to deploy an enterprise portal providing a unified platform for all existing websites by examining issues, complexities, and organizational factors associated with the existing environment, business drivers, requirements, and constraints.
- **Intelligence Center | Military Client:** Managed a diverse, over 50-person team including technical and senior-level representatives from major military contractors and other vendors to build and demonstrate a major military contractor's $42M high-performance computing proposed system.

Senior Systems Architect | Program Manager Systems Integration   1992 - 1993
Middle Sized Technology Contractor | Washington, DC

Led Up to 75-Person Teams | Contract Awards up to $42M

Directed and delivered support to several key IT military projects by leading, mentoring, and guiding up to 75-person teams with representatives from major technology companies and military contractors.

- **High Performance and Scientific Computing:** Drove successful design, construction, demonstration, benchmarking, and post-award work for cluster system for a Patriot Missile Simulation system, which led to a $42M contract award.
- **Integrated Digital Distribution System and Engineering Decision Support Software Development:** Enabled engineers to assess target vulnerability, susceptibility, and threat mechanisms and to evaluate alternative scenarios for decreasing each target's specific overall vulnerabilities by creating advanced interactive models.

Technical Director | Systems Architect   1987 - 1992
Large Military Contracting Company | Washington, DC

Directed and delivered support to several key projects by using project management, leadership, and IT expertise, including projects for several government agencies, providing systems to manage documents and engineering drawings still in use today.

EDUCATION

Master of Science (MS) in Information Systems
Georgia Institute of Technology | Atlanta, GA

Bachelor of Science (BS) in Management Information Systems
Georgia State College | Atlanta, GA

PROFESSIONAL MEMBERSHIPS

Project Management Institute (PMI)
Armed Forces Communications and Electronics Association (AFCA)

PROFESSIONAL COMMUNITY SERVICE

President (Elected)   2003 - 2017
Atlanta Property Owners Association Board of Directors | Atlanta, GA

$175,000 Annual Income
~ $500,000 Assets (not including ~25 Common Properties)
Board Composition: 5 Directors / 2 Managers
The property included a **Retail Shopping Center**
Supported: Management Company / Law, CPA, and Audit Firms
Publications Manager

Managed fiscal, governance, infrastructure maintenance, and community activities for a large property owners association, which included approximately 4,000 residents and governed multiple retail, hotel, office, and residential sub-associations and member classes on a ~457-acre complex. Developed and delivered annual operating and capital budgets to ensure the availability of the right resources.

KEY HIGHLIGHTS:
- Built and enhanced the community's internal and external brand and image
- Enabled improved customer experience, web platform, signage, traffic, and finances for retail management company
- Created a professional community publication and web presence
- Returned thousands of dollars to the community with a correct infrastructure

133

Contributed by Robin Schlinger, Founder, Robin's Resumes (https://robinresumes.com/). Robin holds the following credentials: Master Career Director (MCD), Certified Master Resume Writer (CMRW), Certified Federal Resume Writer (CFRW), and Certified Electronic Career Coach (CECC) from Career Directors International; Certified Professional Resume Writer (CPRW) from the Professional Association of Resume Writers and Career Coaches; 360 Reach Branding Analyst, and Job and Career Transition Coach (JCTC).

Background on Mike Douglas' Resume

Situation: The client owned a company that provides technology services to large federal government agencies. He had lost his last contract during a rebid and no longer had new work coming in so he wanted out of the government space. Mr. Douglas networked with a large retail company seeking a Chief Digital/Technology Officer position and wanted Robin to construct a resume to meet that goal.

Formatting the resume: After speaking with the client, Robin found that when he first set up his company in the 1990s, he had done some consulting for two firms providing IT services. She listed them on the first page and did a summary and job explanation that matched the company's advertisement and branding on their webpage. She also added highlighted words to draw the eye of a recruiter to the page, choosing colors that matched the company's colors and listed major successes of the client in the government workplace on the second and third pages. Many of these related to skills and technologies the company was looking for (it was a long job announcement). Robin also added some of the client's earlier success since it was a major leadership role for a large retail chain and mentioned his outside property leadership since he supported a retail management firm.

Result: The client got the interview with the retail company but decided, after interviewing, that he was not a fit. Instead, he got another contract with the government.

JANE MARIE DOE

"Creativity is my superpower."
New York, NY • 111.222.3333 • email@email.com

❧ SENIOR VICE PRESIDENT OF DESIGN ❧
BRAND BUILDING EXPERT | FASHION AND FABRIC INNOVATOR

Recognized as a World Class Designer by Vogue Magazine, WWD and the Intimate Apparel Industry.
Notably recognized at Bergdorf Goodman, Henri Bendel, Lord & Taylor, Victoria's Secret and specialty stores across the country.

Purposeful Visionary inspired and energized by fashion trends around the world. Builds collections mindful of sustainable design and practices. Partners with the best and brightest creative thinkers at Tommy Bahama, Robert Graham, Nautica, Anne Klein, Carole Hochman, Cuddleduds, DKNY, Halston, Oscar de la Renta and Stan Herman QVC. Inspiration comes from people, travel, music, architecture, nature, New York City's energy and old things with a history and a story. Energetic, perceptive communicator who is not afraid to challenge the status quo and builds deep trust at every level. Leads by example with style and poise.

EXPERTISE

Agile Innovation / Brand Identity / Print & Fabric Development / Athleisure-Loungewear / Intimate Apparel
Sustainable Fabrics / Consumer Needs Assessment / Creative Idea Generation / Entrepreneurship / European R&D Exceptional
Presentations / Product Development / Strategic Vision / Time Management / Trend Direction / Global Travel

HIGHLIGHTS OF DISTINCTION

- **Design Lead,** successfully launched Nautica Women's Sleep & Lounge Collection, including DTC, a **multi-million dollar** division. Took this iconic VF brand to a higher aesthetic and corporate rebranding strategy.
- **Launched Kolmar** into the Men's Furnishings category with Tommy Bahama and Robert Graham lifestyle brands.
- **Generated millions** in revenue developing key items for Costco US and International under Tommy Bahama men's brand.
- **Generated millions** in revenue securing annual Costco and Sam's Club key item programs for Anne Klein, Oscar de la Renta, DKNY, Carole Hochman and Cuddleduds.
- **Created specific, highly-successful products** for QVC, QVC International, Saks Fifth Avenue, Neiman Marcus, Amazon, Dillard's, Steinmart, Belk, Boscov's, MMX and other OPP retailers.
- **Developed a successful** Ulta Cosmetics GWP Holiday program that includes Women's Spa, Fashion and Men's Robes and added a Plush Home Throw that added **millions** in revenue.

EXPERIENCE AND CONTRIBUTIONS

ABC APPAREL, New York, NY   2004 to 2019
Vice President of Design

- **Design Lead** at this apparel powerhouse. Managed multiple design teams, developed key item volume programs for major retailers in a multi-channel distribution setting that resulted in exponential volume growth and revenue.
- **Concept and Brand Identity Expert** for Tommy Bahama Men's and Women's, Robert Graham, Nautica, Anne Klein, Carole Hochman, Cuddleduds, DKNY, Halston, Oscar de la Renta and Stan Herman QVC.
- **Maximized productivity and margin goals** with suppliers and production teams and utilized strategic negotiations to reduce costs without sacrificing innovation.

LANEWOOD MANUFACTURING, INC., New York, NY   1998 to 2004
Director of Merchandising and Product Development

- Enhanced corporate brands due to fabric diversification.
- Consistently achieved growth across all accounts and channels of distribution.
- Developed unique new products in Turkey, Mexico, Pakistan and Korea.

WORLD CLASS DESIGNS, INC., New York, NY
Chief Creative Officer
- → **Recognized as a World Class Designer** by Vogue Magazine, WWD and the Intimate Apparel industry as a lifestyle brand of fine lingerie and as an early innovator of multipurpose dressing, taking lingerie out of the bedroom and onto the street.
- → **Earned notable recognition** at Bergdorf Goodman, Henri Bendel, Lord & Taylor, Victoria's Secret and a variety of specialty and major department stores across the country.
- → Managed the firm's flagship retail store on Wooster Street, Soho, NY.

MS JONIE, INC., New York, NY, *Director of Private Label Design, Sleepwear*

SLEEPWEAR FOR HER, INC., New York, NY, *Creative Director, Intimate Apparel*

AVON PRODUCTS, New York, NY, *Apparel Design Consultant, Women's and Children's Apparel*

THE EXECUTIVE DESIGN GROUP, New York, NY, *Designer, Intimate Apparel*

JANE SMITH FOR SMITHSPORT, New York, NY, *Designer, Sportswear*

ADDITIONAL ACCOMPLISHMENTS

- → Developed high-volume seasonal key item programs that consistently drove the bottom line.
- → Streamlined the development process, reduced shipping costs and successfully negotiated zero sample and fabric costs.
- → Made factory samples that reduced the number of fittings and prototypes and saved a significant amount of time.
- → Influenced and inspired design teams to create new concepts that were well-received and came in on budget.
- → Contributed to sustainable practices by developing a recycled fabric made from plastic bottles for a key item robe program.

EDUCATION

PARSON'S SCHOOL OF DESIGN, New York, NY
Bachelor of Fine Arts, Fashion Illustration

FASHION INSTITUTE OF TECHNOLOGY, New York, NY
Associate of Applied Science, Fashion Illustration

PROFESSIONAL ASSOCIATIONS
UnderFashion Club
LIM Fashion Camp

LANGUAGES
Conversational Spanish, French, Italian

CAREER MEMORIES
Bergdorf Goodman - Having a key branded designer shop of silk lingerie.
Bergdorf Goodman - Branded Christmas Windows on 57th street.
Elizabeth Taylor's personal stylist purchased a Purple silk gown ensemble for her personal wardrobe from a design.

Contributed by **Laura Slawson.** Certified Professional Resume Writer and Credentialed Career Manager, owner of The Creative Edge. Laura, who specializes in resume, LinkedIn profile and career document writing, contributed four resume samples to this edition.

Background of Jane Doe's Resume

SENIOR VICE PRESIDENT OF DESIGN

Needs and Objectives

The client's objective was to obtain a position as a Senior Vice President of Design. Jane requested a resume that showed, "femininity, a dash of color with an organic, modern, clean feel." She loves the color lavender and was blown away with this design, especially after she immediately received compliments and calls for interviews.

Summary of Strategy

In the Professional Branding Statement, awards were showcased up front, as well as descriptions of what she does, her passion for her work, how she gets her inspiration and what she has to offer a potential hiring manager.

Important information is bolded to draw the reader's eye. An interesting twist is a section highlighting three unique career memories. This client worked with Elizabeth Taylor's personal stylist and felt that was important to mention. She also created the only sustainable fabric made completely from recycled plastic bottles that created a best seller!

Since earlier career experience is more than 25 years ago, dates were left off, but career progression is evident beginning as a *Sportswear Designer* to *Vice President of Design*.

JOHN JOSEPH
"Skilled Master in the Art of the PR Pitch."

New York, NY 44444 | 111.222.3332 | email@email.com

✶ AWARD-WINNING ✶
DIRECTOR OF PUBLIC RELATIONS AND DIGITAL CONTENT

Public Relations Trailblazer *who values the creative approach and has talent, vision and foresight to capitalize on rapidly changing markets. A belief that creative communication comes from careful thought, thorough research and the ability to drill down and speak with people to uncover key information to create a compelling story. Builds a stronger brand, networks to acquire new business and creates world-class content. Leads by example to mentor, inspire and empower others to be creative. Tech savvy. SEO smart.*

- **Creative Storyteller** who knows how to generate big concepts and innovative PR pitches connecting the dots.
- **Artisan Designer and Word Crafter** who effectively uses compelling verbiage and digitally savvy content.
- **Creative Thought Leader** with superb critical thinking skills that can creatively outdo the competition.
- **Forward-Thinking Innovator** easily recognizing and quickly capitalizing on rapidly emerging markets.

✶ AWARDS ✶
Award-Winner in Broadcasting, Public Relations and World Class Content Development.
Northeast Talk Radio "Best Innovative Content"
New Jersey Ad Club Award
Creative Gold Award

EXPERTISE
Account Management / Broadcast Media Production / Business Development / Creative Brainstorming & Storytelling
Customer Service / Digital Broadcasting / Media Relations / Training & Pitching / Product & Company Launches
Sales Management / SEO Optimization / Social Media / Speeches & Presentations / Strategic Partnerships
Talent Development / Writing & Content Development

PROFESSIONAL EXPERIENCE

THE ENGAGED CREATIVE GROUP, Anytown, NY   2006 to Present
Senior Creative Director
- Creative Director of a highly-successful Public Relations / Digital Marketing firm focusing on the "art of the media pitch."
- Collaborate with an exceptionally creative team working in a culture completely dedicated to developing unique business solutions, exceptional marketing and communications campaigns.
- Develop and implement formulas and templates that "connect the dots."

Accomplishments
- Early innovator in developing new media content freeing up companies to creatively expand their messages.

FUSION PUBLIC RELATIONS, Anytown, NY   2000 to 2006
Director of Accounts
Directed, trained and managed a team of 15 who excel securing top-tier trade press.
- Oversaw and developed educational and creativity sessions for the staff to focus on refining creativity and PR skills.

Accomplishments
- Led business development efforts across the US and Canada - increased revenue in the **millions.**
- Developed, oversaw and pitched highly creative PR campaigns in *B to B Magazine, PR News Week* and *Technology Marketing Magazine.*

138

THE NEW BANK, Anytown, NJ

1999 to 2000

Vice President and Marketing Director
- Managed agencies that produced advertising, websites, direct mail campaigns and annual reports.

Accomplishments
- Oversaw the marketing department's efforts that led to outstanding asset growth of **38.7%** .
- Established the first in-house PR function - increased press coverage **120%.**
- Introduced a new technology, and increased efficiency of the marketing department **25%.**

ADDITIONAL CONTRIBUTIONS

- **Increased Revenue:** Acquired four new accounts and increased income **$30K** per month in the first year.
- **Reduced Expenses:** Developed a new podcast design using the latest technology - reduced recording costs **60%.**
- **Saved Time:** Used innovative technology for producing podcasts - saved costly studio production time.
- **Streamlined Operations:** Worked with remote staff - made work easier and more cost efficient.
- **Millennial Leadership:** For the Podcast Division, created credibility by partnering with a world-class team to develop high-end digital content for millennials.
- **Business Expansion:** Created niche focus in a variety of verticals with branded podcasts that targeted Canadian companies - and successfully secured five high-end clients.

EARLIER EXPERIENCE

COMMUNITY COMMUNICATIONS, Anytown, NJ

Account Supervisor
- Created and implemented communications plans for financial technology firms that were seeking to market enterprise risk evaluation systems, internet websites and securities trading processing systems.

MID-HUDSON BANK, Anytown, NY

Vice President and Marketing Director
- Skillfully garnered outstanding TV and print media coverage that enhanced introduction of new financial products and PC home banking products and increased awareness of the organization exponentially.

EDUCATION
Fairleigh Dickinson University, Teaneck, NJ
Master of Business Administration, Marketing

Drew University, Madison, NJ
Bachelor of Arts, Political Science

TECHNICAL PROFICIENCIES
Desktop Publishing
Photoshop / SEO Optimization

139

Contributed by Laura Slawson. Certified Professional Resume Writer and Credentialed Career Manager, owner of The Creative Edge. Laura, who specializes in resume, LinkedIn profile and career document writing, contributed four resume examples to this edition.

Background on John Joseph's Resume

AWARD-WINNING DIRECTOR OF PUBLIC RELATIONS

Client's Needs and Objectives
John's objective was to obtain a "next step" position as a Director of Public Relations and Digital Content.

Summary of Strategy
The tagline was captured from the client's questionnaire … it fit perfectly!

In the Professional Branding Statement, John's expertise in creative storytelling, word crafting, and innovation is shown right up front as are his many awards.

Important concepts are bolded to draw the reader's eye. In addition, an Additional Contributions section was created to show how the client increased revenue, reduced expenses, saved time, streamlined operations, expanded business and is interested in the next generation of innovators, Millennials.

An Earlier Career section rounds out the resume with education and technical proficiencies. This resume garnered many interviews as soon as it was distributed.

140

THOMAS L. SMITHSON

Extensive experience managing Multi-Million Dollar Enterprise Initiatives.

Anytown, NJ 12345 | 111.222.3333 | email@email.com

VICE PRESIDENT - DIRECTOR
OMNICHANNEL - CUSTOMER SERVICE

➡ **Executive Leader of People.** Extensive expertise in Wholesale, Retail, Ecommerce Operations, Store Operations, Contact Center Management, Financial Services and Omnichannel Initiatives.

➡ **Business Transformer.** Identifies and implements operational improvements, increases organizational effectiveness and drives profits while simultaneously creating a positive, enjoyable, idea-generating atmosphere.

➡ **Interpersonal Communicator.** Leads effectively, listens actively, collaborates expansively to exceed goals and objectives.

➡ **Consensus Builder.** Actively engages cross-functional teams to grow, develop and deliver growth and profits.

SKILLS AND COMMITMENT TO EXCELLENCE

Manhattan Associates Distribution Order Management System (DOM)
Analytical Abilities / Business Process Reengineering / Consensus Building / Cross-Functional Team Leadership
Customer-Driven Management / Efficiency Improvements / Executive Presentations / Financial Management
Logistics / Loss Prevention / Multi-Site Operations / Policy & Procedure Development / Profit & Growth Initiatives

---

PROFESSIONAL EXPERIENCE

The New Store Place, Anytown, NJ   **2010 to 2020**

Vice President, Store Operations and Omnichannel Initiatives

As Vice President for the largest pure-play children's specialty apparel retailer in North America, and key member of the management team for several critical role, successfully contributed to significant company growth and profitability.

- ➤ Led the Store Operations Team of 30 to manage daily, strategic operations for **800+** retail locations across North America.
- ➤ Directly controlled Standard Operating Policies and Procedures, Omnichannel Operations, Support and Loss Prevention.
- ➤ Collaborated with Planning, Allocation, Merchandising, IT, Logistics, Marketing, Real Estate, Ecommerce and Finance teams.
- ➤ Led implementation, management, reporting and system updates for all Omnichannel use cases.

Leadership Successes

- ➤ Business Lead for a **multi-million dollar** project that impacted every aspect of store technology for the entire fleet.
- ➤ Replaced primary internet in all stores from T1s to Broadband. **Result:** improved speed, efficiency and visibility to expenses.
- ➤ Enabled mobile technology/Wi-Fi access through all stores and mobile checkout **grew 40% within 6 months** of launch.
- ➤ Managed replacement of approximately **2,000** fixed POS registers with new state-of-the-art HP touch screens.
- ➤ Replaced the old telephony system with VOIP and saved **millions** in annual telecom expenses.
- ➤ Business Lead for one of the **company's largest projects** - replaced in-store POS software in **less than 2 years**, and replaced 20-year old technology with new integrated software in **less than 2 years** from RFP to successful implementation, in addition trained the entire team of Associates and Support Centers simultaneously.

Vice President, Ecommerce and Business Transformation (2013 to 2017)

- ➤ Managed operations for the digital offering, Customer Service, Ecommerce Production and the Digital Analytics team.
- ➤ Strategic Business Lead for digital releases (desktop, tablet, mobile web/app) all enhancing the customer experience.
- ➤ Partnered with IT and Marketing to identify the user experience and directed product and vendor improvements.
- ➤ As a member of the Business Transformation Office, managed a portfolio of large-scale enterprise projects including:

Leadership Successes

- ➤ Complete website redesign and re-platform that moved from a traditional CODE to a headless architecture.
- ➤ Launched eReceipts fleetwide – improved the customer service experience and generated new email connections.
- ➤ Led the company's **largest, most critical project** that revolutionized the gap between the digital and in-store experience.

Director, Customer Service and Ecommerce (2012 to 2013)

- ⋏ Managed customer service, budgets, forecasts, quality, KPIs, trends, satisfaction surveys, website FAQs and improvements.
- ⋏ Directed all aspects of Ecommerce/Digital Platform and successfully led a variety of cross-functional teams.
- ⋏ Oversaw users/web developers who ensured website/mobile updates matched Ecom promotions, sales and floor changes.
- ⋏ Partnered with Ecom Merchants and Creative Design to market specialty shop creation, SEO and free shipping promotions.

Leadership Successes

- ⋏ Managed a strategic relationship with a third-party partner and moved Call Center Operations to a lower cost center, which was near-shore location as inbound volume **more than doubled** in 4 years with an hourly rate savings of **more than 58%.**

Director of Customer Service (2010 to 2013)

- ⋏ Managed the Customer Service team responsible for inbound contacts and a **multimillion dollar** budget.
- ⋏ Project Manager - trained all teams on an initiative to launch a new loyalty program, myPLACE Rewards.

Leadership Successes

- ⋏ Outsourced calls/emails to a third-party vendor **within 4 months,** met consumer demands due to expansion of Ecommerce.
- ⋏ Optimized the Case Management System and process flow, reduced average handle time (AHT) and improved productivity.

The Watch Group, LLC, Anytown, NJ   **2006 to 2010**
Director of Customer Service

*Managed the US Customer Service Call Center that responded to **1,000+** calls per day to ensure consumers received outstanding customer service for repairs, orders and problem resolution.*

- ⋏ Created and managed a **multi-million dollar** customer service budget.
- ⋏ Project Manager for The Watch Group's online order entry website launched to **20+** retailers.

Leadership Successes

- ⋏ Improved service quality and job knowledge through enhanced training for new hires and experienced associates
- ⋏ Collaborated with after sales service, distribution, IT and sales, reduced costs and improved customer satisfaction.
- ⋏ Introduced an incentive program for associates to motivate and reward productivity and quality efforts.
- ⋏ Redesigned the Movado Service website - reduced inbound calls and delivered outstanding service.
- ⋏ Increased consumer usage of Online Repair Processing website **400%+ within six months.**
- ⋏ Spearheaded an online consumer satisfaction survey to gauge consumer satisfaction - obtained a **25%+** response rate
- ⋏ Selected as a Power User for the development/ launch of a new ERP System, SAP.

EDUCATION
Muhlenberg College, Allentown, PA
Bachelor of Arts
Economics and Philosophy - summa cum laude

142

Contributed by Laura Slawson. Certified Professional Resume Writer and Credentialed Career Manager, owner of The Creative Edge. Laura, who specializes in resume, LinkedIn profile and career document writing, contributed four resume examples to this edition.

Background on Thomas Smithson's Resume

VICE PRESIDENT – DIRECTOR, OMNI-CHANNEL – CUSTOMER SERVICE

Client's Needs and Objectives

In the personal branding statement, Thomas wanted to showcase his diverse experience in wholesale, retail, e-commerce and store operations coupled with contact center management, financial services and omnichannel initiatives. He is also an expert at transforming businesses, building consensus and buy-in through is approachable style of communicating. Quantifiable leadership successes are bolded for emphasis.

JOANNE CONVERSE

Holmes, MD| 555.955.95555 | jconverse123@gmail.com | https://careerwebfolio.com/joanneconverse123/

CLIENT SERVICES & OPERATIONS LEADER

Transforming Operations • Forging Strategic Alliances • Boosting Customer Satisfaction

Results-oriented Client Services & Operations Executive – with extensive experience in audit compliance and delivering customized life insurance solutions for financing nonqualified benefit liabilities. Adept at driving collaboration across internal and external functions. Strategic thinker with success leading large-scale business operations, integration of new products, and implementation of policies. A trusted leader achieving shared vision and goals.

CORE COMPETENCIES

- High-Performing Team Development
- Service Delivery Optimization
- Project Management & Execution
- Collaborative, Cross-Functional Leadership
- Customer Engagement Strategies
- Transformation & Change Management
- Strategic Partnerships
- Solution Implementation
- Coaching & Mentoring

PROFESSIONAL EXPERIENCE

Zee Systems | Queens, NY   2007 – 2020
One of the largest global providers of annuities, employee benefit programs, and insurance with over 90 million clients.

Vice President of Client Services & Operations | 2013-2020
Oversaw servicing and operations for 1,000+ nonqualified benefit plans with more than $20 billion in assets, $465 million in sales, $282 million in revenue, and $93 million in annual earnings. Led a team of 30 employees in client services, operational support, and financial management through three direct reports. Supervised an offshore team of five in India.

Cultivating High Performance

- **$240 billion spinoff divestiture completion supported** by overseeing the migration of $2 billion in COLI policies under the transition service agreement.
- **Maximized account management performance** through improved audit finding by documenting over 400 end-to-end procedures across 36 products and five lines of business.
- **Enriched team morale and engagement** through cascading goals to align strategies and enhance collaboration among three departments.
- **Enabled new sales** by writing business specifications for additional products, implementing new cases on systems, creating client reporting and administration, and training client executives on new products and procedures.

Improving Customer Experience

- **96% customer satisfaction rating** and a 91% ease-of-doing-business score achieved by implementing metrics, standardizing turnaround times, and championing the voice of the customer survey.
- **Delivered competitive advantage** in a key product marketplace by leading audit certification.
- **50% reduction in installation time** attained by improving implementation of large product cases and enhancing customer satisfaction via gap analysis.
- **Bolstered customer experience** by building an online portal for participants to access information on demand.
- **24/7 access to reports-on-demand accomplished** to enhance customer satisfaction by introducing reporting and self-service transactional capabilities via a website portal for brokers and corporate clients.

Optimizing Operational Efficiencies

- **Decreased U.S. headcount** by transitioning 20 processes to the global operations service center in India.
- **Improved operating efficiencies and cut costs** by migrating multiple products from legacy systems of acquired firms into the corporate administrative platform.
- **Increased productivity** and operational efficiencies for client services by originating a web-based workflow system.
- **Complied with FINRA regulations** by managing registered representatives.
- **Enhanced performance and efficiency** by devising and continuously improving standardized metrics.
- **Optimized resources and created efficiencies** by realigning departments and restructuring financial management under client services.

Assistant Vice President | 2007-2013

Led delivery of policyholder services for corporate clients, specialty brokers, agents, and high net worth individuals. Managed a team of 30 performing death claim administration for all lines of business.

Maximizing Resources & Results

- **10-day turnaround time** realized for 85% of deaths by conducting death claim administration for all business lines in adherence with state requirements and company policies.
- **Maximized internal resources** by expeditiously resolving issues related to accounting, administration, legal operations, pricing, tax, and underwriting.
- **Facilitated meeting sales plans** by overseeing the business and providing RFP support for nonqualified executive benefit plans, deferred compensation plans, and financing benefit liabilities to the sales brokers.
- **Accelerated profit growth** while reaching client and asset retention goals by leading successful delivery of policyholder services for corporate clients, agents, specialty brokers, and high net worth individuals.
- **Improved benefit plan management** by applying critical policy, insurance, and investment account guidance to support decision making for the CFO and treasury staff for corporate and bank-owned insurance products.

Leading High-Performance Teams

- **Propelled human capital efficiency** through capacity models by analyzing and identifying optimal performance based on work volume.
- **Met market segment needs** by collaborating with sales, actuarial staff, and product management to evaluate products for development based on market demand.
- **Augmented process efficiency** by originating an internal case information and pricing system within Salesforce to manage clients across multiple departments.
- **Optimized resources and value** by reorganizing the department in alignment with enterprise objectives.

EDUCATION & PROFESSIONAL DEVELOPMENT

Bachelor of Science
in Economics
University of Illinois

FINRA Series 6 and 26

SALES & OPERATIONS EXECUTIVE

Senior sales and operations executive with extensive experience. Maximizing sales and gross profits by building sustainable revenue pipelines, forging strong customer relationships, and implementing best practices to improve overall service and performance.

Driving Revenue & Profitability with a Focus on Customer Satisfaction & Quality

A dedicated leader skilled in delivering customized solutions and devising robust operational processes to attain corporate goals and objectives. A performance-driven motivational leader with a background in facilitating training and development, coaching, and mentoring programs.

Strategic Planning | Sales Management | Field Operations Leadership

Customer Relationship Management | Sales Forecasting | Revenue Generation

Finance & Budget Administration | Talent Acquisition & Retention | Performance Improvement

EXPERIENCE

SOUTH HILL CORPORATION   Cass, WV
A distributor and service provider of sunglasses, cell phone accessories, apparel, and general merchandise to convenience stores nationwide.

Senior Vice President of Field Operations | 2019-2020
Oversaw service to more than 40,000 convenience stores across the U.S. through a team of five district managers, 30 area managers, and over 400 service representatives generated $275 million in 2020.

- **$14.3 million in sales generated**, a 51% increase in one year by adding 417 new stores.
- **$7.5 million in residual sales** and $5.2 million in gross profits projected for 2021 by leading the planning and establishment of a new division within 90 days, installing 288 programs in two months.
- **$3 million decrease in expenses** by merging the field service team.
- **$1 million in additional sales** accomplished while reducing excess inventory by adding over 16,000 programs in four years.
- **24% rep turnover achieved**, down from 56% by identifying factors negatively impacting morale and instituting changes including revised incentives, route ride scoreboards, and improved training.

Vice President of Sales & Service | 2007-2019

Led a team of five regional and 15 district managers. Managed several major corporate accounts. Completed weekly service schedules, staying within budget, and ensuring platinum-level customer service and high-scoring compliance audits.

- **$21.6 million in additional sales cultivated** over nine years by designing and introducing the "top dog" sales contest to foster comradery and motivate competition among the route service reps.

- **Bolstered productivity and operational efficiencies** by implementing a new compensation plan based on updated payroll laws, replacing sales commission with a quarterly audit incentive, and rolling out a sales spiff program.

- **94% service audit scores** and on-time deliveries reached across 450 sales/service reps and 40,000 customer doors to drive customer satisfaction and retention as well as sales by integrating two sales teams post-merger through leadership, training, and a focus on quality.

Regional Sales Manager | 2003-2007

Managed a team of ten district managers to ensure route sales goals and support of route service reps (RSRs). Oversaw sales, service, and profitability for 100+ RSRs. Maintained relationships with six key accounts. Insulated customers from the competition and added new programs.

- **$300+ million in sales** attained over three or four years, a $35 million annual surge by hiring, training, and leading a team of new business development reps to build a new business pipeline.

- **Earned "Regional Manager of the Year"** award for three consecutive years.

- **$2 million in total sales** for four years realized by selling five large new chains with over 500 stores.

Additional Experience with Soth Hill Corporation: District Manager and Route Sales Representative

PROFESSIONAL DEVELOPMENT

Franklin Covey, Six Critical Points of Management & Speed of Trust

RACI | Five Choices | The Four Disciplines of Execution

Sam Wilson

Green, WV | 555.555.5555| swilson1432@gmail.com | https://careerwebfolio.com/swilson123/

C-LEVEL MARKETING & SALES EXECUTIVE

Crisis Mastery • Startup Expertise • Change Fulfillment

A Success-Proven Management Professional with extensive domestic and international experience, starting and driving businesses to record achievement - bringing consumer products to the retail marketplace. Visionary in identifying growth opportunities. Strategic and dynamic leading creative groups, sales teams, and production units in maximizing results. Spent decades generating profitable output from offshore suppliers, overcoming cross-cultural friction, and creating responsive and productive relationships. Firm believer in the team as the greatest asset of the organization. Willing and able to accept responsibility for moving a company from where it is to where it needs to be, overcoming challenges, and delivering heartening ROIs.

CORE COMPETENCIES

Sales & Marketing Management | P&L Responsibility | Strategic & Tactical Leadership
Product Design, Creation & Launch | Entrepreneurial Acumen | Business / Brand Development
Team Training, Coaching & Mentoring | Operational Intelligence | Collaboration / Negotiation / Closing
Clear, Concise, Persuasive Communication | Cross-Functional Partnerships | Client / Vendor Relationships
Complex Supply Chain Dynamics

PROFESSIONAL EXPERIENCE

WarrenInternational, Inc. | Grass Lick, WV   1997 – 20

A $50 million design house, importer, and distributor of home decor and outdoor living products to major and independent retailers and through e-commerce channels in the U.S. and Canada.

President

In addition to collaborating on daily activities in the West Virginia and foreign corporate offices, focused on product development, marketing, sales-force leadership, building and strengthening customer relationships, and fostering employee well-being.

Grew the Top Line

- **$8 million in a single account's volume produced** by leading the development of an adult version of a traditional child-oriented brand and promoting consumer acceptance at the retail level.

- **Consistently exceeded all core financial goals** by reinforcing customer relationships through stressing the adequacy of the company's systems and resources to meet demands of growth and user inquiry.

- **Explained to a major US retail chain**, through statistical and practical evidence, the causes of an unnecessarily poor selling season and provided actionable solutions that secured the position of future partner.

- **Earned the rights to market an extensive package of luxury items** branded with the image of a popular home-improvement TV series that broadened sales channels and raised volume 50% YOY.

- **$7 million in first-year sales** of a recently added product line aided by gaining exposure on a televised shopping service including two highlight positions that sold out faster than expected.

Built the Company's Inner Strengths

- **20% over the annual revenue forecast** and a reduction in selling expenses achieved by hiring, guiding, and working in conjunction with a best-in-class sales team.

- **Built the firm into an industry leader** by compiling a mix of customers that included large and mid-sized retailers, wholesale distributors, and e-commerce outlets.

- **Forged reliable quality, production, and timely delivery standards** within a group of Asian factories resulting in the company earning the valued reputation of a dependable supplier.

- **Invested in ERP systems and procedures** and trained US-based design and offshore development teams to collaborate in ways that ensured visibility of documentation and timelines to all pertinent parties.

- **Reduced inter-cultural frustration and delay among creative staffers** by bringing the domestic design group to Asia to meet with colleagues in business and social gatherings.

Solved the Big Problems

- **10 million units of an eccentric product sold** in less than ten years by agreeing to give a concept that did not fit the business plan the attention and investment necessary to qualify for market introduction.

- **Avoided significant economic damage** from the 2008 crash by shifting selling strategy from independent retailers to major chains, closing showrooms, and selling off $2 million (92%) of excessive inventory.

- **Negotiated a change in international contract manufacturers' terms of sale** that gave the company five days for in-bound inspection prior to payment ensuring quality customer deliveries and eliminating reliance on line-of-credit financing.

- **Averted a potential sales catastrophe** by swiftly converting a surprise product problem into a chance to demonstrate good faith to an existing customer and add a new large retailer to the base.

-PREVIOUS EXPERIENCE-

Reasoable Corporation | Grass Lick, WV

A $100+ million importer of home decor, with offices in Little Rock, Charlotte, New York, and China. Of the more than 3,000 multi-national employees, ≈500 held sales positions.

Vice President of Sales

Managed five employed US sales managers and five independent representative groups. Facilitated large retailer accounts that generated $16-$20 million annually in domestic business. Coordinated daily in-store service performance with the division vice president.

- **$60 million five-year top-line increase accomplished** by changing from a totally independent to a nearly all-employee sales team with the ability to apply dedicated effort to building sustainable, profitable growth.

- **Diversified the customer base** by gaining the confidence of the marketing team that retailers not carrying the company's current line would buy more elaborate, higher-priced items from the firm.

- **Guided acquisition of a manufacturer** with expertise facilitating expansion of the company's product line and managed an introductory sales campaign that overcame the loss of $16 million in revenue occasioned by the closing of two major outlets.

- **Improved the company's process for budgeting** and managing sales, operations, tradeshow, and entertainment expenses. Never exceeded budgets despite increasing annual revenue up to 27% annually.

- **Satisfied a key customer's request for additional service** without incurring net margin erosion by increasing support in "a" and "b" stores, with increased sales growth, while reducing visits in "c" and "d" stores.

ASSOCIATIONS / PRESENTATIONS / LANGUAGE SKILLS

Business Network International, Officer • "International Business in China"; Elmira University Guest

Lecturer | Speak Mandarin well enough to navigate

Jim Douglas

Los Angeles, CA • Jdouglas9865 @gmail.com • 555.555.5555 • https://careerwebfolio.com/imdouglas123/

Strategic Growth & Business Operations Leader
Transforming Organizations • Driving Consultative Solutions • Cultivating Strategic Relationships
Leveraging relationships by influencing people through a consultative approach

EXECUTIVE SUMMARY

CORE COMPETENCIES
- Client Relationships
- Strategic Partnerships
- Business Operations
- Cross-Functional Leadership
- High-Performance Teams
- Business Development
- Strategic Planning
- Leveraging Technology

A transformative business leader with extensive experience in driving organizational growth and change via strategic relationships. Maximizing customer experience, revenue, and profitability through negotiation, value propositions, and superior knowledge in technology solutions. Delivering results in challenging environments.

Focused on Growing Businesses Strategically & Tactically

A trusted advisor and strategist to company leaders, management teams, clients, organizational partners, and staff. Inspiring identification of hidden opportunities and development of innovative solutions by collaborating with key stakeholders. Building individuals and groups into teams driven to achieve aggressive goals and objectives.

PROFESSIONAL EXPERIENCE

ACME — Denver, CC
An industry-leading provider of consulting and business services with over $44 billion in revenues and 500,000 staff.

SALES & SOLUTIONS EXECUTIVE   2016 – 2019

Oversaw sales, negotiations, client relationship management, big deal pursuits, solution architecting, and budget management. Led new business development support teams of up to 30 responsible for $35+ million in sales goals.

- **$100+ million in contracts closed** by negotiating with lawyers, business agents, and procurement leads to finalize complex contractual agreements.
- **Increased sales** and earned a promotion by building client trust and confidence through demonstration of superior knowledge in technology solutions and a passion for the business.
- **$100 million sales pipeline constructed** by developing multi-partner value propositions.
- **Leveraged the full value of the company** and drafted strong business cases for unsolicited proposals to drive the big deal sales teams.
- **70% business development win ratio** won by creating a sales tool and implementing a robust deal close plan.

COSIGN CORPORATION — Charleston, WV
A multinational corporation with 138,000 employees generating $20 billion in IT services and consulting.

GENERAL MANAGER, MANUFACTURING INDUSTRY   2014 – 2016

Managed a portfolio of $250 million in annual new business. Drove sales growth and supported a team of 100.

- **100% improvement in forecast accuracy** and a 50% uptick in efficiency attained by proactively devising new forecasting tools and processes.
- **Augmented company credibility** in the industry and with customers while minimizing reliance on external marketing resources by crafting content utilizing unique value propositions for articles and video interviews.
- **20% surge in employee satisfaction** reached by awarding bonuses, bestowing timely promotions, and seeking staff input on client challenges.
- **12% YOY revenue growth** realized by focusing on client needs, developing trusting relationships, and understanding the competitive landscape.
- **Drove sales, exceeded performance metrics,** and doubled scope of responsibilities by forging relationships with customers and internal leaders to gain trust.
- **25% increase in the sales pipeline** and a 10% boost in annual revenue accomplished by innovating solutions to meet client demands.

RSVP CORPORTION — Huntington, WV

A leader in technology services generating $9 billion in annual revenues with 175,000 global employees.

GLOBAL CLIENT PARTNER   2009 – 2012

Forged, maintained, and improved client relationships, managed flagship accounts, transformed delivery, and lead a global team of nearly 400.

Business Development

$150 million in unsolicited contract renewal work acquired over five years by changing support metrics to a business-oriented model in a client service contract.

Generated organization recognition in the industry by showcasing corporate value proposition and transformation in an article that won "contract of the year" with the National Outsourcing Association.

Positioned the firm as an industry leader and emphasized the client's ability to transform its business model by contributing content on a partner-centric business arrangement featured in multiple publications.

$40 million in annual revenues fostered, a 50% escalation, by delivering on existing promises and addressing client issues with emergent solutions.

Strategic Planning

50% reduction in staff attrition obtained by designing advancement opportunities, demonstrating employee relevance and value, connecting staff performance to client results, introducing a recognition program, and meeting regularly with the global team.

25% rise in a client's net promoter score by using IT solutions aligned to end-user satisfaction.

Earned "Best Global Client Partner" award and advanced business goals by forming strategic partnerships that balanced the needs of the company, client, and team to realize mutually beneficial goals.

5% decrease in costs cultivated by conducting P&L tasks to enhance knowledge and management of expenses and revenue streams.

GLOBAL INTERESTS CORPORATION   South Fork, VA

A $90 billion technology products and services provider with more than 300,000 staff around the world.

LEAD CONSULTING PARTNER   Pre-2000 – 2008

Managed a high-value client in the automotive industry to enrich client relationships, grow revenue and profitability, build, and manage a sales pipeline, develop proposals, monitor P&L, negotiate contracts, manage vendors. Supported $50 million in business through a team of 30 consultants.

$50 million in revenue nurtured at one of the largest automotive accounts by listening to and comprehending client needs, using innovation for improvements, and securing the trust of a highly valued partner.

- **Millions of dollars saved for clients** by collaborating with various strategic partners to introduce technologies and innovative solutions.

- **Extended the company influence** with the client by facilitating executive-level meetings, formulating internal cross-functional cadence, and leading international coordination with colleagues.

- **800% growth in client relationships** secured by bridging the knowledge gap between emergent technologies and business results.

Improved client service by enriching consulting staff skills through mentoring, engagement, encouragement, career pathing, and building rapport. Achievement statement

- **80%-win rate** reaped by authoring hundreds of high-value proposals through active listening to client needs.

EDUCATION, CERTIFICATION, & PROFFESSIONAL AFFILIATION

Master of Business Administration in International Business – Marshall University

Bachelor of Computer Science - University of Wisconsin

Project Management Professional (PMP), Project Management Institute

Toastmasters International, Distinguished Member & President

In the process of conducting workshops for the General Officer Transition Assistance Program (GOTAP), I met Brigadier General John C. Millard. JC worked with the Stewart, Cooper & Coon branding team and the example resumes that follow are his original "before" and our reworked "after" version of that document. I wish to thank JC for allowing us to use his document in the fourth edition of *Ready, Aim, Hired.*

John (J.C.) Millard

Metropolitan City | 999-223-12347| john.c.millard@mail123.outlook.com | www.linkedin.com/in/profile

Accomplished senior-level executive and U.S. Air Force veteran, culminating in the rank of *Brigadier General,* with 28 years of global leadership and management experience across a various set of fields: aviation operations, logistics, strategic planning, cyber integration, and risk management. Currently holds a *Top-Secret Security Clearance*.

Servant leader with proven success building cohesive teams to identify and solve complex problems. Led large organizations, *2,300 personnel and a $430 million budget*, and lean high-performance teams. Passionate about delivering technology-enhanced innovative strategies with a mindset of continuous process improvement. Have an inclusive approach in creating enduring strategic partnerships to achieve organizational goals and meet financial targets. Successful in diverse cultures including the Department of Defense, White House, Department of State, as well as Internationally.

Key Accomplishments

- ❖ Voting member on Air Mobility Command's governing board. Guided *$389 million* on infrastructure investment.
  - ➤ *Set policy on Headquarters reorganization, cloud migration, and $1.2 million for unmanned aircraft systems.*
- ❖ Initiated two critical innovation efforts: Fuel Efficiency process improvements and the Electronic Flight Book.
  - ➤ *Saved an estimated $3.6 million/year in aviation fuel and reduced purchasing of flight publications by $1.2 million/year through improved aircraft and FAA policies and procedures.*
- ❖ Led the most complex Defense Department restructure in the Central Asian States after 13 years of operations.
  - ➤ *Executed a 3-phase plan/1,600 key tasks, 11 international contracts; achieved a 30-day accelerated timeline.*
- ❖ Reengineered government funding and reimbursement process with U.S. Treasury for Air Force activities.
  - ➤ *Eliminated payment latency and debt collection role for 34 Federal agencies. Reduced finance staff by 33%.*

Professional Experience

Chief Compliance and Risk Officer *(Inspector General, HQ Air Mobility Command)* Belleville, IL   2019 - present

Executive strategist for the Chief Executive Officer (**4-Star Commanding General**) of Air Mobility Command. Leads a selectively-hired, 90-***person*** staff implementing policy, conducting inspections, continuous process improvement, and risk management on *67* organizations. Directly impacting the organizational effectiveness and readiness of *124,000* personnel. Executes a *$3.7 million* operational budget.

- ➤ *Drove a fundamental shift to operational readiness with the Air Force Inspection model to highlight undetected risk. Led reduction of inspection requirements by over 50% and reduced reporting by 29%.*
- ➤ *Analyzed data trends from 37 inspections, directed over 100 corrective actions across enterprise.*

Senior Vice President *(Deputy Director - Strategic Plans, Requirements, and Programs)* Belleville, IL   2018 - 2019

Senior Executive for 169 military and civilian personnel across five divisions. Developed the strategic budget for all mobility concepts, planned Air Mobility Command's force structure as well as established future aircraft requirements. Budgeting advocate to Headquarters Air Force/Pentagon for the nation's air mobility enterprise.

- ➤ *Shaped Command's funding strategy of $180 million for global air operations center planning system and $105 million VIP/Executive inflight communication requirements.*
- ➤ *Led mobility command's cross-functional team to onboard the KC-46 the USAF newest air refueling aircraft; coordinated staff policy, force laydown, aircrew and maintenance training.*

Senior Program Manager/Innovation Team Lead *(U.S. Transportation Command)* Belleville, IL 2017 - 2018

Led a *12-person* innovation team thru test and acquisition of a commercial-off-the-shelf world-wide transportation system. The goal, to link disconnected nodes (aerial/seaports, distribution hubs and staging bases) across the Joint Deployment and Distribution Enterprise with a common platform.

- ➤ *Produced a 120-day Proof of Principle concept across two major lines of business, addressed 38 distinct capabilities and successfully closed 9 of the 12 multi-modal operational gaps.*
- ➤ *Rapidly deployed an innovation contract for a $50 million Transportation Management System. Merged government software with an enterprise resource planning system. Awarded in 12 weeks.*

Executive Director (*Executive Officer to the Commander, U.S. Transportation Command*) Belleville, IL   2016 - 2017

Directed the inner-command staff (C-Suite) and administration actions to guide the Chief Executive Officer (**4-Star Commanding General**) of U.S. Transportation Command across strategic engagements, communications, and staff actions to achieve strategic and operational objectives. Facilitated rapid decision-making processes with the Office of the Secretary of Defense and Joint Staff.

> ➢ *Integrated commander's intent, priorities, and enterprise innovation initiatives through the organization and **150,000-person** workforce.*
> ➢ *Coordinated staff actions to execute CEO's strategic plan and engagement strategy with Congress, International Heads of State, Industry Leaders, and eight Combatant Commands.*

Chief Executive Officer (*Commander, 89th Airlift Wing*) National Capitol Region   2014 - 2016

Led the nation's highest-visible airlift organization of *1,200 personnel* with an annual *$180 million* budget charged with the exclusive task of transporting the **President of the United States** as well as providing executive airlift and airborne communications support for the Vice President, Congressional leadership, and foreign dignitaries. In addition, managed the logistics port and a *$350 million* aircraft maintenance contract.

> ➢ *Notable missions: The President's historic visit to Cuba and the repatriation of prisoners from Iran and N. Korea. All total, **114 Nations** with a **98.4%** aircraft reliability and overcame a **20%** reduction in aircraft availability with a diverse fleet of 19 aircraft.*
> ➢ *Created organization's first strategic alignment and communications plan; won the Installation Excellence Award for quality of life, environmental stewardship, public relations, and safety.*

President, Chief Operations Officer, and Senior Director (*U.S. Air Force*) Various   2011 - 2014

Led an international military organization of *2,300 personnel* with an annual budget of *$430 million* managing a multi-national logistics center. Simultaneously supported the U.S. Embassy with humanitarian and social-cultural programs. Commander of largest Operations Group led *1,000 personnel* in five organizations to include an aircrew training center to conduct global air logistics. Directed *80 employees* in the USAF's largest air transportation center; integrated over *900 daily* global missions with a diverse fleet of *1,400* aircraft.

> ➢ *Led combat operations with the first KC-135 air refueling aircraft task force in Afghanistan. Reduced tanker response times by **66%** while simultaneously increasing fuel availability by **21%**.*
> ➢ *Guided 90 military engagement events in concert with the U.S. Embassy. Delivered over **$1.4 million** in humanitarian aid and 51 support programs and projects in Kyrgyzstan.*
> ➢ *Developed Western U.S. consortium of nine organizations to overcome a **30%** reduction in flying hours; increased aircrew training by **20%**, simultaneously improved graduation rates by **31%**.*
> ➢ *Managed inter-staff team to fix the KC-10 enterprise's global secure communications capability. Wrote new training program, procedures, and coordinated staff efforts for **$2.4 million** in funding.*
> ➢ *Directed initial emergency humanitarian response to the Japanese tsunami executing **40 missions** transporting search and rescue teams; **70 operations** supporting the devastating Pakistani floods.*

Professional Development

Corporate Board Directorship Certification, National Association of Corporate Directors   Washington, DC
Safety and Accident Investigation Board President's Course, USAF Safety Center   Montgomery, AL
Green Belt - Lean/Six Sigma Facilitator Course | Air Force Smart Operations 21   Fairfield, CA
Leadership Development Program, Center for Creative Leadership   Greensboro, NC

Education

Master of National Security and Strategic Studies, Naval War College   Newport, RI
Master of Military Operational Art and Science, Air Command and Staff College   Montgomery, AL
Master of Arts in Business Administration and Management, Webster University   St Louis, MO
Bachelor of Arts in Geography, University of New Mexico   Albuquerque, NM

JOHN (J.C.) Millard

Metropolitan City | 999-223-12347| john.c.millard@mail123.outlook.com | www.linkedin.com/in/profile

Senior Managing Director: Logistics / Operations

Supply Chain / Logistics • IT Integration • Strategy Development • Change Management • Risk Management

Accomplish the Mission, No Matter the Challenge

A decisive, **senior operations leader** and former military general officer with the United States Air Force. Adept at resolving complex problems, integrating advanced technologies, and leading team performance through change management, strategy development, and enterprise risk management.
Security Clearance: Top Secret / SCI

Creating Vision & Strategy to Lead Teams in Solving Complex Business Problems

Energetic with keen decision-making skills, the ability to manage risk, and willingness to adapt to change within dynamic, fast-paced environments. A proven mentor and coach to propel team development. Effectual communication skills to clarify information, align objectives, and improve decision making. Driven to realize objectives and succeed despite obstacles.

CORE COMPETENCIES
- Multi-Departmental Leadership
- Strategy Development & Planning
- Supply Chain / Logistics
- IT Business Integration
- Global Operations
- Program & Project Management
- Enterprise Budgeting
- Risk Mitigation
- Public Speaking / Communications
- Change Management
- Operations Management
- Teamwork / Teambuilding

PROFESSIONAL EXPERIENCE

Chief Compliance & Risk Officer | Inspector General | Belleville, IL   2019 - Present
Serve as the executive strategist for the 4-Star Commanding General of the Air Mobility Command. Responsible for leading selectively hired 90-person staff to implement policy, conduct inspections, continuously improve processes, and oversee risk management for 67 organizations. Maintain a direct impact on organizational effectiveness and readiness of more than 124,000 USAF personnel. Manage a $3.7 million operational budget.

- **50% decrease in inspection requirements and a 29% reduction in reporting** by transforming the Air Force inspection model's focus on operational readiness and simultaneously reduced 1,200 labor hours per unit inspection.
- **Assessed undetected risk/non-compliance data trends** from 37+ inspections and directed more than 240 corrective actions enterprise-wide to improve unit capability.

Senior Vice President | Deputy Director of Strategic Plans, Requirements, Programs | Belleville, IL   2018 - 2019
Oversaw 169 military and civilian staff in five divisions. Devised the strategic budget, planned the force structure, and set future aircraft requirements. Advocated for the nation's air mobility budget to Air Force headquarters / Pentagon.

- **Fashioned the $180 million funding strategy** for a global air operations center planning system and the $105 million VIP / executive inflight communication requirements.
- **Steered the mobility command's cross-functional team** to onboard the newest air refueling aircraft including orchestrating staff policy, force laydown, and training for aircrew and maintenance.

Senior Program Manager | Innovation Team Lead | Belleville, IL   2017 - 2018
Led a 12-member innovation team through test and acquisition of a commercial off-the-shelf worldwide transportation system to link aerial / seaports, distribution hubs, and staging bases with a common platform.

- **$50 million transportation management system contract deployed within 12 weeks** by merging government software with an enterprise resource planning (ERP) platform.
- **Conceived a 120-day proof of principle concept** across two major lines of business, addressed 38 unique capabilities and successfully closed nine of the twelve multi-modal operational gaps.

Executive Director | Executive Officer to the Commander | U.S. Transportation Command | Belleville, IL 2016 - 2017
Led c-suite staff and administration actions to guide the 4-Star Commanding General of the U.S. Transportation Command through strategic engagements, communications, and personnel actions to realize strategic and operational goals. Expedited rapid decision-making processes with the Office of the Secretary of Defense and Joint Staff.

- **Orchestrated team activities to execute the strategic plan** and engagement tactics with Congress, international heads of state, industry leaders, and eight combatant commands.
- **Integrated the Chief Executive Officer's plan, priorities, and innovation efforts** through the 150,000-member workforce and organization.

Chief Executive Officer | Commander, 89th Airlift Wing | National Capital Region   2014 - 2016
Directly supported the President of the United States. Managed the country's highest visible airlift unit comprised of 1,200 staff and a $180 million annual budget accountable for the exclusive function of transporting the President on Air Force One and providing executive airlift and airborne communications support for the Vice President, Congressional leaders, and foreign dignitaries. Administered the logistics port and a $350 million aircraft maintenance contract.

- **Spearheaded significant missions such as the president's historic visit to Cuba** and the repatriation of prisoners from Iran and North Korea. Completed missions to 114 countries with a 98.4% aircraft reliability while surmounting a 20% decline in aircraft availability with a diverse fleet of 19 aircraft.
- **Conceptualized the first strategic alignment and communications plan** to earn the installation excellence award for quality of life, environmental stewardship, public relations, and safety.

President | Chief Operations Officer | Senior Director | Various Locations   2011 - 2014
Commanded a global organization of 2,300 personnel with a $430 million annual budget to oversee a multinational logistics center. Concurrently supported the U.S. Embassy with humanitarian and social-cultural programs. Led a team of 1,000 staff in five organizations and an aircrew training center to perform global air logistics. Guided a team of 80 employees in the largest air transportation center, integrated more than 900 daily worldwide missions via a fleet of 1,400 aircraft.

Operational Performance

- **Directed the most complex DOD restructure** in the Central Asian States, executing a three-phase plan with 1,600 critical tasks and eleven international contracts to complete a 30-day accelerated timeline.
- **66% reduction in tanker aircraft response times while boosting fuel availability 21%** while leading combat operations with the first KC-135 air refueling aircraft taskforce in Afghanistan.
- **31% surge in graduation rates achieved** by escalated aircrew training 20% to trounce a 30% decline in flying hours by creating a consortium of nine organizations.

Program / Project Leadership

- **Guided $389 million infrastructure investment** and set policy on reorganization, enterprise cloud migration, and $1.2 million for unmanned aircraft systems as a voting member on Air Mobility Command's governing board.
- **$1.4 million in humanitarian aid delivered** along with 51 support programs by direction 90 military engagement events with the United States Embassy.
- **Oversaw a team to enrich global secure communications proficiency**, authored the new training program, and coordinated personnel actions for $2.4 million in funding.

IT Integration & Innovation

- **$3.6 million in annual** aviation fuel savings and a $1.2 million decrease in purchases of flight publications initiated by improving aircraft fuel efficiency procedures and FAA policies while championing the Electronic Flight Book initiative.
- **Reengineered the government funding and reimbursement process** with the U.S. Treasury by implementing an IT solution that eliminated payment latency and debt collection for 34 federal agencies, curtailing finance staff 33%.

EDUCATION & PROFESSIONAL DEVELOPMENT

Master of National Security & Strategic Studies, Naval War College
Master of Military Operational Art & Science, Air Command & Staff College
Master of Arts in Business Administration & Management, Webster University
Bachelor of Arts in Geography, University of New Mexico

- **Corporate Board Directorship**, National Association of Corporate Directors
- **Lean / Six Sigma Green Belt Facilitator Course**, Air Force Smart Operations 21
- **Leadership Development Program**, Center for Creative Leadership

CHAPTER 6
COVER LETTERS

Cover letters, or letters of application, are simply letters that accompany your application materials. They introduce you to the reader and reinforce, but don't repeat exactly, what is on your resume. Cover letters should be highly organized and just the right length to show off your writing skills. Remember, potential employers are looking for the message under the message (in this case, your best writing skills). In this chapter, I'll will:

- Show you a quick and easy format
- Go over a few mechanics of creating the letter
- Explain how to practice "word economy" so your letter will be read

Before beginning your letter, consider first the purpose of a cover letter and how an employer will see it.

GENERAL CONSIDERATIONS

Do yourself a big favor: don't make the same mistake most people make by simply restating in your cover letter what is already in your resume. If you do, you will harm your candidacy.

The purpose of the cover letter is to tell the hiring authority *why* you should be the only candidate for consideration for this position. What is the answer to this question? The answer is simple: You are a problem solver! You not only have researched problems they are likely having, but you are also able to provide solutions.

Many people make the mistake of writing the letter from the top down. However, to improve the organization of this important document, you should first think about two specific reasons *this* organization would want to hire *you*. **Write one paragraph about each of the two reasons FIRST,** *then* **work on your introduction and conclusion.**

Remember, almost all resumes go through applicant tracking software (ATS) that will look for words that match the job description. *People* don't look at it first, so a cover letter that says "See Resume" is useless. Reread the job description and ask yourself what the organization is really looking for in a candidate. What would *you* be looking for? What hard and soft skills are the most important? What proof do you have that you are the best qualified candidate?

Your cover letter must gain attention, so dust off your best writing skills or seek help if you need it. Be self-critical and ask for others' opinions. Have at least three people who are excellent writers read your cover letter.

Create a unique letter for each application. Remember, the ATS has no sympathy; if you don't hit the right keywords for the job description, you have just been overlooked, period.

Also, don't skip sending a cover letter as not doing so will be interpreted as a sign of laziness. John Lees, a UK-based career strategist and author of Knockout CV, agrees. "Even if only one in two cover letters gets read, that's still a 50% chance that including one could help you.

EASY, ORGANIZED, COVER LETTER FORMAT

You can quickly write and tailor any business letter using this standard format. Use the same font style for your letter and resume, but create variety and style by changing type size, and using bold where appropriate. **See the explanation of the various parts of the cover letter following this sample.**

Your Full Name

Email address

Website address

Phone number

Date

Recipient's full name

Title

Organization

Address

(do not include phone number in an address)

Dear Mr., Ms., Dr.: (if you *absolutely* can't get his/her name, use To whom it may concern:)

Attention-getting opening sentence. Tie in sentence. Preview sentence with reference to position (preview 2 reasons to hire you).

Clear intro sentence about first reason they should hire you followed by supporting sentences with number, testimonial, or the like. Don't repeat resume. Seven lines max for this paragraph.

Same for second reason they should hire you. This one can be converted to a *SHORT* SHARE story highlighting how you solved a problem they need solved. Seven lines MAX.

Short closing paragraph with action statement, contact info and thank you.

Sincerely,

Your signature (write neatly)

Your name

Title*

*As an option your title can go in your heading under your name.

Don't go on to a second page.

YOUR FULL NAME

Place your full name at the top of your letter. That is, use your first name and middle initial or name, and last name. ***Don't*** label the parts of your header (i.e., Name:, Email:, etc.). No nicknames. Use 14-point, bold font.

YOUR ADDRESS

Mailing addresses are optional these days. Most communication with a potential employer will occur through email and phone but, since many employers prefer to hire locals, adding your address can't hurt. I have chosen to leave it off some examples. Unfortunately, these days security concerns must also be taken into consideration.

YOUR EMAIL ADDRESS

Your email address should be professional and a reflection of your name. If you have been using <u>hotlvr@dmail.net</u>, it's time for a change. Use 12-point, bold font for your email address.

YOUR WEBSITE

You should have a professional website or e-portfolio that also reflects your name. Place it under your email address. Use 12-point, bold font. Place a few extra spaces between your website address and your phone number if necessary to make it stand out.

DATE

You have seen many ways to express dates but, though you may wish to alter it if applying internationally, stick to month (write out entire word), day and year. October 9, 2021, looks better than 10/9/21.

INSIDE ADDRESS

First, find your contact's name. "To whom it may concern" smacks of pure laziness. There is always a way to get a name. Use social media, website research, or phone the company and ask the name of the HR manager. This is particularly important for executive cover letters.

The name, title, organization and address of the person to whom you are writing is called the inside address and it should appear 2 spaces below the date. Triple check for accuracy of spelling, courtesy title, etc. Remember the message under the message. An inside address on a letter to me would be as follows:

Fred Coon
Chairman, CEO
Stewart, Cooper and Coon, Inc.
PO Box 50099
Phoenix, AZ 85076

SALUTATION

The opening of your letter, the salutation, gives you a chance to establish that you know who the addressee is and how to properly address him or her. Dear Mr. or Ms. (never Mrs.) is usually the appropriate salutation. Always use the salutation, "Honorable" or "Doctor" where appropriate. Some people take great stock in their titles. They spent years earning them and you should respect them by getting them right. You can easily look up courtesy titles online. Finally, if flushing left, use a colon (:), not a comma.

Write your two middle paragraphs first, focusing on reasons they should hire you. Then, create an introduction. Typically, the introduction is the most difficult part to write, so here are a few ideas for how to begin.

ATTENTION-GETTING INTRODUCTION

The opening of your cover letter should consist of a powerful attention grabber, followed by a sentence that ties the attention grabber to a preview of two reasons to hire you. **Remember, you should write the first paragraph of your letter AFTER you have written the two paragraphs in the body that describe your skills.** Once you have clearly expressed why *they* should hire *you*, then you can return to the beginning and work on gaining their attention using one of these recommended methods.

Your ability to create an interesting opening is key to enticing them to read the whole letter, so avoid neutral, boring, overused statements like, "I read at X that you have a position opening in your widget department and I'd like to be considered."

The **most *boring*** cover letters begin like this:

The purpose of this letter...

I am writing this letter...

This letter is intended to...

These show that the message under your message is that you are unimaginative. By the same token, you don't want to sound desperate or hokey, so also **avoid** phrases like this:

Sales down? Need the best person to being them up?

Looking for the best person to fill your X position?

Instead of using meaningless phrases, gain a potential employer's attention by using short quotes, references to others working in the organization, or meaningful statistics and references to field-specific trends.

SHORT QUOTES AND TESTIMONIALS

Short quotes of famous people are one of the most interesting ways to begin a letter. You can easily look up quotes on specific industries, or by famous people. Be sure the quote is short, that it can easily be tied into the job, and that you indicate who said it. Try, for instance, this: Bill Gates once said, "If you think your teacher is tough, wait until you get a boss."

If you have found the perfect quote, but fear the reader won't know the author, add his or her title. For example, you may say, "The great myth of our times is that technology is communication." Composer Libby Larsen.

Tying the quote to the job and your qualifications is critical or the quote will seem disjointed. If you are applying for a teaching job, for example, you might do this:

Bill Gates once said, "If you think your teacher is tough, wait until you get a boss."Gates knows that great teaching means setting high but achievable standards that will prepare students for today's competitive workplace. My 28 years of experience empowering students to achieve their goals, and track record of developing curriculum that anticipates the employment needs of Pennsylvania industry are two reasons you should consider me for the full-time, tenure-track position at X University.

Verbatim testimonials from clients and coworkers can also be effective in gaining attention. Be sure the person you are quoting knows that potential employers may call for more information. Testimonials can be worked into your first paragraph just like other quotes.

REFERENCES TO MUTUAL ACQUAINTANCES

Earlier in this book I indicated that, according to Richard Bolles author of *What Color is Your Parachute?*[20] employers often ask trusted employees for recommendations of candidates to fill positions. If a friend or acquaintance has mentioned an opening, send your materials at once and refer to him or her in the introductory paragraph of your cover letter. Here is an example of how to do so:

*Your Director of International Sales, Philip Esposito, just informed me that you have an opening for a buyer at ABC Coffee Roasting Company. I've just spent three years touring South American coffee plantations assessing quality and developing contracts for XYZ Company as Lead Buyer. My **experience** and **knowledge base** will fit perfectly with your system as you expand operations.*

Now you've set yourself apart. You've shown experience, expertise and ability, and are the object of respect.

INDUSTRY-SPECIFIC TRENDS AND STATISTICS

Referring to industry-specific trends and statistics shows you are current in your knowledge and can react to changes in your field. If I were applying for a job in hospital administration, I may begin my cover letter like this:

Seventy-five million Baby Boomers are moving into their geriatric years. As demand for medical services increases, so does the need for strong strategic planning and administrative skills in the organizations challenged with caring for this population.

---

20   Bolles, R. (2019). *What color is your parachute: A practical manual for job-hunters and career-changers.* Ten Speed Press.

PREVIEW OF REASONS TO HIRE YOU

Stating clearly in the beginning of the letter why they should hire you does two things. First, doing so reinforces your brand and value. Second, a clear structure for the letter is established. The two reasons to hire are appear in bold in this example.

> *Seventy-five million Baby Boomers are moving into their geriatric years. As demand for medical services increases, so does the need for* **strong strategic planning** *and* **administrative skills** *in the organizations challenged caring for this population.*

The second and third paragraphs of your cover letter (the body) will explain and exemplify the reasons to hire you listed in your introduction. See? Clear, organized structure.

THE BODY

Focus on writing the body of your letter first. The body of your cover letter should include two paragraphs not to exceed five to seven lines each (four is better). A well-written, concise, action-packed letter is highly effective, so don't overload the reader with the story of your life. Conne once received a 3-page, single-spaced letter of application detailing the candidate's personal journey through life and career, including childbearing. She still uses it as an example of what *not* to do when creating a cover letter. Your cover letter should fit on ONE page.

Also beware of beginning *too many* sentences with "I," which can make you seem self-focused. Eliminate a few of them by beginning sentences with nouns or pronouns, or the adjective "my." For example, "I have extensive knowledge of the X industry, which enables me to…" could be expressed, "My extensive knowledge of the X industry enables me to…"

The first paragraph *in the body of your letter* is the second paragraph of the document (after your introduction, of course). It is about *one thing only*: the first reason they should hire you. Don't be tempted to go off on tangents or repeat what is in your resume. Think of the job description as it relates to your brand, experience and accomplishments, and emotional intelligence. Work in some hard numbers that demonstrate your success (see the example letter). Make sure your references can verify that your claims are true.

The second paragraph *of the body of your letter* addresses only the second reason they should hire you and should accomplish everything the first paragraph does. Remember, stay on track with the point of each paragraph. You can give them the whole enchilada in your resume.

CLOSING PARAGRAPH

Your close should be brief and include an action step. Will you send a follow up letter, email, or other form of correspondence? Will you call or a visit them? Whatever you say you will do, do it when you tell them you will do it! I recommend the following language for your close:

> *Please review my resume. I will call you on [date—give them a week] to discuss the possibility of scheduling an interview. You can contact me at (XXX) XXX-XXXX or* <u>DKillick@dmail.com</u> *if you have any questions in the meantime. Thank you.*

Avoid excess words in your close. Phrases like "questions or concerns" and "thank you for your time and consideration" are wordy and add length with no value. Also, if you provide a specific date and/or time, then make sure you keep your commitment.

SIGNATURE BLOCK

The most commonly used close in business is "sincerely." Don't try to get cute here with phrases like "Profitably yours" or "In sincerest hope" and so forth.

Space two lines down from your closing paragraph (remember, you're still flushed left). Type Sincerely, (note the comma) and space down three lines for your signature. Then, type your name. This time, you can use a nickname if you wish, like Dan instead of Daniel. Directly under your name, type in your title and, under that, if appropriate, your organization.

ADDITIONAL ADVICE

Here is a brief list of mechanical suggestions for your cover letter. See also the formatted example.

- Block your letter left side of page. Do not use the letterhead of the organization for which you are currently working.
- Always use the middle initial of the person to whom you are writing. If you have to call someone to get it, then do so. It is a proper professional touch.
- Use 1" margins all around, but you can fudge them a little if you need one more line.
- No more than four paragraphs with no more than seven lines per paragraph.
- Don't abbreviate anything but the state in the inside address (ex. NY or CA) and the courtesy title (Dr., Mr., Ms.).
- Use 11- to 12-point font that matches your resume.
- Your phone number should be clear and stand out (use bold).
- Your email and website addresses must be on all correspondence.
- Under no circumstances mention or even allude to the fact that you may not be qualified.
- Humor is great after you have the job or in the interview, but avoid it in a cover letter.
- Avoid trite statements such as, "I'm confident my skills and abilities will be beneficial to your company, blah, blah and blah." EVERYONE applying for this position says the same thing. Your job is to set yourself above the crowd.
- Eliminate grammar and spelling mistakes. I guarantee that, if either your resume or cover letter contains mistakes, it will be cast aside, regardless of how well-qualified you may be. Remember, "tin" and "ten" will both pass muster in spell check programs.
- Reread everything at least three times, once backwards. Read it out loud to your search partner. Read it to your mom. Read it to my mom. Give it to someone who can write well. Let them review it and read it back to you. Hearing your work read out loud is magical for picking up awkwardness and error.
- Be sure to use key words from the job description.

SUCCESS STORY: SHORTER IS SWEETER

CONTRIBUTED BY CONNE REECE, CO-AUTHOR AND EDITOR

Megan was an exceptional student with excellent job search materials. With a major in communication and a minor in biology, she worked as a naturalist and interpretive park ranger before moving into communication specialist roles.

I worked with Megan on her resume and cover letters as they evolved and noticed that she had a tendency to be wordy. One cover letter exceeded 450 words.

In her rewrite, Megan focused on organizing the cover letter into four short paragraphs that provided two reasons to hire her. She cut out a lot of "fluff" and used concrete, descriptive words to convey her value. This approach reduced the number of words in her cover letter to about 250.

Megan says that she has used this format for all her cover letters and has been told by many potential employers that they "appreciate the quick yet highly informative read that concisely organizes her former experiences and their direct relation to the job posting."

ADDITIONAL RESOURCES

- Alred, G.J., Brusaw, C.T., & Oliv, W.E. (2018). *The business writer's handbook* (12th ed.). Bedford/St. Martin's.
- Gallo, A. (2020, December 23). *How to write a cover letter*. Harvard Business Review. https://hbr.org/2014/02/how-to-write-a-cover-letter/
- Thill, J. & Bovee, C. (2021). *Excellence in business communication* (12th ed.). Pearson.

SAMPLE COVER LETTER

Daniel T. Killick
DanKillick@dmail.com
www.DanKillick.com
(555) 444-3333

October 9, 2021
Julia Crowe
General Manager
Awesome Electronics
44 Mall Circle Drive
Townupnorth, ME 00000

Dear Ms. Crowe:

Bill Gates once said, "If your culture doesn't like geeks, you're in real trouble." Like Gates, I am proud to be called a "computer geek." I grew up plugged in and will use my knowledge of technological problem solving and my success as a sales rep to build lasting relationships with customers as a sales associate at Awesome Electronics.

Though I possess broad knowledge of all electronics, I excel in cell phone sales, set up and service. I'm fluent in iPhone, Samsung, LG, Sony and more, and can quickly solve customers' problems. My positive and personal approach to fulfilling customer needs at Portland Cell earned me a promotion to assistant manager in just 6 months.

My track record in sales has also consistently exceeded expectations. As a sales associate at Portland Cell, I used upselling techniques to boost the bottom line and had a 10% higher than average record over the past year. In addition, my position at Portland has enabled me to develop managerial skills such as leadership, problem solving and customer service.

Please review my resume. I will call you on Monday, October 25 to discuss the possibility of an interview. In the meantime, please contact me at (555) 444-3333 if you have any questions. Thank you.

Sincerely,

Dan Killick

Daniel T. Killick
Assistant Manager
Portland Cell

CHAPTER 7
CREATING AN ONLINE PRESENCE

The greater your online presence, depending upon your specific rung on the employment hierarchy, the better you will do in a job search. However, the *quality* of your electronic presence will make or break your credibility. Here are the online options I'll be going over in this chapter:

- The use of common sense and social media "scrubbers" to clean up past mistakes
- An e-portfolio/Career WebFolio© with video resume
- A **professionally written** LinkedIn account and profile
- A Facebook account or a cleaned-up version of your current Facebook account
- A Twitter (and possibly other) social media account

Over 70% of potential employers are Googling you (some studies have shown that number to be over 90%). They are cruising your social media and making decisions about your character, judgement, communication skills, personal focus and more. Surprisingly, many people still believe that their social media, with the right control, is private.

Conne once had the human resources director of an international company speak to her class about hiring practices. They questioned his words of caution about their use of social media, but fell silent when he said, "I work for a multi-billion dollar international company. How big of a deal do you think it is for us to spend $10,000 on a social media investigator?" **You only *think* they can't see everything**.

Interestingly, a positive social media presence can work to your benefit. A 2018 CareerBuilder survey indicated that, "Nearly half of employers (47 percent) say that if they can't find a job candidate online, they are *less* likely to call that person in for an interview."[21]

CLEAN UP YOUR SOCIAL MEDIA

Pretend you are a boss looking to hire the right person for a job. Then, looking through his/her eyes, Google yourself. Google every name you might have placed information, posts and pictures under and see what you find.

Every person thinking of hiring you is doing so because they think you can make them money or solve a problem. When you get a job, YOU BECOME THE ORGANIZATION. Therefore, employers want to know that you will represent their company well and that you have the judgment not to embarrass them. They want to know that you have common sense.

A 2017 CareerBuilder survey[22] revealed that "...more than half of employers (54 percent) have found content on social media that caused them not to hire a candidate for an open role. The survey indicated the percent of employers who decided not to hire a candidate based on their social media profile issues. Here are the results:

- Candidate posted provocative/inappropriate photos, videos or information: 39%
- Candidate posted information about them drinking or using drugs: 38%
- Candidate had discriminatory comments related to race, gender, religion: 32%
- Candidate bad-mouthed their previous company or fellow employee: 30%
- Candidate lied about qualifications: 27%
- Candidate had poor communication skills: 27%

---

21 CareerBuilder (2018). More than half of employers have found content on social media that caused them not to hire a candidate. Retrieved August 6, 2020 from http://press.careerbuilder.com/2018-08-09-More-Than-Half-of-Employers-Have-Found-Content-on-Social-Media-That-Caused-Them-NOT-to-Hire-a-Candidate-According-to-Recent-CareerBuilder-Survey/

22 CareerBuilder (2017). *Number of employers using social media to screen candidates at all-time high.* Retrieved August 6, 2020 from http://press.careerbuilder.com/2017-06-15-Number-of-Employers-Using-Social-Media-to-Screen-Candidates-at-All-Time-High-Finds-Latest-CareerBuilder-Study/

- Candidate was linked to criminal behavior: 26%
- Candidate shared confidential information from previous employers: 23%
- Candidate's screen name was unprofessional: 22%
- Candidate lied about an absence: 17%
- Candidate posted too frequently: 17%"

Some people don't have common sense. How many times have you seen an inappropriate social media post, tweet or picture? Take an honest look at your accounts. Would an employer be proud to hire you? Part of developing your online presence involves cleaning up past mistakes you have made with your social media. You can do much yourself by simply deleting items you think will work against you.

Another thing that will turn off potential employers is being too self-focused. If your Facebook page included nothing but selfie after selfie, you are likely to be looked at as narcissistic. **Be especially careful not to use face-altering apps**, which will make you seem underconfident and superficial. Imagine a hiring manager's surprise when you walk in their door looking entirely different from your pictures! Ask your friends not to post compromising pictures of you either.

If you think you have some hidden skeletons on your social media, purchase a social media scrubber. A social media scrubber is a program that searches your social media and alerts you to posts and pictures that may be offensive. There are many brands of scrubbers, including Brandyourself.com, Scrubber.Social and more. These programs are worth their small monthly fee if you think your past social media choices have not been the best.

CREATE AN E-PORTFOLIO OR CAREER WEBFOLIO©

You may remember that, in Chapter 2, I asked you to gather some materials. These included work samples, testimonials, reference letters, performance reviews, photographs (a *professional* head shot and other action shots of you working or volunteering) and videos (short, professional clips that show off your speaking or other relevant skills like understanding of technology). A reread of Chapter 2 is recommended because these items will be used to build your e-portfolio.

An e-portfolio (electronic portfolio, also called a Career WebFolio©), is a one-stop-shopping website that includes "artifacts" that reinforce your brand and prove to potential employers that you are the right person for the job. Please remember that the style of your e-portfolio will depend on your career focus and brand, but **MOST job seekers do not have e-portfolios so, DONE RIGHT, they are magic for gaining employment.**

Let's discuss DONE RIGHT. Remember the message under the message? If you think your resume and cover letter are sending messages under the messages, understand that your e-portfolio is doing so by 100-fold. Every aspect of this website must be planned and critiqued with great attention to detail. Poor work examples and testimonials that seem contrived will decrease your chance of getting hired.

Conne had a student who created a fabulous e-portfolio. It got noticed in the university system and the student was asked to present it to the Pennsylvania State Board of Governors before graduating. After graduation, her career progressed swiftly, and she was told by *two* hiring managers that it was because of her e-portfolio.

My clients rave about their online Stewart, Cooper & Coon Career WebFolios. Recruiters and hiring managers like them as well because our Career WebFolios are visual, concise, clear and present *value*. Value is what all companies want.

An internet search will reveal many programs you can use to create a website for free. Most will offer you a subscription, which I highly recommend because you can choose your own domain name. If you are using a service for free, potential employers will see something like this: http://dk1234.site.com/dankillick/ instead of cleaner-looking danielkillick. com. The second reason to get a subscription is that you get more options if you pay. Most website services are in the $20 per month range.

If you feel that building a website is too much for you, hire someone to do it for you. My firm, for example, offers this service.

To see examples of executive-level E-Portfolios, go to:

StewartCooperCoon.com and type Career WebFolio in the search bar.

Typically, your portfolio will include tabs or links through which others can see your resume, a video resume, work samples, videos (perhaps of you giving presentations if that is part of your job), testimonials, SHARE© Stories, a gallery (which would ONLY include action shots related to your work or volunteer activities if appropriate), links to your social media, publications, and anything else that is germane to what you do. It could include your (brief) philosophy about your profession, for example, or a personal mission. Be sure to make your contact information stand out.

Don't overpopulate the site with lengthy videos or documents. Instead, give them samples. Don't forget the message under the message. If you need good writing skills (and who doesn't?), give them a brief writing sample, not a 40-page document. You may include a FAQ page answering questions such as whether you are willing to relocate, but leave out personal details (age, marital status, etc.).

Now is the time to have a professional head shot done. Most photographers will take several shots, perhaps a few that are formal and a few that are casual. When choosing a photographer, look at his or her previous work. Whose style captures who you are? Should you consider a black and white photo? An outdoor setting? An action shot in which you are looking off-camera? You may be able to work more than one picture into your website. Just be careful not to seem *too* self-focused.

Remember, above all, your BRAND. How does each artifact contribute to promoting who you say you are and what you say you can do? Your website isn't meant to include everything you have ever done. Be selective. Show them your *best* work! To that end, *revise* work you have done previously. Want to include an executive summary you wrote last year to show off your business writing skills? Revise it until it is perfect. Picture not in focus? Re-take it.

Conne tells me that those seeking entry-level positions hearing this for the first time often say, "What if I don't have this stuff?" She says, "If you don't have it, GET IT! Don't have any pictures of yourself volunteering at that event? First, ask around. If you can't find any, put on your Special Olympics t-shirt, go back to the track and have someone take a few snaps of you looking active. If you haven't kept recordings of yourself making presentations, get some friends together and stage one." Some of the pictures of Conne teaching that appear on her university's website were taken by a colleague in an empty classroom. As long as you aren't deceiving anyone about your skills, activities or abilities, go for it. THINK ACTION SHOTS, NOT SELFIES.

Here are a few additional pieces of advice for building your portfolio:

1. **Avoid template language**. EVERYONE'S profile is going to say, "Hi, I'm Dan and I want to show you...". Language like that is too informal and cutesy. Plus, you don't want to take the chance that someone else's portfolio will be the same. Using third person language that reflects your brand is preferred. Try this:

   ***Dan Killick**, M.A. is a social media analyst with 9+ years of experience creating data-driven strategy that builds customer traffic and increases return on investment.*

2. **Align your portfolio with what is on your resume**. You want to *reinforce* what you can do and make it easy for someone interested in you to talk to people who know your work, so **create tabs that reflect your resume's major sections**. Ask the references you provide on your resume to write testimonials and make sure those testimonials reinforce your brand. Post those to your online portfolio.

3. **Don't include a collage of unrelated skill sets**. You're a computer software specialist who does a little photography on the side? Don't confuse a potential employer by not focusing on the skills related to your chosen profession. Make two websites.

4. **Find ways to relate your soft skills and emotional intelligence.** Testimonials and SHARE© stories are a great way to do this. Pictures that show you helping others is another excellent way to promote likability.

5. **Add an Employer Attraction Recording (EAR)**. Employer Attraction Recordings (EARs), sometimes called video resumes, are short videos through which you relate to potential employers your qualifications for a job. You may have several EARs, each targeted at a specific industry or skill set. There is no cookie-cutter method for making an EAR, but yours should reflect your resume and personality without being unprofessional. Here are some suggestions for how to begin:

- Think of a unique reason your viewer would want to hire you more than anyone else in your field (that part is important). This "reason to hire you" should already be reflected on your resume, so draw from that document. Begin by introducing yourself and providing your contact information and current job title or job goal. Use some graphics or still pictures to illustrate numbers that appear on your resume. In the video, you can explain what they mean and how you succeeded.

- Create a SHARE© Story that exemplifies your skills and accomplishments. Remember: You need to be able to tell the story just like you would in an interview without reading it off cue cards. Try to blend it into the video. Say, for example, you had a great experience during your tenure at Company X and you want to tell your related SHARE© story. You can't just start talking about it. Connect your thoughts with transitions like this: "I really developed my managerial skills while working at X. For example, …"

- Design an introduction and a close for your video. Slowly and clearly say your name, what your profession is, etc. Don't give your age. Think of yourself as a professional, not a college student, if you have recently graduated. Explain experience that directly relates to the job you want. Subtitle it with contact information and don't forget to say thank you at the end.

- Language is critical. Don't refer to your EAR as an EAR. Potential employers don't know that phrase. In fact, you can just talk to them as though they are in the room with you. For example, you might say, "Today I'd like to share with you some of the work I have been doing in events planning. Specifically, I'll be telling you about an open house I planned for the Scranton Pennsylvania Chamber of Commerce and about some challenges I faced during the planning process." Avoid saying "reasons to hire me" or anything else that sounds hokey.

- Stay animated and smile. Read the section in this book on body language and verbal expression in interviews for tips. Use gestures. Vary your expressions. Enunciate.

- Lighting is critical. Dark videos look fuzzy and unprofessional.

- Add some professional-looking animation, pictures, video, etc. You can talk over the pictures, etc. NO BACKGROUND MUSIC.

- Aim for a total of 1 to 2 minutes *tops*. DO NOT EXCEED 2 MINUTES. Pace is important. Give the viewer enough time to absorb what you are saying without allowing them to get bored. That's about 150 words per minute. Don't speak slower than 140 wpm or faster than 160 wpm.

- Tie everything together with your resume. Your EAR has to be just as focused as your written documents.

Once you have decided what you will say in your EAR, practice, but don't memorize and don't read off of cue cards. It is critical to sound natural and articulate, not staged. Practice smiling, looking into the camera and using gestures. Be humble, but confident.

Make a test video to see how you look and sound (dress appropriately even for your first take). Share it with friends, family, former employers and professors and get their feedback. Tweak your video until it is perfect.

I highly recommend hiring a professional videographer. If you can't afford it, contact your local university media department and see if a student would be willing to help you for a reduced rate. Students usually have access to the specialized equipment needed for a project like this.

JOIN OR MAINTAIN LINKEDIN

This section, on LinkedIn, will be the most detailed section in this chapter, as it is by far the most powerful online networking for working professionals. However, a full explanation of how to maximize its use is beyond the scope of this book. In *Leveraging LinkedIn for Job Search Success,*[23] Andrew Ko, Kelly Stewart and I provide a detailed step-by-step guide for building a LinkedIn profile.

Currently, there are more than 660 million LinkedIn members in 200 countries, including executives from each company on Forbes' Fortune 500 list. In fact, one would be hard pressed to find a Fortune 500 executive who is not an active LinkedIn member. The use of LinkedIn is critical in aligning job seekers with hiring authorities since both use it.

In straightforward terms, if you are not on LinkedIn, you will certainly not be visible to potential employers, recruiters, and clients. Moreover, a noticeable lack of presence on the network can even translate into a form of uncertainly regarding your professional legitimacy and technical competence.

Building a basic personal profile is the first step toward gathering the extensive benefits of LinkedIn. Your profile should spotlight your strengths, accomplishments, talents, and education. These elements will allow you to be noticed by colleagues and decision makers. The following are guidelines for creating a results-driven profile on LinkedIn.

---

23   Coon, F., Ko, A. & Stewart, K. (2019). *Leveraging LinkedIn for job search success.* GAFF publishing.

UNDERSTANDING THE BASICS

LinkedIn, as a social media platform, should be thought of as a corporate boardroom (even if that's not exactly where you work). It does not have the informal feel of Facebook and the kind of information you post on it should be professional, not personal. Use LinkedIn to build your brand such that others see you as an expert. Make connections with those with whom you can build a mutually beneficial professional relationship. To make the most out of using LinkedIn, you should focus on four strategies. You should be:

- Intentional—Understand and relate how your work experience translates to new positions
- Professional—Select relevant, compelling information
- Proficient—Craft your profile with a clear target in mind
- Prolific—Leverage networks and refresh your connections

Your goal with LinkedIn is to achieve 100% profile completeness. The more complete your profile is, the greater the chance you stand of appearing higher in searches. It is impossible to achieve a complete profile without including a profile photo, filling in information in each section, and receiving three recommendations.

Your LinkedIn profile page offers the chance to *expand* the information that already exists on your resume. Therefore, in addition to merely uploading your resume, take advantage of the opportunities to add relevant documents, publications, and even supporting videos which can help you project your value to prospective employers. LinkedIn users should ensure that they take full advantage of each section that applies to them and express their personal brand accordingly.

Be sure to include a *professionally taken* photograph. Poke around on a few LinkedIn profiles. You can easily tell the difference between a professionally taken headshot and a picture taken with a phone. There is no comparison. Professional portraits say you are serious about your career.

When performing a LinkedIn search for prospective candidates, recruiters and employers rely heavily on industry-specific words and phrases. For instance, a search for a project manager may include keywords such as "engineering," "analytics," "proactive management," or "operational proficiency." Even if you are among the top in your field, you are likely to remain under the radar if you do not place the right keywords within your profile. In fact, your profile must be rich in keywords so the search engine will match you to someone who needs your skills.

Keep your LinkedIn profile positive. Professionals seeking employment—or any other type of meaningful business connection—should refrain from sharing overly personal details or specifics that could be seen as negative.

Consistency of "voice" is also important, but whether you use first (I am...) or third person (Dan Killick is...) isn't important. Even leading experts on LinkedIn vary in their opinions about whether to use first person, third person or a mix. The goal is to have a consistent feel from section to section but writing in third person is particularly effective in the About section (see my profile).

Regularly update your status. Your status updates will remain on all your connections' homepages until cleared out by more recent information. A constant flow of status updates guarantees a constant presence in front of your connections.

Each section of a LinkedIn profile has a character limit. As this isn't a resume and space is not an issue, use as many of the allotted characters as possible. Again, you want to make your profile rich in content. Create powerful, action-packed sentences.

Make your profile 100% visible to the public, regardless of whether they are a connection. The whole purpose of LinkedIn is for prospective employers and business professionals to be able to get a look at who you are. Select *all* contact settings, as this will increase your chance of showing up in a search. If someone searches for an "Expertise Request," and you do not have that option selected, the number of people who are able to view your profile is limited.

TIPS FOR YOUR LINKEDIN ACCOUNT SETUP

Basic memberships on LinkedIn are free, but you can upgrade for a fee at any time. Go to LinkedIn.com and follow the instructions for setting up an account. This section of this book is not meant to provide step-by-step instructions. Rather, I'm alerting you to a few choices you will make in following LinkedIn's instructions for account set up. You can skip some steps and go back later if you want.

Use your personal email address or a specially created email just for LinkedIn. Your email address should contain your name and not be something like BigDogLover@dmail.com.

During the set-up process, you will be asked to verify your email and enter a 6-digit code. Then, you'll be asked whether you want to send connection requests to people you have communicated with using the email you are using for LinkedIn. **I recommend skipping this step for now, since you won't have a chance to write a personalized message.**

You will be asked to upload a photo to your profile. **ABSOLUTELY DO NOT SKIP THIS STEP.** Have a professional head shot taken (re-read the chapter on branding). Update your photo every few years or any time your appearance changes a lot.

Eventually, LinkedIn will take you through a systematic process to build your profile. Be aware that the first few steps are designed to allow LinkedIn to mine data so they can connect you to others using your address and other personal information. *You can skip these steps for now but go back later when you are ready to control your information and use it to your benefit.* Instead, we will focus on inputting professional background information, building your network and following sources of news and other information.

Your professional background information is conveyed through your LinkedIn profile. As you build your profile you can add sections tailored to your brand and career. Here, I have provided a few suggestions.

HEADLINE (220-CHARACTER LIMIT BUT IT KEEPS CHANGING)

The goal of the headline section is to define who you are. Hard hitting and short is best. Target 120 characters. Try to include your most valuable information, including current job title, industries or product lines, and information that puts you at an advantage. If you are at entry-level, create a descriptive "title" that does not mislead readers into thinking you are currently employed under that title. Examples include, Social Media Specialist, Computer Programmer and the like. You can go up to 220, but make it count.

EXAMPLE 1:

John Smith

VP of Business Development

Executive leader who builds motivated and goal-oriented teams, grows existing markets, develops new territory, and maximizes company profits.

EXAMPLE 2:

Jane Smith

Chief Marketing Officer

E-Marketing | Corporate Branding | Market Penetration | New Product Launch | Traditional Media specialist who applies creative strategies to grow top and bottom lines.

SUMMARY (2000-CHARACTER LIMIT)

The goal of the Summary section of your LinkedIn profile is to strategically position yourself as an expert in the reader's eye. Use short paragraphs, bullet points, and list specific accomplishments and other impressive information. You can view my LinkedIn profile at https://www.linkedin.com/in/fredcoon/.

My summary contains 1961 characters but changes as I modify it periodically. Note the first-person tense that I mentioned earlier. It is more personal and reads better.

My profile includes my licenses and credentials. Please understand, mine is written to promote my company, so it will look different than yours in the respect that I list my company's operating divisions. My books are also listed, as well as my speaking engagements and other materials. I also state my purpose for being on LinkedIn.

EXPERIENCE (1988-CHARACTER LIMIT PER POSITION):

You will have a limited amount of space in this section. However, if you have developed your resume according to the instructions in this book, posting it in your LinkedIn profile should be a snap.

Your goal for the Experience section of your LinkedIn profile is to write keyword-rich content. The majority of the content should be accomplishment-focused, but also take into account your roles and responsibilities. In this section, you are not as restricted by a character limit and, like a resume, limited by space on the page. Include all positions and companies, as you never know who you might connect with. Additionally, this paints a picture of not only what you have done, but what you are capable of doing.

Use a combination of paragraphs and single-line items. By doing this you can dictate where you want the reader's eyes to go on the page.

EDUCATION

This section is not just for the colleges or universities you attended. Include additional credentials, certificates, webinars, seminars, academic honors, awards and other related qualifications and accomplishments. The more of these you include, the more you showcase your abilities, AND the more you connect with others who have attended the same type of training or hold the same certifications.

You should also consider listing your educational knowledge by topics, especially if you have recently graduated. DO NOT list the titles of courses as they can be misleading. Instead, think about relevant skills you learned. Don't list the date you graduated.

HONORS AND AWARDS

In the Honors and Awards section, you can highlight any distinguishing recognition that you have received over the course of your career. List articles you have had published, publications in which you have been quoted and any expertise you have that wouldn't fit into other sections of your profile. Cite commendations you have received from professional organizations or volunteer work. Many of us don't think of being specially selected to do something as an award, but listing such items is another way to boost your credibility. For example, if you were invited to speak, singled out for your high performance, or asked to fill an interim position, work it in to this section.

RECOMMENDATIONS FROM OTHERS

Receiving recommendations through LinkedIn is essential because you will not have a complete profile without them, and because they show that people who have first-hand experience with you in a professional setting are willing to put their reputations on the line by recommending you.

You MUST have at least three recommendations on LinkedIn, otherwise your profile will not be considered "complete." Complete profiles are weighted higher in search results, so it is essential that you have a complete profile.

At a minimum, strive to obtain recommendations from 10% of your LinkedIn connections. LinkedIn experts agree that this is the optimal ratio for this section so, if you have 90 connections on LinkedIn, you should have a minimum of 9 recommendations. This can be achieved by following these steps:

1. Go to the LinkedIn profile of the person from whom you're requesting a recommendation. You must be a first-level connection of that person to request a recommendation.

2. Click the "More..." button below their profile picture and select "Request a Recommendation" from the drop-down menu.

3. Select your relationship to the recommender and your position at the time you worked together.

4. Write a brief note about what you would like the recommender to say and click the "Send" button.

Try to have one recommendation for each position held. This demonstrates a consistent pattern of success from job-to-job. Your recommendations should come from peers, those you reported to, those who reported to you, and others who are knowledgeable about your skills in key areas.

LinkedIn will directly send you a final version of the text. This permits you to either reject or accept/post the recommendation. While members can leave you endorsements at their own volition, requesting them from connections whose presence would make a positive impact on your professional standing is certainly recommended.

CHARACTERS THAT CAN BE USED WITH LINKEDIN

Sometimes LinkedIn profiles can be spiced up by adding special characters. **DO NOT use characters like these on your resume as they are not applicant tracking software friendly.** You can always copy and paste characters you like from another profile, or use the more popular ones below:

- Phone: ✆ ☏
- Scissors: ✁ ✃✄
- Music: ♪♫♩♬♭♮♯° ø
- Write: ✎✏ ✐
- Stars: ⋆✢✣✤✥❋✦✧☆ ⌞☆⌝ ✪✫✬✭✮✯☆ ★✱✲ ✪✳✴✵✶✷✸✹✺✻✼ ❄❅ ❆❇❈
- Money: € £ ¥ ₴$ ₰¢ ₤¥ ₳₲₪₵元₣ ₱฿¤ ₡₮₭₩ﾅ円₢₥₫ ₦z ł ﷼₠₧₯₰RsK č ₹
- Hand: ☜☞ ☚☛☟
- Copyrights: ™ ℠© ® ℗
- Yes: ✓ √
- No: ☐☒☮ ✗✘✕✕
- Weather :☼ ☾☽ ☇☈⊙☉℃ ℉ ° ❄❅ϟ
- Flower: ✽✾✿❀❁❃❊❋
- Triangles: ▲▼◀▶ ◣◢◥◤◥▴▾ ◂▸△▽◁▷◿▻◅▵▹◃▿
- Flags: ⚐⚑
- Recycle: ♲ ♳♴♵♶♷♸♹♺♻♼
- Miscellaneous:
- Ratios: ½⅓⅕⅙⅛⅔⅖⅚⅜¾⅗⅝⅞⅘
- Compare: ≂≃≄≅≆≇≈ ≉≊≋≌≍≎≏≐≑≒≓≔≕≖≗≘≙≚≛≜≝≞≟≠ ≡≢≣≤ ≥ ≦≧≨≩≴≵≶≷
- Roman: I II III IV V VI VII VIII IX X XI XII L C D M i ii iii iv v vi vii viii ix x xi xii l c d m
- Circled: ①②③④⑤⑥⑦⑧⑨⑩➊➋➌➍➎➏➐➑➒➓ⒶⒷⒸⒹⒺⒻⒼⒽⒾⒿⓀⓁ ⓃⓄⓅⓆⓇⓈⓉⓊⓋⓌⓍⓎⓏⓐⓑⓒⓓⓔⓕⓖⓗⓘⓙⓚⓛⓜⓝⓞⓟⓠⓡⓢⓣⓤⓥⓦⓧⓨⓩ
- Functional: ␛␡␚␟␘␠␤␋␌␍␎␏␐␑␒␓␔␕␖␗␙␜␝␞
- Quotes: ❝❞« » ‟‹ › ⟨⟩„ ‵‶‘ ’ ‚ ‷ ” ‴‴″
- Round: ◉○◌◍◎●◐◑◒◓◔◕◖ ◗❂ ⊗⊙ ◘◙◍
- Boxes: ❏❐❑❒▀▁▂▃▄▅▆▇▉▊▋█▌▍▎▏▐░▒▓▔ ▕■□▢▣▤▥▦▧▨▩ ▬▭▮▯☰☱☲☳☴☵☶☷☐
- Pointers: ➝ ➢➣➤➥➦➧➨➚➘➙➛➜➔➝➞➟ ➠➡➢➣➤➥➦➧➨➩➪➫➬➭➮➯➱←↑→↓↔ ↚↛↜↝↞↟↠↡↢↣↤↥↦↧↨⇦⇨⇨⇨⇨⇨⇨⇨ ↫↬↭↮↯↰↱↲↳↴↵↶↷↸↹↺↻↼↽↾↿⇀⇁⇂⇃⇄⇅⇆⇇⇈⇉⇊⇋⇌⇍⇎⇏⇐⇑⇒⇓⇔⇕⇖⇗⇘⇙⇚⇛⇜⇝ ⇞⇟⇠⇡⇢⇣⇤⇥⇦⇧⇨⇩⇪⌦⌧⌫

LEVERAGING LINKEDIN

Your ability to use LinkedIn to your best advantage is critical to your job search. Social media is all about building relationships (a.k.a. networking) and LinkedIn is the perfect tool no matter what your level or profession.

CONNECT WITH OTHER MEMBERS

Once you join LinkedIn and build a profile, you will have the opportunity to search through the site's vast database and send invitations to connect with individuals who would be advantageous to have in your professional network. In addition, LinkedIn offers the prospect of synchronizing your personal account with your email account(s) to connect with other members. The more you work to develop your professional network, the more connections will become available to you. For instance, if upon entering the job market, you notice that a former college classmate is in a network with an HR professional or recruiter, you have the perfect chance to reach out to this individual who may be of assistance in your job search.

CONTRIBUTE TO YOUR NETWORK

Are you an authority on a specific subject relating to your industry or field? Have you come across an informative article that may be beneficial to others within your network? Keep in mind that while creating an inclusive LinkedIn profile is critical, regularly sharing ideas and engaging in meaningful dialogue with fellow members is also necessary to expand your network, build your reputation as a respected thought leader, and make valuable employment connections.

LinkedIn members should also remember that the fundamental purpose of any networking site is to "see and be seen." The interviews and meetings that result from having the right industry leaders view your LinkedIn page are dependent upon the quality of your content, contribution to relevant groups, and representation of your personal brand.

JOIN GROUPS

This is by far the most crucial section of your LinkedIn profile. Joining groups allows you to see the names and email addresses of everyone who asks to join your group and you can save that contact information for future outreach. You can also shape the group's focus by inviting people in your area of interest. As the group grows, you create a network that helps you find work and enhance your career. You create goodwill that pays you back in unforeseen ways. The more LinkedIn groups you join, the more professionals you can connect with directly.

Before creating a group, do a LinkedIn Groups Directory search to see if another similar group exists. If another such group is large and active, you may not want to create your own. If you decide to create a group, click the Create a Group button and follow the steps.

Join groups that demonstrate professional, industry and personal involvement and contribution. Be ACTIVE in each group you join. This could mean posting links to interesting articles, starting conversations in the discussions forum or introducing yourself to other members. The level of participation by group members is paramount to its success. If it's not seeded with posts early on, and builds in activity, it will wither and die, so don't just get people to join. Encourage them to post news, updates, jobs, respond to discussions, etc.

Join as many groups as possible. You are allowed by LinkedIn to be a member of 50 groups at any given time, and with more than 100,000 groups to choose from, maxing out your groups should not be difficult.

Once you have established a presence on LinkedIn, ask yourself several strategic questions to make certain your profile page is as effective as possible. Use these as a check sheet for success.

- Can my target demographic can view my profile?
- What would encourage another member to want to be part of my professional network and why?
- Have I articulated my professional value to recruiters and potential employers?
- What can I expect companies to draw from my LinkedIn profile?

BUILD A LINKEDIN CONTACT LIST

One of the benefits of LinkedIn is that it gives you access to those who may be looking for someone with your skills. You should, therefore, use it to build a contact list. Sign up for auto connecting extensions like LinkedIn Helper or We-Connect. Create a targeted list on LinkedIn, save it and setup your campaign to send bulk connection requests. You can even automate follow-ups after your connection request is accepted. I would, however, strongly suggest you read LinkedIn's policy on this before doing so.

Another way to build a contact list on LinkedIn is to search for a company name. Look at the titles of people who work there. Send them a message or request a link with them. If you request a link with them, give them a good reason to do so. It is getting harder and harder these days to secure first level links with members so make your explanation a good one.

Once you have established a link with someone, try to learn something about the person by looking at his or her profile, past blogposts, and so forth so you can tailor your communication. How you approach matters. Be brief and think about what would intrigue the recipient. Don't mention a job-hunting need the first time you reach out. Focus on how you can help them and cite a common point of interest (same industry niche, location, alma mater, etc.).

Regardless of field or industry, job seekers must remember that LinkedIn is only as effective its user. A profile that meets the essential criteria will greatly increase the likelihood of shortening your job search and garnering more opportunities.

FACEBOOK

Facebook has gone through substantial changes since its inception in 2004. Originally just for use by college students, it rapidly expanded to include city, state, and organizational networks. However, over the past few years, Facebook has exploded into not only the largest social network in the world, but into the driving force behind change in the new media industry, setting the pace for all future improvements and enhancements.

Facebook is no longer targeted toward the 8–25-year-old. In 2020, the average age of Facebook users was about 50.[24] An entire new string of capabilities has opened up, including being able to market yourself, a product or a business.

Facebook is often overlooked as a medium for professional networking even though it usually appears among the first results in most personal internet searches. More than simply an opportunity to post pictures of your last vacation, Facebook contains a myriad of professional groups to be searched and used. By creating a dynamic profile that shows only your most applicable characteristics, you can begin to connect with companies of interest. In fact, in February 2017, Facebook launched a job search tool through which companies can post current openings, easily accessed by users of the site.

If you are on Facebook solely for personal use, **do not** accept friend requests from professional contacts. If this occurs, simply reply with a message stating that you manage your

---

24 Clements, J. (2020). *Twitter usage reach in the United States in 2019 by age group.* Retrieved January 18, 2021 from https://www.statista.com/statistics/265647/SHARE©-of-us-internet-users-who-use-twitter-by-age-group/

professional network through LinkedIn, and include a link to your profile, as well as an invitation to join your network.

The key is to find a good mix between personal and professional. Develop a profile that you would be comfortable showing to your boss.

FACEBOOK CONTENT

The content of your social media pages is critical. Seeing or hearing about someone who was turned down for a job due to social media content is commonplace. Posting damaging information on Facebook will hinder your job search.

Facebook allows you to merge your professional self with your personal self. It gives you the opportunity to post photos, a personal bio, favorite quotations and information about personal interests, but this should be done with an eye to what a potential boss might want to see.

Since organizations are attracted to people who do volunteer work, you *can* use Facebook to show that you are trying to make the world a better place. However, Facebook should be used with caution. Interested employers are trying to make a connection between who you are as a person and whether you will be a good fit with their organization. Your social media, including Facebook, should *not* be a just collection of selfies and vacation pics. It should be a reflection of what you contribute to society.

Conne was once on a hiring committee for a faculty member to teach social media skills. "When the committee examined her Facebook, it was riddled with pictures of the candidate drinking at parties, in a bikini and so forth. What a terrible impression for someone applying to teach social media strategies to create! It made us cringe to think of our students seeing that," Conne said.

While it might be fun to connect with old college friends and reminisce about "that one party," it isn't wise to leave those conversations up on your wall for the rest of your connections to see. Just as you would with any conversation, if there is certain information that you don't want broadcast to a broad audience, hold that conversation via a personal message, sparing you and the other party possible embarrassment or worse.

On Facebook, set your default privacy settings to where only accepted friends can view your personal information. From there, you can edit specifics, including which of your "friends" you want to view all content, and which you would just like to have as a connection. However, one of the most common gaffes with Facebook is people thinking their profile is private, and only your accepted friends can view its content. This is NOT the case. Facebook has detailed privacy settings that you can adjust to fit your profile. You can have certain people as accepted friends but make those same individuals only able to view certain, basic information. Also be aware that organizations can and do hire social media forensic analysts who can look beyond your settings.

USING FACEBOOK GROUPS AND SETTINGS

Facebook puts a cap on the number of groups you can join. Unlike LinkedIn, you do not have to be as selective when joining a group, as the majority are fun and recreational. Additionally, Facebook also has pages that you can become a "fan" of, and those pages will show up in your profile. You can create groups and Fan Pages for products, services, events, businesses or even people and, depending on your career, this can be a tremendous marketing tactic. Just remember to be judicious. **Stay away from politics, religion and hot social issues for now**.

USING STATUS UPDATES TO PROMOTE YOURSELF

One of the key features of Facebook is status updates. You can update your status to include anything from where you ate lunch to an informative article you read. If you are unemployed and searching for a new career, you can use your Facebook status update as a marketing tactic. As with LinkedIn, you should regularly update your status, as it will show up on your connections' news feeds. However, remember to keep your status updates targeted toward your ultimate goal, whether that is finding a new job or establishing yourself as an expert in your field.

TWITTER

Twitter offers users the ability to say what is on their mind in quick, 280-character bursts known as "tweets." It is used by 38% of those age 18-29 and 27% of those age 30-45.[25] Clearly it is a powerful took for marketing your brand. Many hiring authorities will check

25   Clements, J. (2020). *Twitter usage reach in the United States in 2019 by age group.* Retrieved January 18, 2021 from https://www.statista.com/statistics/265647/SHARE©-of-us-internet-users-who-use-twitter-by-age-group/

your Twitter activity, but Twitter users don't realize its full potential. Use it to do good, be honest, and share factual truth, not supposition. This section includes a few ways to use Twitter to solidify your brand.

If you are engaging enough, the brevity of Twitter assures that others will take the time to read your posts. The platform also makes it easy to reach out to those you admire in your field. Furthermore, recruiters and employers make use of Twitter by posting jobs directly to the site. By following the right companies and searching applicable hashtags, job seekers can apply to many open positions.

The more you become engaged, expand your network and contribute to your field, the more you are seen as an expert. On Twitter, you can follow an unlimited number of people and also have an unlimited number of followers and, since each post, or "tweet," can be only a maximum of 280 characters, it is easy to make regular contributions to your Twitter account. Connect with as many industry leaders as you can and find ways to encourage others to follow you. Post information that is new and useful and you'll be looked at as an expert in no time.

Social networking has changed the face of recruiting. Recruiters are using sites such as Twitter and LinkedIn more often to find the right candidate. If you do a simple internet search, you can find networks for recruiters, as well as lists of the top recruiters on Twitter. Once you have that information, and once your profile is complete, don't hesitate to engage with recruiters. That is what sets social networking, and Twitter, apart from other media; it is acceptable to engage others in conversation, especially when it revolves around their line of work.

A Twitter profile is not as complex or detailed as LinkedIn or Facebook profiles. However, your Twitter profile still needs to be optimized. Twitter offers a dual name feature on which you can list your username, as well as your Twitter name. Here's an example:

Twitter Name: FredCoonSCC Username: @FredCoon

Also, make your Twitter bio as powerful as possible by using a high-impact statement. There is a 280-character limit, so use powerful, action-oriented language.

Ask 100 Twitter experts about what is the most important part of your Twitter profile and nearly all of them will say effectively communicating your brand. There are many ways to create a brand, but the best way is to be consistent throughout your social networks.

Rereading the chapter on branding may help you. It doesn't do you any good to have one underlying brand message on your LinkedIn profile and a different brand message on your Facebook or Twitter profiles.

In this chapter I have covered e-portfolios, LinkedIn and Twitter, but certainly you should take advantage of other media such as Instagram, Snapchat and YouTube if you think they will push your brand forward. If you take one thing away from this chapter it is that you must remain *engaged*. Simply optimizing your profiles and joining select networks will not get you where you need to go. You must **be a regular contributor to your industry**. Make the right connections, join new social networks and groups, and always keep yourself aware of changes in new media, as you never know how they will benefit your career.

SUCCESS STORY: LINKEDIN WIN

CONTRIBUTED BY BARBARA LIMMER, FORMER EXECUTIVE COACH, STEWART, COOPER & COON

Bob J. left his job in the automotive industry after 20 years because a reduction and reorganization of its workforce would necessitate relocation – an unwanted move. After numerous in-depth interviews in related industry sectors, Bob applied for a senior managment role at a desirable company.

Bob knew his online application might not be enough to gain traction, so he used his LinkedIn network to reach out to an acquaintance who worked at the organization. Within a few days, he entered into a series of interviews and challenges that included an hour-long simulation and having to write an essay on a relevant topic, as well as many meetings with senior-level executives.

Finally offered a position with the company as Senior Manager for Technical Program Management, Bob is making an even higher salary than expected. His success resulted in the following:

- A 30% higher salary than he had in his last position
- Working remotely 3 days per week
- *Not having to move*

Networking on LinkedIn lead to more money and life satisfaction for Bob.

ADDITIONAL RESOURCES

- Coon, F., Ko, A. & Stewart, K. (2019). Leveraging LinkedIn for job search success. GAFF publishing.
- Levinson, J.C. (2011). *Guerrilla marketing for job hunters 3.0: How to stand out from the crowd and tap into the hidden job market using social media and 999 other tactics today* (3rd ed.). Wiley.

CHAPTER 8

SECURING AN INTERVIEW: RESEARCHING COMPANIES, NETWORKING AND ANSWERING JOB ADS

You have now no doubt put many hours into perfecting your resume, cover letter and social media presence. Your next natural inclination will be to go on Monster or Indeed and look for openings. My late friend and the author of *What Color is Your Parachute?* Richard Bolles indicates that this strategy only works 4% of the time. Why not spend your time more effectively? Bolles indicates that the top three most efficient ways of finding a job are to 1) ask friends, colleagues and social media contacts for job leads (works 33% of the time), 2) physically visit organizations for which you want to work (works 47% of the time but is best for smaller employers) and 3) use the (online) yellow pages or other search engines to identify companies of interest to you and set up appointments with decision makers. This method is successful **65%** of the time.[26]

This chapter will focus on:

---

26   Bolles, R. (2019). *What color is your parachute: A practical manual for job-hunters and career-changers.* Ten Speed Press.

- Researching companies and people of interest to you
- Networking effectively
- Answering job ads

In Chapters 2 and 3 you focused on your preferences for company characteristics, fellow worker traits, geographical locations, and other likes and dislikes. As you search companies, don't lose sight of those preferences. Also, don't forget the forms you filled out that included information about you and your past work. These forms hold the keys to your transferable skills. Your job is to transcend the "he/she hasn't worked in this field" barriers and move on with your career.

Also, there are two major market segments. These include the published, or visible/advertised jobs, and those that are "hidden." The visible market consists of jobs posted by recruiters, associations, newspapers, journals, magazines, internet and other forms of printed media. The hidden job market is accessed by networking, direct mail and contact, and event opportunities. Use both.

Once you have used the suggestions that follow to select a few companies of interest, renew your commitment to spending time making contacts. Barbara Limmer, Senior Job and Career Transition Coach, Stewart, Cooper Coon, recommends thinking of yourself as an investigate reporter constantly looking for the next lead.

RESEARCHING ORGANIZATIONS OF INTEREST

Your first assignment is to identify a minimum of 100 desirable organizations and decision makers within those organizations. If you are unable to move, the list may be shorter. Concentrate on closely matching criteria you developed from earlier exercises and remember that just because a company is based in New York State doesn't mean that it doesn't have branches elsewhere.

There are many issues to consider when selecting an organization to target. Start reading all you can about companies of interest in the Wall Street Journal, national business and news magazines, special journals, and any other reliable sources of current, authoritative information. This activity will allow you to identify organizations that are stable and, preferably, growing.

Next, ask yourself why you want to work for one company versus another. What makes one viable and others less so? You also must consider the technological revolution and repercussions of the COVID pandemic. The ability to adapt will drive some companies to greatness and bury others. Research trends, statistics and meaningful company data and then make the best choice you can. If you've done this, you've done your best.

At this point you may be saying, "I don't have time to research every company I may want to work for. I'll just look for openings on the internet." Stop! Remember that this method alone is highly ineffective. LinkedIn author Lou Adler indicates that up to 85% of jobs are found through networking, so you need to *simultaneously* build your network while researching organizations that may be a good fit for you.[27]

Most people in the workforce are changing jobs every 3-5 years now. You don't want to have to start all over again. Doing this work now is an investment in your future. "To effectively target organizations where you have a good chance of getting hired, you should know and be able to easily communicate what value you have to offer. If you have experience managing research programs in the pharmaceutical industry, for example, your target list should be comprised of biopharma companies or suppliers to those companies," says Susan Peppercorn, Executive Career Coach.

Good research is critical, but where do you begin? You begin with a search of the North American Industry Classification System (NAICS) codes (formerly known as the Standard Industrial Classification—SIC—codes). As the name implies, the NAICS classifies every industry and organization using a numerical code. You will look both for industries you have experience in *and* for industries in which you can apply your transferrable skills. You will look for broader categories, called sectors, and for industry sub-sectors that you previously may not have thought of as being appropriate for you.

For example, perhaps you have just lost your job working in the production division of a pet food manufacturing plant. You are looking for similar work and you know your skills are transferable to other types of food manufacturing. You can use NAICS codes to find companies that might want to hire you. Use the following steps:

1. Go to www.NAICS.com

2. Look for the dial down feature.

---

27 Adler, L. (2016). *New survey reveals 85% of all jobs are filled via networking.* Retrieved September 10, 2020 from https://www.linkedin.com/pulse/new-survey-reveals-85-all-jobs-filled-via-networking-lou-adler/

3. In NAICS search, type manufacturing. You'll find that manufacturing has a code of 31-33.

4. Now do an SIC search for production. You'll find that there are almost 638,000 manufacturing plants. In fact, there are 311,500 cheese manufacturing facilities.

5. Check out the list of the top cheese manufacturing plants by geographic location.

6. Identify 10 industry sectors with 10 sub-sectors for each and begin your search of those specific organizations.

A list of major NAISC/SIC codes appears at the end of this chapter.

SEARCH ENGINE TIPS

The following thoughts about internet searching are provided by recruiter Shally Steckerl.[28] First, don't depend on any single search engine for results. The overlap between Google, Live, BING, Yahoo, etc., even for the exact same search string is quite low and rankings prove it.

Second, don't just look at firms in your industry (e.g., many accountants, attorneys, etc., work in places other than accounting and law firms). Consider targeting companies in growth industries or economically un(der)affected industries such as healthcare, education, energy, defense and so on, or startups being funded by incubators. Look at the annually compiled lists of growing companies overall (www.inc.com) or by location (e.g., Boston Globe's "Growth 50" within Globe 100 (www.boston.com).

Third, look to competitors. Not every company in the same industry is laying off. Analyze the media for trigger events that show growth in an industry or organization. In your search, use words like company expansion, expands, growth, hiring, won contract, profit, etc.

GOOGLE SEARCHING AND BOOLEAN TECHNIQUES

I know you know how to use Google, but do you *really* know how to make the most of your search? Boolean search techniques can be used to broaden or narrow your search as necessary. Think of a Boolean search as a Google search that uses AND, OR, and NOT to retrieve particular information on the internet. Special characters are also used to simplify and maximize effectiveness, thereby reducing the time it takes you to find what you want.

---

28   Personal communication (2013).

Use "and" to expand your search. Public relations **and** videographer will give you jobs for each. Use "or" to reduce your search. "Not" is a useful search word when you want to look for jobs that include some responsibilities but not others. For instance, you might try "public relations not social media" if you want a PR job, but don't want to do social media.

Special operators and characters that instruct Google to use keywords in a search string can also be used. You don't need to learn about all the operators to become successful in your searches but adding a few operators will help. Here, I'll cover some operators that I think are a must. Brian Ardan, Director of Media Services at Lock Haven University of Pennsylvania, offers the following useful tips for maximizing your search:[29]

Plus sign. The plus sign in front of a word tells Google to use exactly this word. This may be useful for two reasons. First, Google typically ignores what they call "stop" words, meaning very common short words like "the" or "in." If you put a plus + in front of "the," it will be included as part of the search. Second, Google "auto stems," which means that it will look for some variations of a word you include; if you search for manager, it will show results with management as well. Put a plus in front of manager, and the results will only include exactly this word.

Minus sign. One especially important special character is the minus "-." If you use it in front of a word with no spaces in between, it means "not." For example, you want to look up client relations but NOT public relations. Try "client -public relations." Use this to *narrow* your search.

Quotation marks. If you put a phrase in quotation marks, Google will look for the whole phrase. For example, you could search for "Database Administrator," and get a great many results. However, Google will recognize the operator OR if you add it within the quotes. You can search for "Database Administrator OR Developer" and you will find pages with either "Database Administrator" OR "Database Developer." Use this to *expand* your search.

The Asterisk (*)—An asterisk after a word tells Google that you are interested in the root of that word and any related words. For example, you are interested in administration, but you know some businesses might use variations of that word, such as administrator.

---

29   Ardan, B. (n.d.). *Communication: Primary research*. Retrieved January 18, 2021 from https://library.lockhaven.edu/c.php?g=413465&p=5188593/

If you search administrate* will find administer, administration, etc. Use this method to *increase* your search.

N, W and Tilde. These are called "proximity operators" in many databases. They are placed between words that are to be searched together such that you are trying to find information that has both key words used in a related way. Let's say, for example, you are trying to find a position in which you can use your knowledge of budgeting and purchasing. If you Google those words without a proximity operator, you will get every job description that includes the word budgeting and every one that includes purchasing. However, if you add N5 for example, you will bring budgeting and purchasing together in the same ad and, because they are only within 5 words of each other, there is a great chance both skills are germane to the position.

Near operator (N) will find the two words within 5 (or whatever number you designate) words of each other regardless of the order in which you typed them. The Within Operator (W) finds words within the number you designate but finds them in the order you place them. Try W for phrases like tax shelter. Use N or W to *decrease* the number of hits.

Sometimes organizations will hide their identity but of course you want to know the name of the company to which you are applying. Pick a phrase from the job description, put it in quotation marks, and search for it on Google. You will land on all web pages that advertise the job. This will also work if you are looking for a job posted by a recruiter, and you are interested in who the client is.

USING GOOGLE TO FIND CONTACTS

Once you have a list of companies you are interested in, search their websites and other sources to discover their organizational structure and contacts. Many company websites include a jobs tab you can use to apply. However, not all jobs are advertised so your real goal is to make contact with one or more hiring managers. Try to find the hiring manager's email address. If the person's name is rare enough, putting it in quotes and Googling it may help. I also use Google advanced image search (https://www.google.com/advanced_image_search) with the "faces" option and often land on the person's blog or homepage. Search LinkedIn as well. If you are looking for an email pattern for a company or are trying to collect email addresses, you can search "email * companyname.com" or "mailto" * companyname.com. Since the symbol typically stands for one word, you can add more asterisks to these strings and get different results ("email * * companyname.com" etc.).

Once you are ready, craft your email carefully. Have 3 people proofread it. The message under the message is critical here and you don't want someone to delete your email because you did not pay attention to detail. Attach your resume and a link to your professional website. Treat your message like a cover letter. Personalize.

NETWORKING

So far, we've developed the product (you) by defining who you are and describing why they should hire you. We've also identified many companies as potential targets and are now ready to take the product to market. Your next step is to begin networking. Networking includes making yourself known to those who may want to employ you and knowing how to act when you are finally make contact. To network effectively, you'll create a list of leads, join some professional organizations, consider job shadowing or participating in an adult internship and, if possible, visit a few job fairs (or other networking gatherings).

Remember that most jobs are obtained through the unpublished or "hidden" job market, so networking is critical.

Networking takes time, but it is the best way to find employment quickly because it puts you in direct contact with businesspersons, especially those in your field. You can't be lazy or shy here. You may have to cut back time spent on things you like to do for a while and refocus your energy on participating in groups with which you are not currently working.

> ### Networking is the most important tool in your job search toolbox.

The first rule of networking is that under no circumstance whatsoever should you approach networking by asking someone to help you find a job. Start by saying that you are considering trying something new and, since they are already in the field, you would like to ask them a couple of questions about their industry. If approached in this way, most people are more than willing to give advice.

MAKE A LIST OF LEADS

The best way to start networking is to make a list everyone that you know and where they work. Most people begin thinking only of business associates. While doing so may serve as a starting point, this approach is too narrow. Don't forget friends, neighbors, house of worship members, merchants or vendors, old college roommates, fraternity brothers or sorority sisters. My barber once introduced me to another of his customers. This man has become an important contact in an industry I wanted to penetrate as a recruiter. An unemployed accountant friend of Conne's met a man in a dog park who knew someone looking for an accountant. She contacted the organization and they offered her a job.

Don't exclude people who are not at your professional level. I know of some very senior level clients who received leads from their barbers, gardeners or other unlikely sources.

Call, visit or video conference with each of your business associates. Graciously absorb everything that they tell you. Take notes. More importantly, find out who they know or would recommend you contact to get more information. I don't recommend reading from a script, but you should think through and practice aloud what you will say. At some point work in the questions, "Does your company employ candidates with my qualifications?" and "Could you suggest three people or companies I can contact that are hiring candidates with similar credentials?"

If you are unemployed and have left your last position on less than stellar terms, you will want to craft how you approach old business associates carefully. Under these circumstances, it is easy to get sucked into airing dirty laundry about your former company or boss. DON'T! Doing so will only make YOU look bad.

Networking can be fun, but it can also be intimidating. Start out with people you know and let them lead you to people they know. As you move farther away from your circle of acquaintances, realize that you will have to sharpen your information-gathering techniques.

Networking is unique in another way. You can use it to continually cultivate information and leads. Keep members of your network informed of your progress. Keep asking them for advice. Send personal thank you notes or buy them an occasional lunch. If working with recruiters, ask them how marketable your skills are. This information will allow you to tweak your career summary, resume and other documents and hone your presentation to fit market conditions.

Beware of getting locked into a networking group that is fun but is offering no new information. Make friends out of the members of this networking group and move to more goal-oriented networking.

Another way of building your network is by reading business articles in newspapers, trade magazines and business journals. These articles usually revolve around four topics: growth, executive change, new product launches, or corporate problems. An executive change indicates that someone might be putting a new team together. If you see an opportunity like this write a "fan" letter to a decision maker. Reference an article that you have read and offer your congratulations on positive events. Briefly present your skills and ask if they would be willing to talk with you about possible employment. If you are responding to an article about company problems, do not reinforce the negative. Point out that you have experienced a similar situation and have the skills to help the company through their current challenge.

JOIN PROFESSIONAL ORGANIZATIONS AND ASSOCIATIONS

Another critical step in developing your networking strategy is to join professional associations. The Encyclopedia of Associations ($20 cost in 2021 or free from your library) contains a wealth of information about current professional, fraternal, non-profit, educational and enthusiast associations and is a valuable tool. This publication is regularly updated. Here are some examples of groups you should target:

- Professional associations or societies
- Chambers of commerce
- Rotary, Lions Club, and many other fine civic organizations
- Toastmasters

The more closely linked the group is to your targeted profession, the sooner you will make meaningful connections. Ask association representatives to pass your credentials along and keep them posted on changes. If possible, attend open meetings. Open conversations, form alliances and strategically let members know of your employment availability. Barbara Limmer, a job and career transition coach, suggests reviewing each contact's background on LinkedIn, then contacting them.[30] Remember, the point of the contact is to build rapport, so begin by asking for their perspective on a topic such as finding a job in the field. After some email contact, ask for a phone appointment. The more you seem like a *person*, the greater your chance of success. Don't lose hope if the association is not willing to pass your credentials on to their members. Simply use the association to gather information on the market.

Don't forget about social and civic associations, your house of worship, college alumni, or sorority or fraternity groups. These non-business associations can often offer excellent opportunities. Several of my clients are West Point graduates. The armed service fraternal organizations are powerful, and they communicate effectively. If you can participate in this group, do so.

If you plan to attend meetings even via web conferencing, polish up your look and manners. Update your professional wardrobe and practice being comfortable and confident introducing yourself to strangers. Learn some conversation starters. My association with my co-author Conne Reece happened because I introduced myself to her in a restaurant.

Once you have your foot in the door and begin building your network, use the Networking Chart at the end of the chapter to manage your referrals and contacts.

JOB SHADOW AND COMPLETE AN ADULT INTERNSHIP

Another way to build your network is to do an adult internship or job shadow. Using the search tools described earlier in this chapter, you should be able to identify organizations and people for whom you would like to work. Don't be afraid to contact them and explain that you are in transition and that you'd like to shadow them for a day to make sure the industry or job is right for you. You will also have success asking to work for free a few hours a week at most organizations. Be up front in your purpose. You want to learn more about the organization and industry in the hope of changing your job or career.

---

30   Coon, F. & Limmer, B. (Hosts). (2018, July 8). Tactics to overcome fear of networking [Audio podcast episode]. In *The US at Work*. Fred Coon Studio. https://theusatwork.com/2 00-tactics-to-overcome-fear-of-networking/

ATTEND ONLINE AND IN PERSON JOB FAIRS

The pandemic of 2020 may have changed the direction of job fairs but, in the hope that by the time you are reading this they will be in the picture again, or even offered virtually, I'll discuss them here. Regardless, **this advice can be used in any networking situation**.

If you've been to a job fair in the past and didn't work it properly, you are probably tempted to skip this section. DON'T. You are probably saying to yourself right now, "I went and didn't find a thing there. What a waste of my time." If a job fair isn't properly worked, it IS a waste of time.

Your role at a job fair is not to interview with the newest HR staff person who got stuck with the assignment for that day. Your purpose in speaking with employers at the job fair is to gain an understanding of the structure of their companies and how you can get in to contact the real decision-makers. The following are some strategies for working a job fair effectively:

Pre-register. Many times, employers attempt to pre-screen applicants. Your name in front of the career fair company representative will secure an audience, which works to your advantage.

Go with a mission. Remember, offers are seldom made at the job fair. A job fair is a place where the process begins. Your mission is to find out as much information as possible, so don't spend all of your time talking to one or two people.

Also, write down exactly what you want to get out of attending each job fair. When you exit the job fair, compare your goal with what you actually accomplished. If you didn't accomplish at least 90% of your target objectives, then review your mistakes and don't repeat them at the next job fair.

If you were a Stewart, Cooper & Coon client, at a minimum you would have the following job fair goals:

• To meet four new target companies with openings in your field
• To practice face-to-face interviewing skills with 6 new companies

Strategize and prepare. You will increase your chance of success by preparing well. After you have set your goals, identify and research the companies with which you want to connect. Analyze the list of attending companies, select your choices in advance and start researching. Call the people whose names you found in your research and suggest meeting them at the job fair.

If they aren't going to be there, ask for the name of the person(s) who will be representing their division. Be able to articulate why you are interested in the company. You WILL be asked this question.

Make a schedule and stick to it. Remember that job fairs tend to be crowded. Prepare an organized 4-item tool kit consisting of business cards, resumes, notebook and manila folder so you don't have to fumble around. Bring a notebook to make notes on EVERY conversation you have. Be relentless in writing down the names of everyone you meet, highlights of your conversation and what you promised to send them. Collect as many business cards as possible.

Having a system for working the floor both inside and outside the main event site is also important. If you are in a large venue such as a hotel, there is likely to be a main room in which organizations have booths set up. However, you never know when you may run in to the right person, so employ your networking skills and work the lobby. Practice your elevator speech and pledge to introduce yourself to at least three people outside of the main event. Go to all the social events no matter how tired you are. It's a lot easier to talk with a company executive while you are standing in a food line than it is to call the office and go through a gatekeeper.

Working the job fair floor is an art. It involves critical time management and customized strategic planning for every company of interest. Leave a resume with every company for which your skills are a match. Don't leave a booth without a business card and a follow-up commitment of some kind. Create a positive "hook" so people will have an easy time remembering you. Remember that lots of jobs are obtained not because of technical qualifications but because of the right chemistry. **Make yourself someone who interacts in a fun manner—someone with an upbeat attitude.**

Polish your appearance and nonverbal communication. One never gets a second chance to make a first impression. Therefore, before you go, have someone evaluate how you look. People are biased about the funniest things. Dress for success. Practice smiling and shaking hands. Practice your verbal "commercial" (review Chapter 4 on branding).

After the job fair, follow up with everyone you meet. Send an email to or call everyone and, here it is folks, **ask for another face-to-face meeting**. They are expecting you to be assertive and employers will be especially attracted to those who reach out to them.

Conne's first job after college was selling radio advertising. "I interviewed with the sales manager, who told me to call Friday afternoon for an answer," she said. "When I did, he said he hadn't made up his mind and to call again Monday morning. I called at 8:00 A.M. He said, 'You did what I asked and showed initiative. You're hired.'"

ANSWERING JOB ADS

While the best way to secure employment is to network, there is no harm in applying for an advertised position. Just don't dedicate too much time to it.

Many ads will direct you to respond to the Human Resources (HR) Department. Their job is to review the hundreds—occasionally thousands—of resumes they receive and select a few candidates to be interviewed.

I don't want to repeat myself too much in this book, but this is an important point. **To narrow the selection, HR compares the resumes coming in against a specific job description.**

Human resources professionals generally do not have in-depth knowledge of many of the categories for which they are screening. As useful as their specialized HR training and education may be in the field of human resources, they are often not qualified to evaluate candidates outside their area of expertise.

You will be more likely to meet with success if you send your ad response to the functional hiring authority instead of the human resources department. You should be able to find the name of the hiring authority, or at least someone of authority in the department to which you are applying, through the organization's website or through calling the department.

Unfortunately, contacting the hiring manager is sometimes perceived as a breach of corporate protocol and this tactic alone may screen you out of contention. My friends who work in HR will not be happy with me when they read this section of the book, but the truth is the truth. You are still better off getting your name in front of a decision maker.

If the company only allows you to apply online, then do so, but continue to try to find out who your potential "boss" will be and send him/her your resume. Be quick to point out that you have applied online as well. Then indicate that, because you see such an ideal match between your qualifications and the job described, you've made a special effort to bring your credentials to his or her attention.

With this technique, you will be penetrating the company at two different levels and increasing the odds of getting a response. Even if the hiring authority forwards your letter to HR, he or she may also request that you be put on the short list for interview scheduling.

One additional advantage to this approach is that it helps differentiate you from the competition. The majority of ad respondents will apply online and just wait for a response. Very few send their responses to the appropriate functional manager. Not only might you gain a strategic advantage, you might gain a numerical one as well. While the HR manager is wading through 300 resumes, the functional manager may only have two or three to review.

You can find many job openings by looking through companies' websites. Medical facilities, universities, utilities, government and other large local organizations employ all kinds of professionals and are a rich source of opportunity for those seeking a career change. These organizations will always post openings on their websites.

Finally, I know it sounds old fashioned but get a paper phonebook and look through the blue (government) and yellow (business) pages. You'll be surprised how many different types of employers are out there. Once you have selected a few targeted organizations, you can do some research to find out who the key players are and make contact.

INTERNET JOB SITES

There are thousands of jobs online today found on various job boards. Jobs for senior management are rarely found in newspapers these days. If you are at the executive level ($150,000+), there are two sites I recommend: Exec-U-Net (www.execunet.com) and www.theladders.com. There are fees, but recruiters and HR people do use those websites to recruit talent, in addition to doing their own Boolean string searches on Google or Firefox, and placements do occur. Indeed, Monster.com, Ziprecruiter and so forth are very useful, but don't forget about the many sites targeted toward certain professions, like the Chronicle of Higher Education or hospitalcareers.com.

PRINT MEDIA ADS

Of all the strategies available, answering newspaper ads exposes you to the most competition. As I said earlier in the book, answering newspaper ads is mostly a waste of time. At senior levels within companies, they are virtually ineffective. However, some people still get jobs from ads, so I've included a discussion about how to run an ad campaign.

Look for job ads in your local newspaper, The Wall Street Journal and trade publications related to your field. Don't forget your state and local employment agencies. If you are lucky, your local paper will categorize their employment ads into specific categories such as technology, health care, purchasing, etc. If this is the case, you should select as many pertinent categories and ads within those categories as possible.

Most ads will direct you to apply online through applicant tracking software. Submit your resume and cover letter and any other relevant materials such as letters of reference. Make reference to where you saw the ad and what position is being advertised in the first paragraph of your cover letter. Then, simply match your skills to the requirements listed. Do not draw attention to areas that do not match.

BLIND ADS

In a blind ad only a method to apply is given. There are some very sound reasons for a company to use blind ads, including company confidentiality, business strategy, or company size (a smaller company may not have application software), but be warned: ads can sometimes be a front for multi-level marketing schemes. Many job seekers avoid responding to these ads. These ads normally generate about 40-60% fewer respondents than ads listing company names.

There is one additional risk to answering a blind ad. The company running the ad may be your current employer. Thus, we recommend that if there is even a remote possibility that the advertiser is your own company, don't answer the ad.

WHEN TO ANSWER ADS

Most job seekers are on the ball bright and early the day after an ad has run. They figure that they are getting a jump on the competition by firing off their response as quickly as possible. However, the person on the receiving end is inundated with hundreds of responses during the first three or four days. How much attention do you think each resume will receive? They are also probably working with an application close date and will look at all of the applications at once when that date comes.

Your response will not arrive too late for consideration unless you miss the deadline. Most companies generally allow a few weeks before the resumes are screened, and an interviewing schedule is set up. The risk you take by delaying your response is very small compared to the competitive edge that you gain by strategizing your application. Be patient and give yourself the time to do it right.

HOW TO ANSWER ADS

Most ads include the company name. Do a little research on the company before you answer the ad. Making a reference in the cover letter that shows that you know a little about the company may set you apart from your competition.

The ad may mention a person to whom you may direct your cover letter and resume. If no name is given, you can send it to the appropriate department head whose name you gleaned from your research.

In addition to looking at ads in which you match 50% or more of the qualifications, you should also be looking for ads that are below your level of expertise. No one is suggesting that you consider moving down in status but, by stating in your cover letter that you are interested in a higher position within the company, you might get your resume passed on to someone at the desired level.

Conversely, you should also be looking for positions that are a *little* higher than your actual level. Your cover letter should indicate that you want to be considered for employment by the successful candidate as he or she begins to put the team together.

You have now developed a fantastic resume, cover letter and website. You've updated your LinkedIn profile and identified 10 industry sectors in which your skills are transferable. Within those industry sectors, you've identified hundreds of potential target companies that you would like to explore. In addition, you have begun building relationships through appropriate groups and scheduled some interviews. The next chapter will show you how to put all of these to work to turn your interview into a job.

SUCCESS STORY: NETWORKING TRIUMPH

CONTRIBUTED BY BILL TEMPLE, EXECUTIVE COACH, STEWART, COOPER & COON

Lesley was a consultant in the garment and fabric industry looking for opportunity and challenge. Her game plan was to create the right role for herself, make herself indispensable and roll the opportunity into a permanent position.

As a master networker, Lesley kept in touch with other players in her industry. An associate of hers introduced her to key players at the right organization and, after meeting Lesley, they knew they needed her consulting services immediately. The organization offered Lesley:

- Transformation and operating model project management office (PMO)
- Coordination and execution of transformation and operating model design projects
- $2,500 per day

Lesley was able to use this engagement to underwrite her consulting business while keeping her options open for other opportunities.

ADDITIONAL RESOURCES

- Coon, F. (n.d.). *Networking advice for vets entering the corporate workforce.* StewartCooperCoon.com. https://stewartcoopercoon.com/networking-advice-for-vets-entering-the-corporate-workforce/
- Moody, K. (2017). *Networking strategies to find jobs in the hidden job market: A recruiter reveals insider secrets for a wildly successful job search.* CreateSpace Independent Publishing.

"WHO NEEDS ME"

NAICS CODE CHART	
Sector	Definition
11	Agriculture, Forestry, Fishing and Hunting
21	Mining, Quarrying, and Oil and Gas Extraction
22	Utilities
23	Construction
31-33	Manufacturing
42	Wholesale Trade
44-45	Retail Trade
48-49	Transportation and Warehousing
51	Information
52	Finance and Insurance
53	Real Estate and Rental and Leasing
54	Professional, Scientific, and Technical Services
55	Management of Companies and Enterprises
56	Administrative and Support and Waste Management and Remediation Services
61	Educational Services
62	Health Care and Social Assistance
71	Arts, Entertainment, and Recreation
72	Accommodation and Food Services
81	Other Services (except Public Administration)
92	Public Administration

MAJOR SIC CODE CHART

AGRICULTURE, FORESTRY, FISHING

(SIC CODE 01-09)

01	Agriculture Production - Crops	07	Agriculture Services
02	Agriculture Production - Livestock and Animal Specialties	08	Forestry
		09	Fishing, Hunting & Trapping

CONSTRUCTION

(SIC CODE 15-17)

15	Building Construction General Contractors and Operative Builders	16	Heavy Construction other than Construction Contractors
		17	Construction Special Trade Contractors

TRANSPORTATION AND PUBLIC UTILITIES

(SIC CODE 01-09)

40	Railroad Transportation	45	Transportation by Air
41	Local, Suburban Transit and Interurban Hwy Pass Transit	46	Pipelines, except Natural Gas
42	Motor Freight Transportation	47	Transportation Services
44	Water Transportation	48	Communication
		49	Electric, Gas and Sanitary Services

WHOLESALE TRADE

(SIC CODE 50-51)

50 Wholesale Trade - Durable Goods

51 Wholesale Trade - Non-Durable Goods

RETAIL TRADE
(SIC CODE 52-59)

52 Building Materials, Hardware, Garden Supplies and Mobile Home Dealers

53 General Merchandise Stores

54 Food Stores

55 Automotive Dealers and Gasoline Service Stations

56 Apparel and Accessory Stores

57 Home Furniture, Furnishings and Equipment Stores

58 Eating and Drinking Places

59 Miscellaneous Retail

SERVICES
(SIC CODE 70-87)

70 Hotels, Rooming Houses, Camps and other Lodging Places

72 Personal Services

73 Business Services

75 Automotive Repair Services and Parking

76 Misc Repair Services

78 Motion Pictures

79 Amusement and Recreation Services

80 Health Services

81 Legal Services

82 Educational Services

83 Social Services

84 Museums, Art Galleries & Botanical & Zoological Gardens

87 Engineering, Accounting, Research Management and Related Services

MINING
(SIC CODE 10-14)

10 Metal Mining

12 Coal/Lignite Mining

13 Oil and Gas Extraction

14 Mining and Quarrying of Nonmetallic Materials, Except Fuels

MANUFACTURING
(SIC CODE 20-39)

20   Food and Kindred Products

21   Tobacco Products

22   Textile Mill Products

23   Apparel and other Finished Products and Similar Materials

24   Lumber and Wood Products, Except Furniture

25   Furniture and Fixtures

26   Paper and Allied Products

27   Printing, Publishing, and Allied Industries

28   Chemicals and Allied Products

29   Petroleum Refining and Related Industries

30   Rubber/Misc. Plastic Products

31   Leather and Leather Products

32   Stone, Clay, Glass and Concrete Products

33   Primary Metal Industries

34   Fabricated Metal Products, Except Machinery and Transportation Equipment

35   Industrial and Commercial Machinery and Computer Equip

36   Electronic and Other Electrical Equipment and Components, Except Computer Equipment

37   Transportation Equipment

38   Measuring, Analyzing, and Controlling Instruments; Photographic, Medical and Optical Goods; Watches and Clocks

39   Misc. Manufacturing Industries

FINANCE, INSURANCE, REAL ESTATE
(SIC CODE 60-67)

60   Depository Institutions

61   Non-Depository Credit Institutions

62   Security and Commodity Brokers, Dealers, Exchanges and Services

63   Insurance Carriers

64   Insurance Agents, Brokers and Service

65   Real Estate

67   Holding and Other Investment Offices

PUBLIC ADMINISTRATION
(SIC CODE 91-99)

91 Executive, Legislative and General Government, Except Finance

92 Justice, Public Order and Safety

93 Public Finance, Taxation and Monetary Policy

94 Administration of Human Resources Programs

95 Administration of Environment, Quality and Housing Programs

96 Administration of Economic Programs

97 National Security and International Affairs

99 Nonclassifiable Establishments

CHAPTER 9
ACING YOUR INTERVIEW PART 1: PREPARATION

More than 2,000 hiring managers and human resources professionals across industries participated in a 2011 poll by CareerBuilder.[31] They shared mistakes job seekers make in the interview process and the errors that turn them off to a candidate. According to these employers, the topmost detrimental blunders candidates make in interviews include the following:

- Appearing disinterested—[indicated by] 55 percent [of those interviewed]
- Dressing inappropriately—53 percent
- Appearing arrogant—53 percent
- Talking negatively about current or previous employers—50 percent
- Answering a cell phone or texting during the interview—49 percent
- Appearing uninformed about the company or role—39 percent
- Not asking good questions—32 percent
- Asking the hiring manager personal questions—17 percent

---

31 CareerBuilder (2011). *Employers reveal outrageous and common mistakes made in job interviews.* Retrieved August 10, 2020 from http://press.careerbuilder.com/2011-01-12-Employers-Reveal-Outrageous-and-Common-Mistakes-Candidates-Made-in-Job-Interviews-According-to-New-CareerBuilder-Survey/

Interviewing is a complicated process. In the next few chapters, I'll break down how to prepare, how to answer questions, and how to use your nonverbal and verbal expression to appear confident and enthusiastic. This chapter will provide you with guidance about the following:

- Understanding the types of interviews
- Scheduling interviews
- Prepping for interviews
- Answering interview questions
- Controlling interviews

Don't let the negative-sounding word "control" throw you. It's an art and it will make the difference between a pocket full of Franklins and the bread line. I will share with you the exact interview control techniques I teach my clients.

IMPORTANT POINTS TO REMEMBER

The interview process is the ultimate competition. You either win or lose. There is no second place and preparation is key.

Your resume has provided them with sufficient background information to justify the interview. They already know you are qualified. Now, they are 1) making sure your personality, goals and values are a good fit, 2) comparing you to other candidates and 3) evaluating your financial worth. Remember, they will only hire you if they stand to gain something given the cost of hiring you.

The purpose of the traditional interview process is to allow the interviewer to justify why they should hire or eliminate you when they compare you with the half-dozen other finalists, any one of whom are qualified to fill the position. **They will be sizing up your manner, appearance, ability to articulate your responses, and skill in painting a picture of what you can do for them.** They are also looking for your judgment, emotional intelligence, and confidence. The other equally important purpose of the interview is for you to size them up and make a good decision.

Everything you do, no matter how seemingly small, will be evaluated. Whenever you send correspondence, interact with support personnel, conduct a telephone screening, they will form an impression of you. Those who seemingly work in the background provide a great source of potential influence. Be nice to everyone you encounter. Remember, the secretary who you just brushed off may very well be related to the owner. At the very least, he or she has the ear of the boss and will undoubtedly have an opinion that could sway the process.

Any materials or correspondence you send to them must be thoroughly checked and rechecked for grammar, spelling, punctuation, syntax, correctness of sentence structure and factual content. You have their attention. Think about everything you say before you say it and always show a positive attitude. Keep conversations professional and friendly in nature. What do you want people to say about you before you report your first day at work? This impression follows you always and can open doors or create barriers.

TYPES OF INTERVIEWS

There are several types of interviews which may be conducted face-to-face or via telephone or video conferencing. Most of the information in this chapter is about face-to-face interviews conducted one-on-one or with a panel, but I'll also provide tips on telephone and video-conferencing interviews and how to deal with human resources and recruiters. All of these concepts for conducting interviews can overlap, so you should familiarize yourself with each.

INFORMATION/REFERRAL INTERVIEWS

The first type of interview commonly conducted is for the purpose of gaining gain information or a referral. As the name implies, the point of this kind of meeting is simply to find out more about a company or ask for advice and leads. **Do NOT use this kind of interview to ask for a job (that comes later).** The info/referral interview usually comes about through a networking contact. To make the most of a meeting like this, follow these steps:

1. Tell your contact you have been referred by so and so and that you are considering a career move. Tell him/her that you have always been interested in either the products or services their company provides and that your networking contact suggested that you meet to get a better feel for the organization or industry.

2. Go prepared with a list of questions. Since this is an info/referral interview only, you cannot immediately start asking questions regarding possible job opportunities. You initially want to ask some of the following:

-   How did you get started in this line of work?
-   Where do you see this industry going over the next 5 to 10 years?
-   What do you like best about this industry and company?
-   Where did you get your training? If you were looking for a new position in this industry, what companies would you approach?
-   Does this industry generally promote from within?
-   What is a typical career path like? Having looked at my background, are there any other options or industries you think I should consider?
-   I am interested in the ABC Company. Do you know anyone there with whom I might speak regarding opportunities?

3. At the end of the interview, ask the most important question, which is "Are there competitors or other companies in related fields at which you know someone who I might contact." If your interaction continues to be positive, you should close the interview by asking if the interviewer would like to be kept appraised of your progress.

4. When you get home, send a thank you note or email recapping your experience, and attaching an executive summary of the meeting and a resume. You never know when your Friday interview will be discussed at Saturday's golf game with your new boss.

TRADITIONAL JOB INTERVIEWS

The second type of interview is a traditional job interview, which can be conducted via telephone, face-to-face or through videoconferencing. Each of these could be conducted one-on-one or with a panel or committee. Here, the objective is simply to sell your skills and set yourself up in a consultant role (see the section on Triangle Theory). For some positions, you may interview with several people or groups throughout the day or on several days. Often just one interview will be enough for a decision to be made, but sometimes a second and even a third interview will be necessary. Being invited to a second interview is a good sign. A third interview is a *very* good sign.

TELEPHONE INTERVIEWS

A traditional interview conducted over the telephone is usually a screening interview and is often done in place of a face-to-face initial interview to save money because no travel is required. Preparation for such an interview is the same as for a face-to-face interview except that *you should spend extra time focusing on vocal dynamics*. Try varying the pitch of your voice so you don't sound monotone. Stay as animated as you can throughout. Sound as enthusiastic and interested as you possibly can because, in a phone interview, you are only a voice. I *highly recommend* recording yourself answering questions and listening to the sound of your voice ahead of time. No one likes the sound of their own voice, but don't let your ego get in the way of success.

FACE-TO-FACE

Being asked to attend a face-to-face interview is usually a sign that you have been selected to be a finalist, perhaps one of three or four candidates they are interested in meeting. Most of this book addresses how to get and do well in face-to-face interviews, so I won't spend much time on it here. The chance that you will be interviewed via videoconferencing (Zoom, Skype, etc.) is much higher now than it was before the COVID pandemic. Many organizations will videoconference with you as a way to screen you and then, depending on the organization, may ask you to come in while observing appropriate precautions.

VIDEOCONFERENCE

The chance that videoconferencing will NOT be a part of your job search is almost 0%. Even before the COVID pandemic, cost-saving videoconferencing interviews using programs such as Skype and Zoom were becoming more prevalent. Now, they are an essential part of functioning as a professional. Unfortunately, many people do not take the time to learn how to make the best of this technology. Let's face it. We'd rather be face to face, but video communication isn't going to go away. Here, I will offer a few suggestions for handling your video interview like a pro.

Create a "studio" that looks like an office. We have all seen the videoconferencing backgrounds that make it look like we are at the beach, but those aren't appropriate for an interview. Also, if you move too fast the fake background may be compromised. Instead, set up a desk or table with a simple, clean, professional-looking background that doesn't show the entire room. Also, now *isn't* the time to show off your autographed poster of Mick Jagger. Consider having a neat bookshelf behind you, or a plain wall with one tasteful painting. You don't want them to even notice the background, but they will if it is distracting. There are exceptions to this rule, though. If you are interviewing for a job as a disc jockey, set yourself up in a studio. Think about your brand. What image are you trying to convey?

Find a quiet place. Do whatever is necessary not to be disturbed during your interview. Kids and pets should be restricted from your space. If you have to, rent a hotel room or go to a friend's house for a few hours. The last thing you want is to be distracted in the middle of your interview. Make sure your phone is turned off.

Position the camera directly in front of you and DO NOT hold your computer on your lap. Obviously, this makes for an unstable picture and a strange angle. The camera lens should be at eye level. Many interviewees make the mistake of putting their computers on the table such that they are looking down into the camera. First, no one wants to look up your nose. Second, it gives you a double chin. Place your computer on something that will bring your camera to face level, maintain eye contact and make sure they can't see the table. They understand that you are going to look at them on the screen but look directly at the camera often when answering questions. It will look like you are looking at them.

Invest in good lighting. There is NOTHING more annoying than not being able to see the face of the person you are interviewing. For about $30 you can buy a light that attaches to your computer. Such lights have adjustable lighting shades (warm, cool) and brightness. The light should be aimed at your face such that it does not create shadows. Also, DO NOT sit in front of a window as the camera on your computer will pick up the background light and create glare.

Position your face in the center of the screen to frame yourself. Conne has a colleague who only ever has the top half of her head visible on screen. It's like looking at a kid at a candy counter. The people interviewing you know you can see what you look like. They are thinking, "If he/she can't do it right in the interview, he/she won't do it right when talking to our clients."

Sit in the right position, not too close, not too far. The interviewer should be able to see you from about the upper rib level. You want them to be able to see your arms and gestures and, of course, your facial expressions. If you sit back too far, they won't be able to see that all-important body language. If you are too close, you look overbearing.

Fix yourself up. Don't dress down just because you are interviewing from home. Wear make-up, fix your hair, shave and dress like you would for an in-person interview.

Educate yourself. The internet is populated with many tutorials for how to look good on video. Watch a few before your interview.

Run a test video. Experiment with your search partner. Make recordings of yourself see how you come across. Be critical. They will be.

Learn the technology. Stay on top of new technology. It communicates that you're innovative, you're practical and you're interested in saving your potential employer money.

Let the interviewer know if you're having difficulty. If you're having trouble hearing or seeing, let the other person know so that it can be addressed and fixed, or even rescheduled. Don't risk blowing an interview because you can't hear the questions clearly.

PANEL/COMMITTEE/GROUP INTERVIEWS

A panel interview is simply an interview conducted by a group rather than an individual. Often members of the panel are members of a hiring committee or interested parties within the organization. If you are being hired by a search committee, you will certainly have a panel interview. Panel interviews are usually set up well in advance, so you'll have plenty of time to prepare, whether they are in person or on video. Ask your contact for the names and titles of the panel members in advance and look them up on LinkedIn or the organization's website before the interview. Then, you will be able to address potential concerns in your responses. If you can't do this ahead of time, ask them to introduce themselves and write down their names and titles on the spot.

Call each panel member by name and secure the correct spelling of each person's name, and his/her title and specific function within the company. You WILL be sending each of them a thank you letter.

Panel interviews can be intimidating, confusing and difficult. You might receive the same question from more than one member. Usually, they are not trying to trap you. It is more likely that one member didn't hear the other's question previously.

Each person on a committee may place importance on a different skill, so don't be surprised if the questions are quite varied. Don't be afraid to ask for clarification if need be. Doing so is better than *not* answering the question they are *really* asking. In a recent interview for a teaching faculty member, Conne asked a candidate to quantify her success. Faculty are usually evaluated by peers, superiors and, most importantly, students. These evaluations are summarized and assigned numerical values. Every evaluated teacher should be able to say, "94% of my students rated me in the top category for..." However, this candidate sidestepped the question 3 times. She had either never focused on quantifying her qualifications, never looked at her evaluations or, worse, was hiding poor evaluations and should have been more direct about it.

Finally, when in a panel interview, make eye contact with each member when answering the questions. Though Interviewer A may have asked the question, they are all listening to your response.

LUNCH INTERVIEWS

A potential employer requesting a lunch with you to discuss possible employment is a good sign. Since your interviewer has chosen to learn about you in a zone separate from the office, you will need to discover the best ways to emphasize your professional accomplishments and strengths while in a non-professional environment. Job candidates should first research the location, and even assess the menu options, so that more time can be spent speaking about your job qualifications rather than deciding on your entrée. Since lunch interviews present a more conversational, even relaxed atmosphere, remember to balance professionalism with a sense of congeniality.

A lunch interview can offer a candidate the opportunity to display the best parts of his or her personality. Relax and enjoy yourself. Be able to make chit chat. Be polite to your server. Brush up on your dining etiquette. Your interviewer might want to know what you will be like when entertaining clients. At the end of the interview, ask the interview what his/her next step will be.

HUMAN RESOURCES INTERVIEWS AND RECRUITER INTERVIEWS

Interviews at a company sometimes begin with someone from the human resources department. Frankly, you are better off focusing on the hiring authority but HR will sometimes be involved. Remember, HR doesn't have the final YES, but they can eliminate you before you even meet the hiring authority.

An interview with HR is a chemistry test to see if you fit into the organization. You almost certainly will be asked the question "Tell me about yourself." In response, you will have prepared your opening statement that briefly describes your past positions and accomplishments. Pick accomplishments that match the position requirements and would be impressive to the interviewer. Don't be afraid to mention the job description and don't forget that you are trying to show them why you meet the criteria better than anyone else they will interview.

Prepare questions for them as well. The type of questions you ask will form their overall opinion of you. Indicate your level of interest in the company, position, and future there. Here are some questions you should feel free to ask HR:

- What is the company trying to accomplish that is new or different from what was done in the past?
- How does the position that we're discussing fit into present and future goals?
- What are the principal skills required to perform effectively in this position?
- What about my resume and background interested you? What are some of the things you are looking for in how the person in this position works with you/your department?

A recruiter is likewise dealing with many people like you and, therefore, won't feel the urgency you feel to get you in front of the right person. They have limited comprehension of the position for which you are applying, but still need to know about your skills. When an HR representative or recruiter calls, your best strategy is to thank them for the call but indicate you cannot talk then. Before you hang up, ask them to provide you with the job description. Confirm your email address and schedule an appointment to talk. This way, you can prepare a conversation about how your skills are a perfect match for the position.

CASE METHOD INTERVIEWS

Case method interviews are now frequently used by some of the largest firms in the U.S. The purpose of case method questions is to assess a job candidate's problem-solving abilities, analytical skills, and creativity. Additionally, case method questions can give employers a better understanding of a candidate's business sense and ability to interpret data. Examples of case method interview questions may include the following:

- An established business wants to expand and develop its online presence. What is your advice?
- A well-known restaurant chain is pulling in less-than-adequate revenue. What are your suggestions for improvement?
- A company discovers that its annual revenue is at an all-time high, although the company still operates at a loss. What could be the reason for this?

If you find yourself participating in a case study interview, take notes, identify and prioritize key issues, and work to stay on topic without becoming side-tracked by real-world industry discussion unless specifically asked to do so. In addition, speak clearly, be ready to justify main points, and recognize that there are no right answers, but simply different approaches to a common goal.

PUZZLE INTERVIEWS

Competitive companies like Google have been known to incorporate what are known as "puzzle" questions when interviewing candidates. For example, a random inquiry such as, "How many people in New York City can be expected to log onto Twitter at 4:00 P.M. on a Friday?" is actually an effective way for an interviewer to determine a candidate's ability to think on his or her feet and thrive under pressure. One would have to know the population of New York City AND 4:00 P.M. Friday Twitter trends and be able to quickly calculate the answer.

Tech related jobs are typically one of the more common industries in which an interviewer may opt for the puzzle approach. To avoid getting flustered, remember that the goal is to exhibit logical analysis, curiosity, and the ability to communicate clearly. In fact, these items may be categorically more important than offering a precise calculation. Essentially, an interviewer wants to identify your capacity to use rational and working strategies to solve a problem, so create a rough outline to assist with computations and estimates. Resist the temptation to jump right in with an answer and don't hesitate to ask for a reasonable amount of time to think. At the very least say, "I would have to know the population of New

York City and the 4:00 P.M. Twitter trends to give you a correct answer." The interviewer will know, then, that you know HOW to solve the problem.

WORKING INTERVIEWS

Some employers prefer a more direct approach. Rather than simply asking you to explain why you are the best match for the position, they want to see you perform. Writers, educators, counselors, salespeople, and engineers are among some of the professionals who may encounter a working interview. For example, a sales manager may say, "Sell me this coffee mug."

Don't panic if you encounter this type of interview as certain strategies can make the working interview a manageable experience. Ask the interviewer how you will be evaluated, how much time you have, and if there is any relevant data available that will improve the quality and accuracy of your response. Since the main goal of the interviewer is to assess your thinking and problem-solving strategies, try not to get engrossed in minor details. Focus, rather, on main ideas with a bullet-point approach.

COMPUTERIZED INTERVIEWS

More and more, organizations are screening job applicants via computer. Computer programs present multiple-choice questions to evaluate experience, education, knowledge and so on. Many computer interviews are video-based and are used to present realistic (behavioral) scenarios to applicants. Candidates record their responses to be viewed later by interviewers.

Computerized interviews have an obvious advantage for companies wanting to save time screening a large number of applicants, but they can be intimidating to interviewees who might freeze up on screen. My best advice is to treat the interview like any other. Be animated, quick, and concise. Practice answering interview questions aloud before beginning to reduce hesitation.

SCHEDULING YOUR INTERVIEW

One of the most intimidating situations in the job search process is calling a hiring manager to ask for an interview. You feel awkward, scared, and afraid of rejection. My best advice is to get over it. You WILL face rejection. It's not personal. All you need is one "yes," though, and you're on your way. Practicing your call ahead of time makes a big difference.

Be prepared to play phone tag, but don't give up. Also, be sure to change your voicemail to something short and professional like, "You've reached Dan Killick. Please leave a message." Use an upbeat tone of voice. People often won't leave a message if you sound too flat or irritated, or if your voicemail only says, "You've reached XXX-XXX-XXXX." Let them know they have reached *you*.

Return calls the same day, using your judgment regarding time of day and time zones. If you can't call the same day, call early the next morning. Return the call even if you know you aren't interested. You never know who the person you are talking to knows in your field. If they like you, they may pass your resume on. *Never* return a call when you are distracted (driving) or there is background noise. Make sure you have a good connection (I still recommend using a land line if possible). Conne told me once that a candidate for a full-time, tenure-track teaching position used her cell phone for an interview. The calls were repeatedly dropped, and a lot of the information was missed despite the candidate insisting that she had a good connection. Her lack of foresight created a very bad impression.

Once you make a connection, your voice is *everything*. Telephone conversations are inherently awkward, so keeping your voice animated is critical to the impression you are making. If you must call someone back, be sure to let him or her know why you are calling. Don't assume a busy person scheduling many interviews will recognize your name or remember why you are calling. Try something like this (remember, *very* cheerful), "Hi! This is Dan Killick. You called me this morning to request an interview for the social media specialist position. I'd be delighted to interview! What date and time are best for you?"

When you schedule the interview, ask how long the interview might last and for the names of everyone who will be present. These questions are important because:

- They allow you time to prepare your interview answers and research the company.
- They allow the company the opportunity to adjust the focus of the job description and duties. Job criteria can change during the interview process. Therefore, you want to be on the later time slot because you will want to interview against the latest criteria, not the earliest.
- Knowing in advance how long the interview should take will help you with your own scheduling but can also tell you whether the interview is going well in the moment. If

you have been scheduled for an hour interview but it ends after 20 minutes, it didn't go well. Ask yourself why. Being at the company for two hours when the original interview was only scheduled for one is a good sign.

PREPARING FOR YOUR INTERVIEW

Once you have an interview scheduled, you must *really* do important homework—both written and verbal—to survive the next phase of this process. Why would you have worked so hard to get this far and then blow it because you thought you could wing it?

Don't try to "wing" your interview.

You will have a new To Do list after the interview is set up. **You must have a full understanding of the job description, organizational history, goals, mission and values, products and competitors, and key players.**

REVIEW THE JOB DESCRIPTION

The job description provides valuable information for planning an interview strategy. Remember, for them it is all about how well your skills match the job. Work as many keywords from the ad as possible into your answers. Determine a salary range and a benefits package based on the job description in case they ask you how much you would expect if you worked for them. You can look up salary averages on www.salary.com or other sites.

Don't forget to look at the soft skills listed in the job ad as they can make or break you. Conne was on a search committee for a new pastor at her church. They were looking to grow membership, so an extroverted personality was essential and, as such, was listed in the description under "desirable characteristics." A great deal of discussion ensued when an otherwise qualified applicant indicated several times in his application materials that he is an introvert. This issue resulted in a mismatch.

Each sentence of the job description provides a clue regarding the types of questions you might be asked in the interview. For example, if the description says the organization is looking for strong leadership skills, you know you will be asked to provide descriptions and examples of your own leadership. Picture each item of the description as the beginning of a question that sounds like "What is your experience with...?" If you don't have direct experience with the skill in question, think of a hypothetical answer. How *would* you handle X if it happened?

Think about how you would use your SHARE© Stories to address the specifics of the job description. For example, if they want someone with supervisory experience, develop a SHARE© Story to fit their need. You will use this in some form or another in your interviews. You can also adjust your SHARE© Stories to fit the company. Your answers should be succinct and never exceed 45-60 seconds in length when spoken. Whatever you do, don't "over SHARE©." Too much information could eliminate you as well. Stick to the question and make your point, then KEEP QUIET! Finally, comb the job description and think of questions you have for *them*.

Examine the sample position descriptions in this chapter. Think of potential interview questions you would ask a candidate applying for these jobs. Next, complete Exercises 9.1 and 9.2, *the Interview Prep and Pre-interview worksheets.*

SAMPLE POSITION DESCRIPTIONS

Note skills, core competencies, behavioral competencies.

EXAMPLE 1: CHIEF STRATEGY & TRANSFORMATION OFFICER

The Chief Strategy & Transformation Officer (CSTO) will report to the CEO and serve as chief strategic advisor to the executive team here at Company. The CSTO will lead creation of all company strategy, an imperative to the business at this stage as we scale from $150mm to $500mm in the next 5 years. As the key partner to the CEO, this person will enable strategy execution, communication, and alignment across the organization, and manage company-wide transformation initiatives to deliver short-term performance improvement and long-term enterprise value. Crucial to this role will be excellent business acumen paired with emotional intelligence, agility, and communication skills. The CSTO will oversee the company's strategic planning, goal setting, KPI management, investment implementation, and business and operating model transformation, in collaboration with a wide range of internal and external stakeholders. This role will also represent Company alongside other global Heads of Transformation within enterprise business unit. This position reports directly to the CEO of Company.

Roles and Responsibilities:

- Drive leadership in the planning, design and implementation of innovative business solutions by defining vision, strategies, and tactics to address market shifts in order to optimize competitive position.
- Measure and manage hard (financial) and soft (cultural) transformation metrics and goals.
- Play a central role in the company's executive governance, including setting meeting agendas, and driving follow up actions.
- Be a master of execution and project management, holding the team accountable and ensuring that deadlines are met across high-priority, cross-functional projects.
- Drive team-wide process for creating and managing investment portfolio and working closely with the finance team to resolve issues as they arise.
- Maintain critical relationships with holding-company stakeholders, including finance and investor relations.
- Work closely with the HR team to evaluate any organizational gaps and lend a hand with influencing the company culture.

Who You Are:

- You have strong business and financial acumen with 10+ years of relevant experience, ideally in a highly analytical role as a management consultant or high-level strategy executive at an organization of similar size.
- You think at a systems level and can distill and convey complex information in a compelling manner.
- You possess detail-oriented organizational and process management skills that allow you to manage a wide range of discrete initiatives.

- You are able to build trust with leadership, as well as with internal and external stakeholders at all levels.

- You are an impeccable communicator in any medium: in presentations and internal memos; in emails and Slack; in person during one-on-ones; and presenting in front of large audiences.

- You thrive in an incredibly fast-paced, ambiguous work environment with action-orientation and drive.

- You possess extreme attention to detail, a sense of urgency, reliability, and commitment to mastering your work.

- You gracefully challenge current wisdom and accept nothing without data and independent analysis.

EXAMPLE 2: PRESIDENT (AD PLACED BY A RECRUITER FOR A MIDDLE MARKET MANUFACTURING COMPANY)

We have been retained to identify the right President for a growing manufacturing business. The company is a leader in the manufacturing & development of furniture & other wood products for their target market. It is well-positioned for increased profitability & poised to grow even more quickly with the leadership & support of the right President.

Requirements include:

- 15+ years of progressive experience, with a demonstrated track record of driving margin improvement & operational efficiency.

- Experience re-engineering internal processes to drive efficiency, increase profitability, & support revenue growth.

- A proven ability to leverage technology & systems to drive operational improvements & profitability.

- Furniture manufacturing industry experience is required.

- A strong early career foundation in operations.

- 3+ years of full P&L experience in middle-market or highly entrepreneurial organizations is required.

- Strong leadership ability, interpersonal skill set, & competitive nature.

- BS/BA required, MBA or relevant advanced degree a plus.

- Acquisition & integration experience strongly preferred.

Reporting to the owner of the Company, the President will be responsible for the broad operational efficiency of the Company, as well as leading the company's overall strategic direction, customer acquisition efforts, and financial performance. He/she will effectively leverage the people, process, & technology necessary to enable this successful, entrepreneurial company to scale while improving profitability levels, customer satisfaction, & the Company's culture.

The President will also play a key role in:

- Advancing the culture of the Company with a strong sense of urgency.
- Mapping, assessing & streamlining complex processes to enable improved profitability, service, & scalability.
- Establishing, improving, & leveraging key metrics & key performance indicators to drive operational performance.
- Reporting operational results in an accurate & reliable fashion.
- Leading annual budgeting of matters under his/her direct control, making periodic re-forecasts as needed.

EXAMPLE 3: SOCIAL MEDIA COORDINATOR (FROM INDEED JOB DESCRIPTION SAMPLES)

The Social Media Coordinator has several duties associated with researching and creating informed campaigns that appeal to a specific target, including:

- Understanding KPI's and defining them specifically for social media.
- Collaborating with designers or copywriters to provide attractive and informative campaigns.
- Monitoring all social media content.
- Tracking the performance of the campaign.
- Keeping up with technologies used in social media.
- Using social media marketing tools.
- Tracking customer engagement and SEO to optimize campaign content.

- Establishing relationships/networks of industry professionals or influencers on social media.
- Hiring and training a motivated team.

Social Media Coordinator skills and qualifications:

- One or more years of experience as a Social Media Coordinator or similar role.
- Proficient in business posts on social media platforms.
- Understand SEO and web traffic data.
- Experience researching buyer and consumer trends.
- Understand social media KPIs.
- Familiar with web page design and publishing.
- Must be able to multitask.
- Critical thinker and problem-solver.
- Works well with a team.
- Organized and self-motivated.
- Excellent time management.
- Exceptional at communication and building relationships.

Social Media Coordinator salary expectations: The average salary for a Social Media Coordinator is $15.57 per hour.

Social Media Coordinator education and training requirements:

Bachelor's degree with coursework in communication, business or public relations. Internships or activities using leadership skills as well as social media management experience. Social Media Coordinator experience requirements: Public relations and marketing experience is required. Candidates may also demonstrate social media knowledge gained by doing research, joining in online forums and participating in online webinars.

STUDY THE ORGANIZATION

The company's website or a google search will tell you about the organization's history, goals, mission, and values. "What do you know about our company?" is a common interview question. Be able to provide a *brief* synopsis of when and why the company was founded, how it has evolved and where it is going.

You should also go into the interview with a basic understanding of what the company does or makes, especially if you are changing focus in your career. Know the services and products the organization provides and who their customers are. Also, find out as much as you can about their competition. Look at it from their point of view. Most people will come into the interview knowing a little about the organization, but very few will have advanced knowledge about the competition. Talk intelligently about how you would beat the competition and the job is yours.

IDENTIFY KEY PLAYERS

You should attempt to secure the names of the President and VP of the company, as well as those in charge of the division in which you will be employed. You may even be able to find an organizational chart that will show you the internal structure of the company. You should attempt to secure the name(s) of the person you will be reporting to and the name of the person they report to, as well.

Most importantly, ask for the names and titles of the people who will be present during the interview. This is not invasive, and a savvy businessperson will recognize that you are trying to do your best to prepare for the interview by asking for names. See if you can glean enough information about their backgrounds to help you form a strategy. Use light questions, not interrogation techniques when talking to your contact or his/her administrative assistant.

KNOW THE INTERVIEW LOCATION

Prior to the actual interview you should plan to do a drive-by or at least check out the directions on a map or GPS. Plot out how much time it will take to get from your location to the interview site with traffic, a few wrong turns, parking and locating the right office in the building.

Nothing is more embarrassing than having to say, "Sorry I'm late." Your interviewer will most certainly think, "You're out because we don't hire careless or unprepared people." A client of ours had four telephone interviews and was finally flown in for a face-to-face interview. When he left the hotel to go to the interview, he asked the desk clerk for directions. You guessed it. They were wrong and he showed up over 30 minutes late, missed his panel interview, and, of course, did not get the job.

Use the pre-interview questionnaire at the end of the chapter. Obtaining critical information will set you head and shoulders above your competition.

PERFECT YOUR INTERVIEW ATTIRE AND LOOK

These days, it seems as though people wear just about anything to work. The rules for interviews, however, have remained largely unchanged: conservative and business formal attire is best in most situations.

Think of it like this. When you are looking for a job, you want to appeal to as wide a range of interviewers as possible. While some may be broader in their view of what you should wear, many old schoolers will think your white socks or short skirt are inappropriate. The person with the broader view will accept your conservative outfit, but the old schooler won't accept your less well thought out ensemble. Therefore, conservative and tasteful is the way to go. Don't worry about dressing better than your interviewer. The worst thing he/she will think is that you are trying to impress him/her and really want the job. Knowing you have the *judgment* to dress like you are at a job interview is going to send the right message.

Here are a few rules I hope you won't break:

Invest in a suit. It doesn't have to be expensive, but a suit by definition is a jacket with matching pants, skirt or dress. That is, usually the fabric is cut out of the same bolt of cloth (some women's suits are the exception). There is research on color. Men should go with dark gray and women with black, but if (women only) you look good in burgundy or brown by all means pick a flattering color. For men, I strongly recommend that avoid either a green or a brown suit. Avoid patterns. Pick something classic, not trendy, and *definitely* not cobbled together. If wearing a skirt, wear stockings (not tights) that match your natural skin tone.

Watch the cut of your clothes. The suit should be tailored, not baggy or tight. Don't go into the interview looking like a stuffed sausage. This may be the trend now, but trends come and go. Skirts should fall between the top of your knee (NO HIGHER) and mid-calf. Remember, your skirt will rise when you sit down. Pants should not touch the floor or be so tight that attention is drawn to your body. Your blazer should also fit properly. You should be able to button it with no gaping or pulling. Wear a dress shirt that matches the suit. Make sure it is not see through or low cut.

Make sure your outfit matches. Your gray pants are not going to look good with a red shirt, lavender blazer and brown shoes.

No cologne or perfume. Many people are allergic to it or just don't like it.

Get a haircut in a style that suits the organization before the interview. Not sure? Look at their website images. The people in the pictures, even if they are stock photos, will represent the organization. Facial hair is OK as long as it is close trimmed and well-shaped. Nothing scraggy. Shave your neck. Consider tying back long hair.

Pay attention to your shoes. They must be polished and not worn looking. Make sure they match your clothes. No sneakers or casual shoes. Women can wear up to a 3-inch heel but should avoid stilettos. A conservative pair of pumps works best.

Keep jewelry conservative. Wedding rings and one other ring are fine. Avoid clanking bracelets, large earrings or necklaces. Watches are fine.

Go low key with cosmetics. Less is more. Avoid bright-colored nail polish and long, fake nails that can be distracting. Leave the false eyelashes at home. You want them to focus on your ideas, not your fashion.

Pay attention to hygiene and grooming. Avoid anything that would make you smell bad, like smoking or drinking.

Leave larger bags such as briefcases and backpacks in the car. Obtain a small portfolio. With a pen and a place for your car key. Don't carry a handbag. Travel lite to the interview.

CREATING A SMASHING FIRST IMPRESSION: THE GUEST/HOST RELATIONSHIP

Think about the last time you met someone. How long did it take you to form a first impression? Research on the length of time it takes to create a first impression varies from 7 to about 90 seconds. That's a big gap, but it's safe to say that in less than two minutes your appearance, way of speaking, body language, manners and much more may either seal or blow the deal. I have addressed attire and grooming already, so here I'll provide some tips for making a good impression through the way you behave.

The interviewer has already determined that you are qualified. Now, he or she is asking "Do I want to work with this person 40+ hours a week?" We all want to work with people who are friendly, cordial and, well, *nice*.

Think of you and your interviewer(s) as having a guest/host relationship. Pretend you are going to a party at the home of someone you want to impress. Perhaps you are attending a holiday party at the company president's house. You have certain expectations of each other. These expectations include warmth, friendliness, excitement about being there, good manners and so on. Imagine the host answered the door with no smile and gave you a weak handshake and an unenthusiastic "Come in." Would you want to stay? If your guest greeted you the same way, would you want him or her to stay?

Job interviews are the same. Your interviewer should treat you like a welcome guest and you should enter the situation with warmth, style and grace. How do you exude these essential characteristics?

First, arrive at the interview 5-10 minutes early...no more, no less. If you arrive too early, you may awkwardly overlap another person's interview. With just a few minutes to spare they might take you early and you will then have more time for your interview session. Too late and, well, that's just rude and will kill your chance of being hired. Pulling into the parking lot with two minutes to spare and bolting for the interviewer's office also isn't a good idea because you will seem flustered. You also don't want to arrive worried about whether you have all of the requisite materials you need. Prepare! Like the old Gillette antiperspirant ads used to say, "Never let them see you sweat." The rest boils down to a firm handshake, a big smile, and impeccable manners.

Next, exude warmth. Your smile is everything. Light humor is okay. If you are interviewing in Detroit in January and it is 10 degrees out you might say, "I see you're having a warm spell."

YOUR HANDSHAKE

Though COVID undoubtedly changed the practice of handshaking, I like to think it will not be a forgotten practice. How you shake hands has direct bearing on whether someone will want to hire you. A study by Stewart, Dustin, Darnold, Barrick and Darnold revealed that, though seemingly superficial, handshakes are important for creating a positive impression.[32] They state, "From a practical perspective, our findings suggest that the effect of the handshake in employment interviews should not be ignored. Interviewers can obtain important information about interviewee traits through the nonverbal cue of the handshake." They also suggest that women need to pay more attention to their handshakes than do men.

One of the biggest mistakes people make when shaking hands is not placing their hand fully into the other person's hand. Rather, they shake with their fingers. When shaking hands, the L (index to thumb) of your hand should touch the L of your partner's. Wrap your fingers around his or her palm, grasp firmly but not *too* firmly and pump gently twice. Shake hands with everyone present at the beginning and end of the interview. **Maintain eye contact and smile.** Not natural for you? PRACTICE! Remember, you may only have seven seconds to impress.

YOUR SMILE

Your smile is the most effective tool in your body language toolbox, and it is especially important when you greet your interviewer. As humans, we react to faces at a subconscious level. When someone is not smiling, we smile less. When a person is smiling, we smile more. To that end, if your interviewer seems a little frosty, you may be able to win him or her over. Conne told me about a student who interviewed for graduate-level entry at an ivy league theological seminary. Competition was stiff and when he got to the entrance meeting his interviewer was tired and unwelcoming. Unrelentingly, he stayed animated, upbeat and enthusiastic and eventually won her over. He got in.

Unfortunately, anyone who has ever been nervous in an interview will tell you that your smile is the first thing to go. You may experience a kind of facial paralysis if nerves overcome you. How do you manage it? *PRACTICE* SMILING. Let your smile reach your eyes! This topic will be addressed again in a later chapter.

---

32   Stewart, G. L., Dustin, S. L., Barrick, M. R., & Darnold, T. C. (2008). Exploring the handshake in employment interviews. *Journal of Applied Psychology,* 93(5), 1139-1146. https://doi.org/10.1037/0021-9010.93.5.1139

YOUR MANNERS

Having good manners in an interview should go without saying, but you'd be surprised at how often nervous interviewees will forget to say "please" or "thank you," or treat the interviewer too familiarly.

Address your interviewer by his or her courtesy title (Mr., Ms., Dr., etc.) until told otherwise. A good interviewer will put you at ease quickly and ask you to call him/her by first name, but some will prefer the professional distance.

Many interviewers will offer you a beverage. I advise against this because the last thing you want to do is spill coffee or have condensation on your hand or the table. If you are in a restaurant, however, go ahead and have a *non-alcoholic* beverage (even if your interviewer has alcohol). Be nice to your server. Your manners toward the server reflect how you treat people in general and that's important to any employer.

Turn off your cell phone before the interview even if your interviewer doesn't. Is any text you will receive more important than what's going on in your meeting?

Dining etiquette is beyond the scope of this book but, if you think you will be going to a restaurant during your interview, brush up. Many interviews include a meal.

Be sure to thank your interviewer for his or her time. Use your thank you to reinforce how right you are for the position. Try something like, "Thank you so much taking the time to meet with me. I really enjoyed hearing how things work here and hope you'll consider me because I know I'm the perfect fit for this position." Shake hands if you haven't and leave. Don't dawdle. There may be another interviewee waiting to come in.

Send a thank you email or note (hand-written notes are still okay if you have nice handwriting) at once after the interview. Even if you don't get the job, they will think of you in a positive light and might want to hire you later. Exercise 9.3 provides a sample thank you letter.

Don't be discouraged if your interview doesn't go perfectly. Immediately write down what they asked you, how you answered and how you could improve. Analyze and reflect.

Finally, be prepared for anything. This book would be 7,000 pages long if Conne and I revealed every crazy thing we have seen in interviews. Don't get rattled if you feel like the interview is not going well. Smile. Exude charm. At the very least, you can tuck the interview into the "live and learn" file. Similarly, don't read in too much if the interview is going well. A good host will make you feel welcome whether he or she wants to hire you or not. Often you will wait weeks—even months—to hear whether you got a job. Busy decisionmakers have other daily priorities. You never know what is going on behind the scenes. Be patient. Every interview is a valuable experience.

The next chapter will address how to answer even the most difficult interview questions. It will allow you to gain advantage by positioning yourself above your competitors.

SUCCESS STORY: INTERVIEW PREP PAYDAY

CONTRIBUTED BY BILL TEMPLE, EXECUTIVE COACH, STEWART, COOPER & COON

Greg was open to new career opportunities when he was contacted by an organization looking to hire someone with his skills. They were impressed with his LinkedIn profile, so Greg began an interview process that lasted over 2 months.

Greg and I discussed what the interview expectations of the company would likely be and how to prepare. We practiced using the conversations to illustrate how his past experiences would have a positive impact on their future. Greg paid particularly close attention to his ability to meet growth objectives as this was a key component of the role.

Though his financial package is confidential, Greg accepted a position as Senior Vice President and Chief Commercial Officer, and was able to secure several important perks:

- A desired commercially focused role
- A corporate culture that aligns with his interests
- Challenges that are in keeping with his experiences and skills

The net result of his preparation for the interviews was that Greg has a position with a company to which he can make great contributions.

ADDITIONAL RESOURCES

- Lock Haven University Center for Career and Professional Development (n.d.). *Dress for success*. Lock Haven University. https://www.lockhaven.edu/career/documents/2018-7-11%20%20Dress%20for%20Success%20brochure_sizing%209x11.5%20for%20DUPL.pdf/
- St. Olaf College (n.d.). Clothes: What do you wear to an interview? St. Olaf College. https://wp.stolaf.edu/pipercenter/how-to-guides/interview-guide/clothes/

EXERCISE 9.1 PRE-INTERVIEW WORKSHEET

Company Name:
Web Address:
Home Office Address:
Local Branch Office Address:

GATHER INFORMATION

Do you have a brochure?
Do you have a 10-k, if available?
Do you have published articles about the business?

KEY CONTACTS

Who are your key contacts at this company? Include anyone with whom you have already spoken.

PRODUCTS AND SERVICES

What are this company's main products and services?
What are the products and services at the locations/divisions that you are contacting?
Competitors
List at least 3 of this company's main competitors.

WHO'S WHO

List the names of the organization's executives and their titles.

NETWORK

Who in your network might have done business with or have contacts with this company?

SUMMARY

Summarize the nature of the company, its position in the market relative to its competitors, and long- and short-term economic factors influencing its lines of business and its management reputation.

JOB DESCRIPTION

List the key qualities and skills the organization needs. Then, compare this list to your own qualifications.

EXERCISE 9.2 INTERVIEW PREP WORKSHEET

Company_____

Date_____ Time_____ Length_____

Location_____

Interviewer(s)_____

Phone_____ Email_____

(attach map or directions; check GPS)

The Week Before

- ☐ Do the pre-interview exercise
- ☐ Have business cards ready
- ☐ Do questions exercise
- ☐ Answer top 20 interview questions
- ☐ Find out about your interviewers
- ☐ Clean and prepare attire
- ☐ Practice SHARE stories
- ☐ Review resume

The Night Before

- ☐ Review job description
- ☐ Review SHARE stories with somebody else
- ☐ Memorize interviewer's name(s)
- ☐ Prepare clothing
- ☐ Shine shoes
- ☐ Check weather forecast

Bring to the Interview

- ☐ SHARE stories
- ☐ 3 resumes
- ☐ Interview questions for them
- ☐ Business cards
- ☐ Folder and notetaking material
- ☐ Umbrella
- ☐ Breath mints or chewing gum

Last Minute Pointers

- ☐ Turn off phone
- ☐ Arrive 5 to 10 minutes early
- ☐ Be nice to receptionist
- ☐ Ask as many questions as they ask you
- ☐ Tell at least 3 SHARE stories

- ☐ Secure a business card from everyone you meet
- ☐ Confirm another meeting or follow-up time

- ☐ Thank the interviewers
- ☐ Thank receptionist

After the Interview is Over

- ☐ Complete the Post Interview Worksheet
- ☐ Write a follow-up thank you letter to everyone you met
- ☐ Write a thank you note to the person who referred you
- ☐ Follow up with a phone call if you committed to do so
- ☐ Review your answers and make a list of items to improve for next time

Do

Dress appropriately
Come prepared
Be on time
Have confidence
Make good eye contact
Speak clearly
Be positive
Have good posture
Learn about the industry
Leave with a sincere thank you
Observe COVID rules

Don't

Shake hands too hard or too soft
Wear too much smell
Be a know-it-all
Act passive
Lack confidence
Talk about past failures
Bad mouth past employer
Make excuses or be evasive
Focus on money or benefits
Be cynical
Have a condescending attitude
Overshare
Be indecisive
Smoke or chew gum
Whine
Lack verbal expression

EXERCISE 9.3   SAMPLE THANK YOU LETTER

Dear Ms. Klausen:

Thank you for including me in your interview schedule for the regional sales manager position. I gained further insight about Oscarmove Solutions and the challenges you face.

As per our conversation, it is somewhat of a surprise that your western territory is generating such low sales volume. Based upon my research of your company, the competitors operating in this arena and the great products you offer, I believe the southwest territory has tremendous growth potential.

At the conclusion of our interview, we agreed that my candidacy is under strong consideration because of my requisite skills and past experiences in increasing sales quickly. Not only can I acquire new clients, but I can deepen your market penetration in this territory and build numerous profitable long-term relationships.

Your company needs, and my skills and proven track history in moving numbers, makes our future working relationship a good match. I would be proud to work for Oscarmove Solutions.

Thank you again for the opportunity to interview with Oscarmove. I look forward to hearing from you soon.

Sincerely,

Dwight Gesson

CHAPTER 10
ACING YOUR INTERVIEW PART 2: HANDLING INTERVIEW QUESTIONS

Prince Machiavelli, a 14th Century Italian diplomat, said that knowledge is power and any person who has it has the potential to control the events surrounding her/his destiny. You are asking right now, "Okay, how do I gain power and control?"

Power and control are not negative terms in this instance. They are tools at your disposal that you can use to get the job and salary you want. To have control, you must gain power (knowledge) and to use this power to your advantage, you must build a two-way street of communication.

Many job seekers, especially at the entry level, view the interview as a situation in which the interviewer has all the power. You may think your job is to answer questions and hope for the best. WRONG. *Look at the interview as a conversation* (referring to it as a meeting might help). You are in the meeting because they know you are qualified. Now, they are looking at your personality, enthusiasm, and desire to learn. They want to see if you have ideas for solving problems and how seriously you have taken the situation by preparing and researching. You already have *some* knowledge and you're going to gain more during the interview. Communication during the interview must flow in two directions. You will answer questions *and* ask questions much the way a consultant does. In this chapter I will emphasize:

- The basics of good communication when interviewing
- How to structure and time your responses
- Types of interview questions
- Commonly asked interview questions

Before reading this information, however, you need to understand that **the way to control your interview and establish yourself as a consultant is through using a method called triangulation.**

TRIANGLE THEORY

Triangle Theory was developed by William Temple ("The Professor"). Bill is one of the most experienced career coaches I know. At the writing of this edition of Ready Aim Hired, Bill Temple had helped hundreds of clients negotiate over $330M in packages and benefits. Bill wrote about Triangle Theory in his book, *Principles of Effective Personal Marketing*©.[33] I present a condensed version here.

Bill's concept of "triangulation" has many applications in personal marketing. Most of us use it every day without really knowing it, or fully understanding its value. It is a critical element of communication, however, when you are conducting information meetings and job interviews. **The triangulation process allows interviewers to view *their* needs and *your* solutions as unifying elements rather than as obstacles created by the "I have the job; you want the job" attitude often present.**

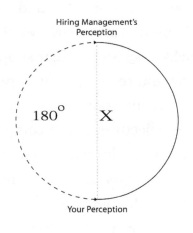

Figure 1 180° Arc

Let's illustrate Triangle Theory. Do you remember your basic geometry? Look at Figure 1. At one end is the employer (here called Hiring Management), at the other end is you, seeking a position represented by the black X in the middle.

You can see that there is a 180° arc between the hiring manager's perception and yours. You and the employer are at opposites on the end of a single line, focused on each other.

---

33   Temple, W. (2001). *Principles of Effective Personal Marketing*. W. Temple.

Getting an offer can become an intellectual tug-of-war between what you want and what they think they want (which, by the way, may not be what they really need).

To help the company make a better decision, and to identify the best opportunities for you, you should interview them while they interview you. You must think like a consultant, evaluating the situation to discover what the real issues are so you can demonstrate from prior experience (your SHARE© stories) that you can find the solutions for those issues. To do this effectively, create a baseline that consists of two points: what you do (your 1-minute commercial) and how what you do fits in to the potential employer's business.

Describing what you do should be easy by now. Incorporate the attributes and functional skills that seem logical for the position. They already have your application materials. What you do will become a "given," and often will not come up again.

Next, ask the interviewer what he or she sees as the organization's objectives. Where do they want to be in 6-12 months? Based on your preparation you should already have a good idea of the answer, and of the steps necessary to get there. Communicate clearly what you would do if hired. Tell some SHARE© Stories that support your ability to meet their goals. You and the employer, represented as "a" and "b," (see Figure 2, Organization-focused Triangle) are altered to focus on X, the objectives of the company, and a triangle is formed. Your tug-of-war loosens as you both focus on what is best for *them* and how *you* can make it happen. You have now gained control of the interview.

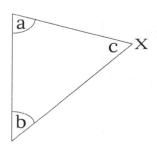

Figure 2 Organization-focused Triangle

Employers will initially see a gap between your capabilities and their needs. The more you can bridge the gap between your past and their future, the more you will appear to line up with their situation and the more tangible you will seem to be as a part of their solution.

As your responses continue, the interviewer will begin to see that you understand and can fulfill the company's needs and his or her perception of you will change favorably. The X (corporate objective) moves closer to the interviewer as you make clear your ability to meet their goals (see Figure 3). In addition, the shape of the triangle changes in that the degree of emotional separation (ex. anxiety) between the hiring manager and the workplace problems he or she needs to solve has been reduced because of you.

Finally, the hiring manager's question about *what* you do changes to how, why and, most important, *when* you can do it.

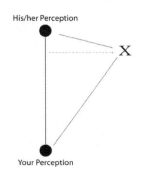

Triangle Theory is the translation of your past experiences into the employer's future opportunities. Go into the interview with the attitude that you already have the job! Your communication strategy then becomes a question of determining where to start to meet the present and future needs of the employer and, in the process, **you are far more likely to demonstrate your value to the hiring managers than your competition**.

Figure 3 Emotional Separation Reduced

ORGANIZATION AND LENGTH OF YOUR ANSWERS

On a search committee once, Conne told a candidate, "Tell us about yourself." He responded with a 20-minute answer not realizing the committee had 36 far more important questions to get through. When interviewing, remember that your interviewer(s) is on a schedule, and nothing is more annoying than an interviewee who can't make a clear, concise point. The interviewer is working and it's likely your interview is not the only thing he/she has to do before going home.

Ask how long your interviewer has and respect that timeframe. Take cues from him or her. If you are not seeing head shaking and attentiveness, chances are you have spoken too long. If your interviewer starts using phrases like *"Briefly* tell us," your answers have been too long. Your best strategy is to tell your interviewer that you plan to provide concise answers but are happy to elaborate when desired. While I'm not suggesting that every answer should be the same, here is a general rule of thumb:

1. Answer directly, saying "yes," "no" or some other direct answer.

2. Briefly explain your response (remember an explanation isn't the same as an example).

3. Provide an example if appropriate (a.k.a. a SHARE© Story).

Let's say you are asked, "What's your superpower?" Answer like this:

*Listening is my superpower (**direct answer**). I can hear both concrete words as well as feelings and that skill makes people feel like they are really being heard (**explanation**). Last week one of my supervisees came to me frustrated about a lack of resources. When she was done speaking, I summed up her comments and told her I understood that she probably felt very frustrated. She thanked me for understanding and knows I'm working on the problem. I'm happy I could put her at ease (**example/SHARE© story**).*

A SHARE© story is not required for every response. Use your judgement. Remember, you're on the clock.

Also, anticipate or at least clarify the *meaning* of the questions. Conne once asked an applicant to list a weakness. The *point* of the question is to determine whether a candidate is self-reflective and actively seeking to improve deficiencies. Not only did the candidate *not* provide an answer, he ended his response with, "None of us are perfect, right?" RED FLAG!!! Think before you speak and ask for clarification if necessary.

TYPES OF INTERVIEW QUESTIONS

Most interviewers, whether they are conducting the meeting over the phone, video or in person, will use a mix of three categories of questions: traditional, behavioral and stress.

TRADITIONAL INTERVIEW QUESTIONS

Traditional interview questions address broad categories like ability to work in teams, meet deadlines and other skills germane to the position. Exercise 10.1 at the end of the chapter will show you a detailed list and suggested answers to commonly asked interview questions like, "Tell us about yourself" and "What are your strengths and weaknesses?" When you are reviewing the questions, think about how a potential employer might tailor them for the position for which you are applying.

BEHAVIORAL INTERVIEW QUESTIONS

Henry Ford had it right many years ago when he said, "I hire the man, not the history." He was likely referring to how people treat others. In other words, he was talking about behavioral competencies 60 years before the concept showed up again in the workplace. Let's focus on the following revision: "I hire the person, not the history."

Remember the section in Chapter 1 about emotional quotient (EQ)? Employers use behavioral questions to determine your EQ. You are in the interview because they know you are qualified, but they still need to know that you are the right person. You may be asking, "What does *right* mean?" It's probably you, but they don't know that yet, so they are going to ask you questions that will assess how you will behave on the job.

They also ask behavioral questions to further explore underlying characteristics that might not be obvious through examination of written materials like your resume. Look at behavioral questions as an opportunity to prove to them that they want to work with you day in and day out more than anyone else.

More companies are moving toward a behavioral approach to their interview programs. The behaviors, competencies, and traits desired in an employee as well as the job skills and knowledge are identified in the job ad. Sometimes these skills are referred to as soft skills.

Here is a list of just a few **behavioral competencies**. Please notice that you do not see technical job skills on the list.Leadership

- Team development
- Exemplary communication
- Motivation
- Integrity
- Trustworthiness
- Adaptability/flexibility
- Creativity/vision
- Analytical, critical, conceptual and innovative thinking
- Strategic decision making
- Interpersonal savvy and diplomacy
- Managing conflicting ideas
- Employee development
- Customer analysis and targeting
- Drive for continuous improvement
- Perceptivity
- Political savvy

Behavioral questions are used by many employers to gain insight into a candidate's past behavior in relatable situations. Whereas in a traditional interview one would answer a series of questions regarding what he or she would do, a behavioral interview might require responses relating to how he or she *has already performed*. This is why SHARE© stories are so important.

Behavioral interviews are based upon validation. Although your experience and skills set may theoretically qualify you for the job, without the ability to substantiate how you put your competencies into action, your descriptive words may be irrelevant.

BEHAVIORAL QUESTIONS AND *CULTURAL FIT*

Listening to the nature of an interviewer's behavioral questions can help *you* determine whether you'd fit in to the organization's culture as well. A company's culture is not based on ideas of how the business should be run, but on how employees interact. A common question I get from clients is "How do I determine a company's culture?" You could be the best person for a position based on your job skills but, if the company's culture does not fit you or your values, there is little doubt that you will be unhappy because you will not be in an atmosphere that's right for you.

Let's say you are interviewing with a company that has the goal of building positive relationships with customers. You want to know *how* they are facilitating that goal because it reflects their culture. You should say, "Give me an example of how customer complaints are handled," or "Describe how or what your salespeople do to find ways to satisfy the customer." Then ask, "What is the level of community involvement of the company and of the sales personnel?" or, more directly, "How would you describe your company's culture?"

Another way to get a handle on a company's culture is to think about your own values as related to theirs. Examine their mission statement, annual reports, website, etc. Do they mirror your values? Also, as you go into the interview, observe the setting. Is it shabby and run down or dirty? Does it appear they care about their employees' work environment?

Also pay attention to the enthusiasm of your interviewer. Is he or she excited about the company and the job? Does he or she complain about the company? Even the way in which they ask you questions is an indicator of culture. Is the process crisp and sharp? Do they seem to know their company? You would be surprised at how many folks do not know what is in their company's annual report. How they answer your questions is a clue about their culture.

Cultures are, in large part, an outgrowth of leadership styles and preferences. However, nothing you ask will help unless you know yourself, so do some self-reflection. If you cannot see the desired characteristics demonstrated around you during an interview, you may want to look elsewhere.

BEHAVIORAL QUESTIONS AND THE *LIKEABILITY FACTOR*

Your "likeability factor" is related to your cultural fit and is based on the interviewer(s) overall perception of what it would be like to work with you day in and day out. Friendliness, genuineness, empathy and similar interests are the key characteristics employers look for according to Tim Sanders, author of *The Likeability Factor*.[34] Sense of humor, humility, warmth, attentiveness, self-deprecation and many other personal characteristics make you more likeable.

The building of your likeability factor is critical. To do this successfully, you must take a skill, such as teamwork, and determine what makes up teamwork in these terms. For instance, to be a good team leader you must be approachable and tuned in to the personal and professional obstacles your team members face. SHARE© Stories that illustrate these qualities will increase your likeability.

Your dependability is also important. If you think about the word "dependability," you might be tempted to conclude that it is weak to sell at high corporate levels. However, if you consider that dependability includes initiation of action on problems, accurate interpretation of a customer's concerns, or providing effective leadership, then it has strength. If you can get these concepts across during an interview, then you are really showing that dependability is part of your emotional intelligence.

PREPARING FOR A BEHAVIORAL INTERVIEW

In matching people with work, employers intuitively assess those underlying factors or competencies that will affect the candidate's success in the job. Often the company wants to know HOW you go about getting things done. For instance, they might ask:

- HOW do you take initiative and ensure results in work assignments?
- HOW do you communicate with those at different levels within the organization?
- HOW do you deal with conflict? What is your personal style of handling conflict?

Analyze the central challenges of the job when preparing for your interview and align them with your competencies and past experiences. Put yourself in the shoes of the

---

34 Sanders, T. (2006). *The likeability factor: How to boost your L factor and achieve your life's dreams*. Currency.

interviewer. What do you think he or she would want to hear? Have no fear of the unknown, because the unknown can only exist if you are not prepared, have not practiced enough, and have not thought about the match between your skills and the job.

Review your resume and the job description with an eye to the experiences you would use to illustrate competencies. Think about the implications of the words you have used to describe yourself and why you chose those words. Use each word as you practice your SHARE© Stories. Doing so will allow you to better demonstrate the use of your key behaviors and traits. For example, many people use the words "manager" and "leader" on their resumes. I have received responses when asking questions about the qualities of managers vs. leaders that have caused me to wonder how well an interviewee knew himself or herself.

As you explore your background, you are likely to discover that there are about 15 to 20 behaviors, habits, and traits that you use to get work done. These represent your key, saleable, personal behavioral strengths; strengths that you want others to know about.

Behavioral interviewing reveals your character and integrity, so ask yourself *why* you are the best. If you do not come up with terms like persistent, credible, motivated, interpersonally savvy, able to identify the needs of others, action oriented, innovative, and approachable, then you do not know why you are effective and, more importantly, who you are.

Finally, to prepare for an interview you need to think about ANY possible inquiry and that means *ANY* type of inquiry. Let your imagination run. Think about the work you do, what skills and knowledge are required, and how it is used. Think about why you are good at what you do. Think of your motivators, about the impact you have had, how you affect the people around you, and how you build relationships. Once you have a clear picture of all of these you are well prepared for behavioral questions.

ANSWERING *BEHAVIORAL QUESTIONS*

During a behavioral interview, you can expect to be questioned in depth because the company is trying to determine whether you have specific behaviors needed for the position. They want to hear the actual behavior in words, so you need to factor those words into an interview answer. The word "hear" is used for a specific reason. For example, if you were demonstrating the use of your command skills, then that term should be used in your answer. Unfortunately, many times the interviewee thinks his or her message is getting across, and that is not a safe assumption. Tell your audience what they want to hear. **Use their language**.

Determine the focus or subject of the question quickly and clarify as needed. You might ask, for example: Your question seems to focus on [specific topic vs. general], is that correct?" or, "I am not sure what you mean by [key word or phrase]; would you clarify that for me?"

You also need to know when the interviewer wants you to provide an example or story and when he/she wants to you speculate or offer a hypothetical answer. Phrases like, "Tell me about a time when," "Can you give us an example of" and so on are clues that they want a glimpse of your past, a specific instance when the behavior came into play in your life. Set up your story with a few key facts like when, where and with whom it happened. Begin your response with, "One time," "In 2020," or "When I..."

Sometimes an interviewer will want you to speculate about what you *would* do in a situation. "Two workers in the plant get into an argument and it's getting heated. What would you do?" Answer these questions chronologically. "First, I would call security. Then, I would..." Interviewers know that you couldn't possibly have faced every situation they might bring up. If you really don't have the experience they want to hear about, it's okay to say, "I don't think that has ever happened to me, but if it did, I would do this..."

Some behavioral questions are aimed at getting you to respond to negative situations. Therefore, you should have examples of negative experiences. Prepare a few SHARE© Stories in which you indicate that you were able to make the best of a situation or, better yet, how you were able to bring about a positive outcome. Keep in mind that all negative experiences are learning situations; be prepared to talk about what you learned.

Refrain from referring to the same accomplishments when describing competencies. Rather, be prepared with at least two or three separate relevant achievements to reach a truly inclusive response to each question. Additionally, active listening, making use of notes, and capturing important keywords are critical to a successful behavioral interview.

In my book *Hire the EQ, Not the IQ: 150+ Questions to Help You Hire the Right Fit*, co-author Ron Venckus and I provide many examples of behavioral questions, which are often deep and complex. For example, instead of saying, "What are your greatest strengths/ weaknesses?" an interviewer may say, "Tell me about a time when a weakness of yours did not allow you to perform up to your capabilities. How did you recognize the roadblock and what was its impact on you and your team?" In the latter version, they are not just looking at your weakness. They are also looking for problem analysis, self-awareness and ability to overcome. They are assessing your ability to see your weaknesses as a roadblock to not only your success but the success of others. One of the key tenets of emotional intelligence is knowing how your actions affect others.

The best way to handle this question is to follow the SHARE© pattern, telling them how you overcame your weakness and briefly stating the impact it had on you...how it changed you. Don't be tempted to talk for too long here. Cut detail and hit the key points of what they are asking. Your response could sound like this:

> *One of my duties when I was a public relations assistant at Hospital X was to supervise student interns who wanted to go into PR. They would write press releases and the like and give them to me to proof. One intern had marginal writing skills and I didn't realize that my negative feedback and lack of direction were roadblocks to her performance. In frustration, she told me she was quitting the program, so I prodded her for more information and had to admit I was not being a good mentor to her. After that we met every other day and her writing improved considerably. I learned that with a little coaching, any employee can become a valuable member of the team. How would you see this training and management approach working for your team?*

Please note that the question I asked to close my answer is open-ended and makes the interviewer provide you with more information and some inkling of his/her acceptance of your answer quality.

You may encounter case method interview questions in behavioral interviewing. Case interview questions require an analysis of a business situation. You could be presented with a question about a firm that is losing market share and is experiencing profitability problems. The interviewer may say, "Give me a picture of how you would go about examining this problem and what actions would you take to turn it around." They are expecting you to use your executive intelligence to provide an on-the-spot analysis.

Executive intelligence (a term appropriate for everyone, not just executives) is the ability to use conceptual thinking. Keep in mind that there are the **four sides of you that you have to sell**: job knowledge or skills; behaviors; conceptual, innovative, analytical thinking; and executive intelligence, or *applying* your knowledge. If you are presented with a case, you need to diagnose, analyze, and clearly communicate a solution to the problem. You should also be able to describe how you would execute your plan. In many cases, the interviewer needs someone with your skills and will give you valuable information about the problem that he/she is trying to solve. You have the opportunity, now, to turn the interview into a consultative sale. You are telling the respective buyer, the hiring authority, how this particular product, YOU, can solve their problem.

When you have exhausted discussing the current problem, ask, "What's the next problem that you want to solve?" and so on. You are now on your way to proving your worth to the interviewer.

Don't be surprised if the case presented to you is based on a reality the organization is facing. Perhaps they are hiring because they know they are having deficits in a certain area. **Go to the interview assuming they want you to present hypothetical solutions or a plan to move forward**. Conne was on a search committee for a new senior pastor for her church. Three candidates were asked how they planned to increase attendance because growing the membership was listed in the job description as a major goal. Not one could answer let alone provide information about how they had done so in the past.

Keep your answers specific and simple when answering behavioral questions. Expect to be asked about anything you have revealed in your search materials.

Hire the EQ, Not the IQ: 150+ Questions to Help You Hire the Right Fit was written for hiring managers so, if you want another look at what questions managers will be asking you, you may wish to obtain your own copy. To purchase a copy, go to **StewartCooperCoon. com and search: "Hire the EQ."**

SUPER TOUGH BEHAVIORAL STRESS QUESTIONS

Interviewers will sometimes ask progressively harder questions. Your answers to these stressful questions reveal who you are and assist the interviewer in deciding whether to move you along in the process. Stress questions explore personality, competencies and skills, functional expertise, flexibility, judgement, leadership, and many more criteria. Interviewers are not only assessing your response; they may be trying to determine how you handle the stress of the interview. They may be looking for irritation or defensiveness or determining how quickly you think on your feet. Remember hiring authorities are looking for "fit."

Watch out for the compound questions known as "minefields." Be sure you know what they are asking before answering. Interviews are a test of your active listening techniques and your ability to provide answers that eliminate your competition. The list below shows low-to-high stress behavioral questions. Think carefully about what they are really asking before you answer these and ask for clarification if necessary.

1. In what areas do you think your last supervisor could have done a better job and why do you feel that way? (low stress question)

2. What is the worst thing that ever happened to you during your career? Why was it the worst thing? (low stress question)

3. What makes you think you are the best qualified candidate for this position? (low stress question)

4. How do you handle tension? (low stress question)

5. What types of decisions are more difficult for you and why? (medium stress question)

6. If you could change any one approach to fixing a serious problem in your last position, what was it, why would you change your approach, and how would you do it differently? (medium stress question)

7. Have you ever worked for or with anyone who demonstrated a lack of integrity in any way and how did you handle the relationship or the situation? (medium stress question)

8. What is your specific process for making a critical decision and please explain what your most important considerations are as you manage that decision and implementation process? (medium stress question)

9. Tell about a time when you were asked to do something that, while it may have been in compliance legally, ethically, and in accordance with policy, made you feel uncomfortable and how did you address this? (high stress question)

10. What is the worst professional mistake you've made in your career? What was the immediate impact of that mistake, what did you learn from that situation, how did it affect your career and how would you handle it now if you were faced once again with that situation? (high stress question)

11. Describe a time when your leadership style met with resistance from subordinates, peers, and superiors, that you led on during project, describe how you dealt with each

of those conflicts, what both the project and personnel resolutions were, and what you would now do differently to create a successful project and leadership outcome, either earlier product delivery or with better results, or both (very high stress question).

Question 11 will create minefield level stress for most people. It contains layers of questions necessitating numerous answers. Therefore, before you go to any interview, it is imperative that you practice answering questions for as many scenarios as possible.

MONEY QUESTIONS

Think back to when you interviewed for your last position. Did your interviewer ask you any of the following questions: "What did your W-4 show for last year?" "What are you currently making or what did you make last year?" or, "What are you looking to make?" All of these mean trouble because most people feel compelled to respond with a number. Answering with a number is detrimental to your fiscal health. **Don't be foolish and give your power away.**

Answer money questions up-front and YOU WILL LOSE and LOSE BIG.

Most of my clients have told me that not only were salary questions asked, but that they found themselves capitulating to company probing and information gathering pressure tactics far too early in the interview process. If you, like them, give in easily, you are giving away not only precious position advantage, but also your power to control your monetary package.

You need to take control of this situation. I highly recommend Jack Chapman's quick to read and high-impact book, *Negotiating Your Salary: How to Make $1000 a Minute.* It is written with great humor and no complex theories, just good solid advice. All of us in career coaching have our own methods of delaying money questions. I've condensed some of Jack's excellent recommendations and included a few of my own. Remember, some interviewers are smart, have been there many times, and may press you for an answer. Try to fend them off two times but go in prepared with a hard number.

DO NOT GO TO AN INTERVIEW WITHOUT LOOKING UP THE SALARY RANGE FOR THE POSITION IN THAT GEOGRAPHICAL AREA. The salary for a senior level accountant in New York City may be higher than in Syracuse, but the cost of living is much more in NYC. Websites like Salary.com are very useful. If you've done your homework beforehand, you already know what a similar position would pay in that geographical area so you will be safe stating a range. Here are some suggestions for answering salary questions. I tell my clients to use response #7 the first time and #10 the second time. If these fail, give a range acceptable to you.

1. Are you making an offer?

2. Well, I'm sure we can come to an equitable agreement in that area since I'm sure you offer a competitive plan. What is your range for this position? That seems in keeping with/lower than my research revealed.

3. If you don't mind, let's hold off on salary discussions until we explore the nature of the position, the responsibilities and whether I'm the right person for the job.

4. I always feel uncomfortable discussing salary so, if you don't mind..., or, I'm happy to discuss my prior salary and packages in a few minutes but, if you don't mind, let's hold off until we decide I'm the right person for the job.

5. I'm glad you asked that. I have researched positions with comparable titles within this geographical area and I'm sure you are within this range. What is your range for this position?

6. In the past, I've been paid fairly for my efforts and skills and I'm sure you will do the same. Before we talk about money, why don't we determine if I'm right for this position and if the company if right for me?

7. I'm sure you and I can agree on a fair and equitable salary when the time comes, but right now, I would like to fully understand the responsibilities of the position and what the criteria are for meeting or exceeding company performance expectations.

8. Don't worry about salary because you and I can easily work that out. Quite frankly, the amount you pay me is not the highest criteria for whether I accept an offer. I am more

concerned whether I can exceed my own performance expectations and be happy working here. Could you tell me more about...?

9. I'm sure you and I are going to agree on salary. If I tell you what I want, you might eliminate me before you even begin to know my capabilities. On the other hand, if you tell me what you want to offer, I might not like it and we both lose. Why don't we postpone this area of discussion until we have a clear understanding of expectations and capabilities? Could you tell me about...?

10. Salary? Well, I expect to receive what others of comparable responsibility in this company are being paid. By the way, what is the range for this position? Well, that's what I thought, and we should have no problem reaching accord in this area. Now, could you tell me about...?

Immediately, upon acceptance of your range comeback, you must use one or more of the questions I provided earlier to engage them in a discussion of the responsibilities they see for the position. Reinforce their perception that you are worth the salary you want by telling a SHARE© Story.

If the question of money comes from a recruiter, discuss your work history and value before you reveal your expected range. The universal rule any salesperson worth their salt will tell you is that he/she who speaks first loses! Therefore, if you mention money first, you lose. They are not going to get mad at you for delaying the discussion. In fact, just the opposite often happens. Respect is earned.

Remember, recruiters are in the business of placing you and, if you fit the criteria for the open job order, they will convince their client to hire you. Recruiters try to get the highest amount for you because they are paid a percentage of your first year's salary. On the other hand, please keep in mind that recruiters have numerous candidates to promote to each company, so don't be greedy about your negotiating position.

SILLY AND ILLEGAL QUESTIONS

Have you ever heard one of these?

*   If you were a tree, what kind would you be and why?
*   What part of a salad are you most like?

- If you could be any animal, what animal would you be?
- Why is a manhole cover round?

These questions can give you the opportunity to talk about yourself. Consider the tree question: a tree that grows tall and wide could be interpreted to mean that you are interested in having a large span of influence.

However, unless your interviewer has an advanced degree in psychoanalysis, there is little point in asking these silly questions. The reality is that some people ask them just to see how cleverly you will respond. Do your best and be able to justify your response.

On a more sinister note, the practice of asking illegal interview questions is alive and well. Asking about age, gender, family or marital status, nationality or citizenship, disability, criminal record and more are illegal. Interviewers CAN ask if there is any reason you can't perform specific duties related to a position. For instance, if the job description involves lifting, the interviewer can ask you if you can lift 50 lbs. **Be aware that an employer may ask you an illegal question just to see how you will react.**

If you think you are being asked an illegal question, you have several options. First, you can choose to answer it. Second, you can ask directly what the question has to do with the job. Finally, you can choose not to take the position if offered.

Here are a few illegal questions you may be asked:

- What arrangements are you able to make for childcare while you work?
- How old are your children?
- When did you graduate from high school?
- Are you a U.S. citizen?
- What does your wife do for a living?
- Where did you live while you were growing up?
- Will you need personal time off for particular religious holidays?
- Are you comfortable working for a female boss?
- There is a large disparity between your age and that of the position's coworkers. Is this a problem for you?
- How long do you plan to work until you retire?
- Have you experienced any serious illnesses in the past year?

You can find a detailed collection of these at: https://www.betterteam.com/ illegal-interview-questions. Familiarize yourself with this list so you don't get caught off guard in an interview.

QUESTIONS TO ASK YOUR INTERVIEWER: GETTING TO YES

Throughout this book I have discussed differences between interviewing with recruiters, human resources representatives and hiring authorities. In most cases, you will eventually be face to face with a hiring authority and your interview strategy should shift. You will be working for this person and he/she must feel comfortable with you and be convinced that the organization is getting its money's worth. In reconciling these issues, hiring managers experience **cognitive dissonance.**

Cognitive dissonance is, in a nutshell, doubt. Your job is to reduce doubt by asking questions that create positive agreement between you and the interviewer. You may not have all of the EXACT qualifications they require. Perhaps you are entering a new career path and they need help seeing how your skills are transferrable. You know, though, that you are the best qualified. If things go awry, and believe me they might, using the following technique will put you ahead of your competition.

Reduce your interviewer's cognitive dissonance by asking lines of questions on six major items: predecessor, job duties, performance measures, support, career path, and personal and growth issues. Order is important, so start with questions about your predecessor and work your way through the list. *Don't ask all these questions as there is usually a finite limit to your interview time.* They have their own agenda, and you should respect it.

Each major question area builds toward a logical conclusion—that you are the right person. These questions will also help you determine whether you want the position and can exceed their expectations.

Another advantage of using this method is that you can refer to the questions when negotiating your package. As you look at each question, a SHARE© Story should come to mind. If you haven't already thought of a suitable one, now's the time.

YOUR PREDECESSOR

- Who occupied this position before?
- What was his or her background?
- How long was he/she in the position?
- What successes did the person have in that position?
- If successful, what caused them to be successful?
- If not successful, what prevented his/her success?
- What kind of personal qualities are you looking for in a person who takes this position?

Ask the interviewer to expand on a particular issue for which you have prepared a SHARE© story. Say, "What is your definition of motivation? Could you be more specific?" Then, when they give you the specifics, hit them with your "employee motivation" story.

THE JOB DUTIES

The duties of a position can change even after the search has begun. Use these to clarify what they will expect of you.

- Please tell me about the job, what this position does and how it fits into the department, product line group, regional structure and company.
- What will my specific duties be (if not clear on the job description)?
- What is the extent of my authority?
- What about my resume, background, or experience caught your attention?
- Do I (acquire new accounts)?
- Where do (they come from)?
- Do I (take over existing accounts and grow that market segment of the business) or do I primarily (look for new business)?
- Tell me about the (type and number of existing accounts).
- What problems seem to be developing with (acquiring accounts)?
- How do you feel the (product or service) stacks up against the competition?
- What do you feel your pricing and product advantage is over your nearest competitor?
- How did your area do compared to last year?
- How did this compare with other similar-sized regions in the company?

- How does the team I work with fit into (accounts management)?
- Is an (account) team already assembled?
- Do I assemble my own (account) team?
- Do I solely (call on the account) or is there a team approach?
- What is your role (in the acquisition) or (management) of my (accounts)?

PERFORMANCE MEASUREMENTS

Understanding how your performance will be measured is critical because you want to know you will be evaluated well and rewarded for your effort. Develop your own questions as they apply to your field.

- What is your expectation for (new account growth) in the next year, two years and five years?
- What (dollar amount or percentage growth) are you looking for?
- What is the (current budget)?
- What factors do you see influencing (expected growth)?
- How do you measure my success with (my accounts)?
- How many (contracts are coming up for renewal?)
- How will I be measured? ($), (relationship), (levels), (account growth)?
- What is the timing for (learning the accounts), (processes), and (core business)?

SUPPORT

You should determine whether the organization is going to give you the tools and resources necessary to succeed. Ask the following:

- Who is currently on the team?
- How long have they been there?
- Tell me about them.
- How do they interact with the rest of the (company, division, accounts, etc.)?
- What resources are available?
- How much money is in the budget for this year?
- What technical resources support this position?

CAREER PATH

Your interview questions should typically not be self-focused. However, in follow-up interviews you may want to ask:

- Is there a comparable position in this area?
- How long have they been with the company?
- How is their career path structured?
- How do you see this position in the company and where do you see it heading?
- Are there other divisions in the company and how are inter-division transfers handled?
- What professional development path do you see for me?

PERSONAL AND GROWTH ISSUES

Be careful not to ask these too soon as you want them to know you are more focused on them than on yourself. Save these for your final interview or even your negotiation.

- What is the company's continuing education policy?
- Is successful completion rewarded by an increase in the package?
- Is there a tiered perks structure?
- Stock option plan?
- 401-K plan?
- Other financial plans?

Again, you are trying to link their answers to these questions with your experience by giving them a short example—a SHARE© Story. For example, when hearing the answer to your employment question, you could say, "Wonderful. I have a lot of experience with that. [Tell a SHARE© Story]. Then ask, "How do you see this fitting into your team?" Use the open-ended, not the closed-ended question structure. Hopefully, they will say yes and BAM...another reason to hire you! In this manner you address all their areas of cognitive dissonance leaving them with no choice but to offer you the position.

Reinforce their positive thinking and force them to rethink their objections. Later, when you sum up your interview session, you will have at least five "agreements" about why they should hire you. If you are told that there is something wrong with your candidacy, you have a concrete foundation to build upon in your attempt to salvage the interview. Moreover, if you sail through without a hitch, you have a basis upon which to build for your package negotiations. Either way, you win.

When you are done addressing each item above say, "Where do we go from here?" Then, you need to do the most difficult thing in the universe: **remain silent.** The adage "He who speaks first loses" is true. By remaining silent, you place pressure on the interviewer to answer your question. If you speak again, you reduce your power to find out what his or her next step will be.

There are no exceptions to this rule. I once sat in a gentleman's office and, after I made my closing statement, we stared at each other for nearly two minutes. Do you know how long that is? It is an eternity when you are trying to sell them on a concept! He finally spoke first and said he knew what I was doing and wanted to see if I would capitulate. Everyone else before me had done so. We signed a $500,000 deal that day which grew to over a million dollars within two years. Believe me, silence works.

DEALING WITH OBJECTIONS

Your interviewer may have some legitimate concerns about hiring you, but that doesn't mean you are not the right person for the job. Your best bet is to deal with the objections strategically. An objection is just a way of expressing a concern—some degree of cognitive dissonance the interviewer is experiencing.

Objections usually have two elements. First, they are concerned that you have a deficiency and, second, they need to know how long it will take you to become proficient. How long will it take you to be worth the money they are paying you? How long will it take you to reduce the dissonance?

When an objection is identified, acknowledge the concern. Then, rephrase it to focus on an offsetting strength and demonstrate that you have that offsetting strength. What follows is a step-by-step method for overcoming objections. In this case, let's say the objection is lack of experience in the employer's industry.

Step #1: Acknowledge the interviewer's objection. Acknowledge the objection, but don't validate it. To accomplish this, you say to the interviewer, "Actually, I'm not surprised you brought that up." Note that you have not indicated agreement with the point being made by the interviewer. You have only indicated that the observation has merit.

Step #2: Surface the real concern and restate it in favorable terms. Shift the focus to the real, underlying concern. In this case, since lack of industry-specific experience is evident, the interviewer's real concern is how long it will take you to become productive. Restate the objection in those terms, like this, "I'm sure that whomever you hire must become productive quickly. Am I right?" It is important to ask a question at the end and get agreement before you proceed.

Step #3: Provide an example SHARE© Story aimed at neutralizing the concern. Once agreement has been reached, provide a story that highlights your ability to meet the challenge and overcome the objection.

What follows is a summary from a coaching session with one of my clients, a regional sales representative with a Fortune 100 company. My wonderful team and I have served over 5,000 clients and we have hundreds of oral, video and written testimonials to prove that what I am telling you works. Here is a client example:

Example: Karen B.

New title:	Senior Vice President (previous position was VP)
Compensation:	$221K base (up $55K or, 33% from previous compensation of $166K)
Bonuses:	$75K signing bonus, negotiated a position to receive a $40K bonus from previous company position, additional $80K at year's end
Additional:	Extra week of paid time off, taking her to 6 wks./yr., plus minimum of two $13K raises during the year

Karen was employed as vice president of an energy company whose owners were going through some personal challenges, making her question both her growth potential and the long-term viability of the company. In addition to overseeing finance, she also managed the MIS, HR and legal divisions. She had been in the same job for 9 years and wasn't sure how to package herself and sell her experience and skills verbally in interviews. She worked on using her SHARE© Stories, controlling and closing the interview using what she termed negative affirmation (i.e., asking whether there were any objections so she could immediately overcome them and close the deal). The following is a summary of comments taken from Karen's post-placement feedback form:

On controlling the interview:

The style of controlling the interview that I learned to implement created urgency and forward movement. I was not left in a state where I waited for a call back. When the interviews ended, I knew the next step and when the next step was to occur. I also learned the importance of creating a natural dialog, being relaxed, being myself, being genuinely humble yet confident. Seems so easy on the surface but it really takes A LOT of work and although it seems that just being natural is the answer, it's the scientific approach of "controlling" the interview with the use of the SC&C method that creates the ability to differentiate oneself during the selection process.

On handling salary questions & closing the interview:

The coaching on the salary questions and closing an interview with a negative affirmation is priceless. During my last week I had 5 interviews, three of which were with company decision makers. In all 5 interviews I was selected to move forward to the next step. The combination of learning how to formulate questions I might ask, mapping those questions to my prior success and closing with the negative affirmation is powerful and magical.

On the overall job transition process:

The entire process begins with the very arduous work of determining one's value, being able to express that in a brand, and negotiate the interviews and negotiations using the SHARE© method. It is critical that one's materials are designed for effect at grabbing the attention of employers and recruiters; in my case this resulted in multiple interviews weekly.

Karen's compensation is 114% higher than her previous year's compensation representing an increase of $189,000 in compensation gain.

CLOSING THE INTERVIEW

You have answered the interviewer's questions, handled his or her objections and asked a few questions of your own. You should still be in control at the end of your interview. Now, it's time to bring everything to a close by asking one final question: "Is there anything that might stand in the way of my consideration as a candidate?" The first reason to ask this question is to dig out any objections that might be in the back of the interviewer's mind. These must be addressed right here, right now! You can be sure the interviewer will address them with others after you've left. However, sometimes simple misunderstandings can occur.

Mack, a client, interviewed with six people while trying to land a consulting position with a major international firm. In every instance, he used the structured interview process presented in this book. In each of the six interviews he used the positive assumptive close, "Looks like a great match! What's the next step?" and was referred on to the next person in the process. Then came interview number seven.

Mack's seventh and last interview was with the Managing General Partner who had total authority over whether Mack got hired. The interview went exactly as the others had, except that when Mack went to close the interview, as he told me later, it came out more like a reverse close. He said, "It looks like a terrific match. Would you agree?"

Within a split second, Mack knew he was in trouble. The MGP paused and said to Mack, "I think you have terrific qualifications, and are really a great guy, Mack, but I need someone with a lot of B2B experience in this position."

Mack nearly fell off his chair. His last 11 years had been spent doing B2B work with AT&T at the most senior levels. The MGP apparently had not read Mack's resume. He assumed that since Mack didn't bring it up, Mack must not have it. Mack assumed that since the MGP did not bring it up, he already knew about Mack's background.

To Mack's credit, he cleared up the misunderstanding immediately. After about 15 minutes of further discussion, Mack asked the MGP if he had any further misgivings about Mack's B2B experience. The MGP said no, and thanked Mack for the clarification. To lighten the mood, Mack leaned back, looked at the MGP and said with a smile, "I'm almost afraid to ask this question, but is there ANYTHING ELSE that might keep me from this position?" There was not and Mack is now a consultant with that company.

The second reason to ask for agreement that you are the right person for the job is to find out how strong your chances are. Another question you can ask is, "How many candidates have you interviewed and how many do you have left to interview? My reason for asking is that I would like to know your opinion of their strengths." Here you are afforded one final chance to tell another SHARE© Story to overcome any perceived weaknesses. Now, you are ready to close the interview. **Bear in mind the time and look for signs that your interviewer is getting impatient.** If not, state the following:

"Mr./Ms. Interviewer, we have covered a lot here today and I wanted to review just to make sure we haven't missed anything. Do you mind if I take a second and review my notes?" Nine times out of ten they will say yes. When they do, briefly mention your SHARE© Stories one by one taking no more than 6-12 seconds to do so. For example, say, "When we started, you said you were looking for (FAST LEARNING CURVE) and you recall our discussion about the short timeframe I was given at XYZ company and the fact that I brought the project in both ahead of schedule and under budget. Then you said you were looking for..." Repeat the above strategy, keeping it under 12 seconds and exactly to the point. **Don't bring up additional information or stories at this point.**

After you have reviewed, look your interviewer in the eye and say, "It seems to me that, based upon the points we've covered, we have a match." Then, **remain silent, again.** Hopefully, they will say, "Yes, it would appear that way."

The very last sentence you will say is, *"Where do we go from here?"* Never leave any interview without asking this question. Otherwise, what have you accomplished? Don't waste their time, or yours, by not asking this question.

The person who speaks first loses!

POST-INTERVIEW FOLLOW-UP

Your interview follow-up is just as important as your prep. After every interview, you should evaluate your performance and build a bridge between you and your interviewer by sending him/her a thank you note.

EVALUATE YOUR PERFORMANCE

Heaving a big sigh of relief and relaxing are tempting after an exhausting interview. Go ahead and pat yourself on the back for the things you did well, but don't stop there. Instead, take 20 minutes to reflect on how the interview went. Write down the questions you were asked and how you answered them. What did you do well? What needs to change? Did you use your SHARE© Stories to your best advantage? Did you talk too much? Too little? How about your appearance, body language and articulation of your responses? Use Exercise 10.3, the Post-interview Worksheet to evaluate your performance.

Next, pretend you are in the interview again and answer again OUT LOUD anything on which you didn't do well. This out loud articulation will help you answer similar questions better in your next interview. Plus, you can review your notes when the time comes.

After you have notes from several interviews, look for patterns of difficulty. Are you having trouble making your point concisely? Not smiling? Zero in on these deficiencies and improve for the next round.

THANK YOUR INTERVIEWER(S)

Next, you'll need to write a short thank you note/email to each person with whom you interviewed. Whether you think your interview went well or not, thanking your interviewer(s) is a sign of respect and good manners. Also, doing so allows you to keep the door open in case they are thinking of hiring someone else. Your note should thank them for considering you, express your continued interest in the position and, most importantly, reinforce any areas that you thought were weak during the interview.

SECOND INTERVIEWS

A second interview can be even more intimidating than the first. Even though you are moving along in the process, and the employer seems to recognize your potential, the pressure is on to provide clear evidence that you are the right person for the position.

Understand that, even though they are clearly interested, the job isn't yours yet. They may have several candidates doing second interviews. Go in with confidence, be professional, but keep your ego in check. Try to get a feel for what it would be like if you did work there.

The higher the position, the more pay involved or the greater the influence you have on others within a corporation, the more interviews you will likely participate in before landing the job. Each interview, from the first to the last, requires the same amount of intense preparation. However, the subsequent preparation for each interview should include learning more about the internal workings and politics of the corporation. This isn't as difficult as it sounds.

If you did your job during the first interview session, you would have uncovered information useful in developing your next round of questions and in directing more research about the organization. Doing a little research on who the other stakeholders are within the organization will benefit you. You may be meeting new people in your second interview. Knowing their professional history with the company shows you are engaged in the process. Examine the details of the position again as well as your notes from the first interview. Think about what *wasn't* said.

During a second interview, you may be presented with vastly different questions than you encountered the first time around. This is a good opportunity for you to demonstrate your character and personality, especially regarding how you cope with difficult situations. While your first interview may have included easy questions, your second may involve more difficult behavioral questions designed to determine, among other things, how you work with a range of personalities. An ideal candidate is one who is not afraid to advocate for his/her own concerns but who is also sensitive to the concerns of others. Also, showing that you can look beyond personalities is a strong indicator that you will not blame others for a lack of progress.

Make a positive impression on everyone you meet. Strive to make connections and demonstrate how helpful you can be in supporting them in their own roles. You will certainly be hired if you are viewed as someone who can make others' jobs easier.

Finally, in the interview, be relaxed, be a good listener, and remember that good interviewing involves building a relationship that leads to trust, then to disclosures (theirs), then to SHARE© Stories (yours). Use the interview to build value and give them a reason to hire *you* as opposed to your competition.

SUCCESS STORY: TRIANGLE THEORY AT WORK

CONTRIBUTED BY VALERIE EL-JAMIL, EXECUTIVE COACH, STEWART, COOPER & COON

Dave was interviewing for a general counsel position with a firm that operated in a highly regulated industry segment. He wanted to focus the interview on trying to eliminate the competition by discussing gaps in their experience and knowledge. I encouraged him to ignore the competition and focus on his value as none of the other candidates had his unique fusion of legal and business experience.

As part of our strategy, we developed simple questions for him to ask that would require the interviewers to provide longer, narrative answers. The nature of the questions led interviewers to dive deeply into the needs and challenges of the organization, thus placing Dave in a problem-solving role.

Dave reported, "I just finished my panel interview and I *killed* it. It went great because you had prepared me on *exactly* the right issues, the way to answer and the way to ask my own strategic questions."

The ability to ask and answer interview questions as a "consultant" resulted in interview success for Dave.

ADDITIONAL RESOURCES

- Coon, F. & Venckus, R. (2017). *Hire the EQ, not the IQ: A 150+ question guide to help you hire the "right" fit*. Gaff Publishing.
- Venckus, R. & Endress, D. (2013). *Why shouldn't we hire you?* CreateSpace Independent Publishing.

EXERCISE 10.1 COMMONLY ASKED INTERVIEW QUESTIONS

These are some of the most commonly asked interview questions. I have provided suggested approaches for answering them that will reinforce your value and reduce the chance you'll get in trouble by providing extreme answers.

1. **Tell me about yourself.**

    This is not an invitation to ramble on. Take time in advance to think about yourself and those aspects of your professional or educational background that you'd like to promote. Write this in about a 90-second to 2-minute format and practice it until delivery is smooth.

2. **What do you look for in a job?**

    State what you want in terms of what you can give to your employer. The key word in the following example is "contribution." "My experience at the XYZ Corporation has shown me that I have a talent for motivating people. That is demonstrated by my team's absenteeism dropping 20 percent, turnover steadying at 10 percent, and production increasing 12 percent. I am looking for an opportunity to continue to make that kind of contribution."

3. **Why are you leaving?**

    You should have an acceptable reason for leaving every job you have held. If you don't, pick one of these seven acceptable reasons: 1) You don't feel there is room to grow professionally in that position or company; 2) Your commute is too long; 3) You are at a dead end in your position; 4) You have excellent skills but there are just too many people ahead of you in line for promotions; 5) You feel, based upon your research, that you are underpaid for your skills; 6) You want to be with a better company; 7) The company does not have the stability you want. For example: "My last company was family-owned. I had gone as far as I was able. It just seems time for me to join a more prestigious company and accept greater challenges."

4. **What can you do for us that someone else cannot do?**

Qualify this question with "What problems are you trying to solve by filling this position?" Then, highlight your skills as they relate to his/her answer. Finish with a question that asks for feedback like, "To what degree are you looking for someone like me?"

5. **Why should we hire you? or Why should we hire you rather than one of the other highly qualified candidates?**

Your answer may be different depending on whether you think they are trying to get you to compare yourself to other equally qualified applicants, or just asking you to reinforce your skills. If you think they are asking for a comparison, begin your response with "Because more so than anyone else, I will/have [list a quality that makes you unique]." Sell it with your body language. Say it like you mean it. Conne asks this question in classroom interview practice sessions. A student once asked her to answer it herself. Without hesitation she looked the student in the eye and said, "A lot of well-educated people think they know everything. I may stop teaching one day, but I will never stop learning. Love for learning is at the heart of great teaching."

If your interviewer simply asks why he/she should hire you, keep your answer short and to the point. Highlight areas from your background that relate to current needs and problems. Recap the interviewer's description of the job, meeting it point by point with your skills. Finish your answer by remarking: "I have the qualifications you need [list a few], I'm a team player, I take direction and I have the desire to be successful."

6. **Can you work under pressure or deadlines?**

You might be tempted to give a simple "yes" or "no" answer, but don't. It reveals nothing and you lose the opportunity to sell your skills and value profiles. Whenever you are asked a closed-ended question, answer the question and add a skill-selling example story.

7. **What have been your most significant accomplishments in your present or last job?**

Keep your answer job-related. You might begin your reply with a statement such as, "Although my most significant achievements are still ahead of me, I am proud of my involvement with [list accomplishment]. I made my contribution as part of that team and learned a lot in the process. We did it with hard work, concentration and an eye for the bottom line."

8. **What is your primary strength?**

Isolate high points from your background and add key values. You might want to demonstrate pride, determination and the ability to stick with a difficult task yet change course rapidly when required.

9. **What is your primary weakness?**

This is a direct invitation to put your head in a noose. Decline the invitation. Design the answer so that your weakness is ultimately a positive characteristic. For example, "I enjoy my work and always give each project my best shot. When I don't feel that others are pulling their weight, I find it a little frustrating. I am aware of that weakness and I try to overcome it with a positive attitude that I hope will catch on."

Also consider the technique of putting a problem in the past. Here, you take a weakness from way back when and show how you overcame it. This technique allows you to answer the question but ends on a positive note. Try this: "When I first got into this field, I always had problems with my paperwork: you know, leaving an adequate paper train. To be honest, I let it slip once or twice. My manager explained the potential trouble such behavior could cause. I really took it to heart and have significantly improved my organization. You only have to tell me something once." With that kind of answer, you also get the added bonus of showing that you accept and act on criticism.

10. **How long would it take you to make a contribution to our firm?**

You are best advised to answer this with, "That is an excellent question. To help me answer, what are your greatest areas of need right now?" Then say, "Let's say I started on Monday the 17th. It will take me a few weeks to settle down and learn the ropes. Do you have a special project in mind that you want me to begin right away?" That response could lead directly to a job offer but, if not, you already have the interviewer thinking of you as an employee.

11. **What do/did you think of your boss?**

People who complain about their employers are recognized as the same people who cause the most disruption in a department. Say something positive.

12. **What features of your previous jobs have you disliked?**

Criticizing a prior employer is a warning flag that you could be a problem employee. No one intentionally hires trouble. Keep your answer short and positive.

13. **Would you describe a few situations in which your work was criticized?**

This is a doubly dangerous question. You are being asked to say how you handle criticism and to detail your faults. If you are asked this question, describe a poor idea that was criticized, not poor work.

14. **How would you evaluate your present firm?**

Always answer positively and keep your real feelings to yourself, whatever they might be. Your answer should be, "Very good" or "Excellent." Then smile and wait for the next question.

15. **What would you like to be doing five years from now?**

The safest answer includes a desire to be regarded as a true professional and team player. As far as promotion, that depends on finding a manager with whom you can grow. Keep your response generic. Try: "In five years, I'd like to have more responsibility than I have right now, because I will have more expertise. I'd like to be working with people who are committed to doing the best work possible to reach the organization's goals."

16. How do you organize and plan for major projects?

"Effective planning requires both forward thinking—who and what am I going to need to get this job done—and backward thinking based on deadlines—steps must be made, and by what time. I'm skilled at both."

17. Describe a difficult problem you've had to deal with.

This is a favorite tough question. It is not so much the difficult problem that's important; it's the approach you take to solving problems in general. It is designed to probe your professional profile, especially your analytical and interpersonal skills.

18. What would your references say?

You have nothing to lose by being positive. If the company checks your references, it must by law have your permission. That permission is usually included in the application form you sign. Use references who can vouch for your work and who will say only positive things about you. Discuss this with your references before your interview.

19. Can we check your references?

This question is frequently asked as a stress question to catch the too-smooth candidate off-guard. It is also one that occasionally is asked in the general course of events. The higher up the corporate ladder you go, the more likely it is that your references will be checked. You should have provided references and reference letters but, if you did not, your answer may include: "Yes, of course you can check my references. However, at present, I would like to keep matters confidential until we have established a serious mutual interest (i.e., an offer). At that time, I will be pleased to furnish you with whatever references you need from <u>prior</u> employers. For now, feel free to call [names] but please wait to check my current employer's references until you have extended me an offer in writing, I have accepted, we have agreed on a start date and I have had the opportunity to resign in a professional manner." *You are under no obligation to give references of a current employer until you have a written offer in hand.* You are also well within your rights to request reference checks of current employers only after you have started your new job.

20. What type of decisions did you make on your last job?

The interviewer may be searching to define your responsibilities, or he/she may want to know that you don't overstep your authority. This is an opportunity to high-light your achievements and detail how the decisions you made resulted in success.

21. How do you handle tension?

This question is different from "Can you handle pressure?" It asks how you handle it. You could reply, "Tension is caused when you let things pile up. I find that, if you break those overwhelming tasks into little pieces, they aren't so overwhelming. I sup-pose I don't so much handle tension as handle the causes of it."

22. How long have you been looking for another position?

If you are employed, your answer isn't that important. If, on the other hand you are unemployed, how you answer becomes more important. If you must talk of months or more, be careful to add something like "I've been looking for about a year now. I've had a number of offers in that time, but I have determined that the job I take and the people with whom I work need to have values with which I can identify."

23. Have you ever been fired?

Say 'no' if you can. If not, act on the advice given with the next question.

24. If so, why were you fired?

If you were laid off as part of general work force reduction, be straightforward and move on to the next topic as quickly as possible. Having been fired creates instant doubt in the mind of the interviewer and greatly increases the chance of your refer-ences being checked. If you have been fired, the first thing to do is bite the bullet and call the person who fired you, find out why it happened and learn what he or she would say about you today. Your aim is to clear the air so, whatever you do, don't be antag-onistic. Explain that you are looking for a new job. Say that you appreciate that the manager had to do what was done and indicate what you learned from the experience. Then ask, "If you were asked as part of a pre- or post-employment reference check, how would you describe my leaving the company? Would you say that I was fired or that I simply resigned?"

If you can find out the employee turnover figures for your former company, voluntary or otherwise, you might add, "Fifteen other people have left so far this year." A combination answer of this nature minimizes the stigma. You have even managed to demonstrate that you take responsibility for your actions, which shows your analytical and listening skills. If one of your past managers will speak well of you, there is nothing to lose and everything to gain by finishing with, "Jill Johnson, at the company, would be a good person to check for a reference on what I have told you."

25. Have you ever been asked to resign?

Being asked to resign is a face-saving gesture on the part of the employer. Rather than embarrassing you by firing you, they simply ask you to voluntarily resign. Because you were given the option though, that employer should not later say, "I had to ask him to resign." Answer the question honestly and refer to the advice given in Question 24.

26. Were you ever dismissed from your job for a reason that seemed unjustified?

The sympathetic phrasing is geared toward getting you to reveal all the sordid details. The cold hard facts are that hardly anyone is fired without cause and you're kidding yourself if you think otherwise. With that in mind, you can quite honestly say "No" and move on to the next topic.

27. In your last job, what were some of the things you spent most of your time on, and why?

Demonstrate good time management and a goal-oriented attitude, which is what this question probes. The interviewer may also be trying to gauge how much experience you have doing particular tasks. Answer in percentages. Say, "I spent about 50% of my time developing content for Facebook, Twitter and Instagram, 30% analyzing our progress and about 10% planning timelines for posts and so forth. The other 10% was spent in meetings and on correspondence."

28. **Do you have any questions?**

A good question. Almost always, this is a sign that the interview is drawing to a close and that you have one more chance to make an impression. Create questions from any of the following:

- Find out why the job is open, who had it last, and what happened to him or her. Did he or she get promoted or fired. How many people have held this position in the last couple of years? What happened to them subsequently?
- Why did the interviewer join the company? How long has he or she been there? What is it about the company that keeps him or her there?
- To whom would you report? Will you get the opportunity to meet that person?
- Where is the job located? What are the travel requirements, if any?
- What type of training is required and how long is it?
- What would your first assignment be?
- What are the skills and attributes most needed to succeed in the company?
- Who will be the company's major competitor over the next few years? How does the interviewer feel the company stacks up against them?
- What has been the growth pattern of the company over the last five years? Is it profitable? How profitable? Is the company privately or publicly held?
- How regularly do performance evaluations occur? What model do they follow?

29. **Rate your work on a scale from one to ten.**

Bear in mind that this is meant to plumb the depths of your self-esteem. If you answer ten, you run the risk of portraying yourself as insufferable. On the other hand, if you say less than seven, you might as well get up and leave. You are probably best claiming to be an eight or nine.

30. **What is the most difficult situation you have faced?**

The question looks for information on two fronts: How do you define difficult? And what was your handling of the situation? You must have a story ready for this one in which the situation both was tough and allowed you to show yourself in a good light.

31. What have you done that shows initiative?

The question probes whether you are a doer. Be sure, however, that your example of initiative does not show a disregard for company policies and procedures.

32. What are some of the things about which you and your supervisor disagreed?

It is safest to state that you did not disagree but, if it was really an issue treat it with a neutral answer such as, "The only thing I can think of is [example], but everyone has different styles of work. Neither of us took it personally and we got along fine."

33. In what areas do you feel your supervisor could have done a better job?

You could reply, "I have always had the highest respect for my supervisor. I have always been so busy learning from Mr. Jones that I don't think he could have done a better job. He has really brought me to the point where I am ready for greater challenges. That's why I'm here."

34. What are some of the things your supervisor did that you disliked?

If you and the interviewer are both nonsmokers and your boss isn't, use it. Apart from that answer, "You know, I've never thought of our relationship in terms of like or dislike. I've always thought our role was to get along together and get the job done."

35. How did your boss get the best out of you?

This is a manageability question, geared to probing whether you are going to be a pain in the neck or not. Whatever you say, it is important for your ongoing happiness that you make it clear you don't appreciate being treated like a dishrag. You can give a short, general answer:

"My last boss got superior effort and performance by treating me like a human being and giving me the same personal respect with which she liked to be treated herself."

36. What personal characteristics are necessary for success in your field?

You might say, "Drive, motivation, energy, confidence, determination, good communication, and analytical skills combined, of course, with the ability to work with others."

37. Do you prefer working with others or alone?

This question is usually used to determine whether you are a team player. Before answering, however, be sure you know whether the job requires you to work alone. Then answer appropriately. Perhaps, you could reply, "I'm quite happy working alone when necessary. I don't need much constant reassurance. However, I prefer to work in a group because better ideas are generated when you have a team working on a problem."

38. Explain your role as a group/team member.

You are being asked to describe yourself as either a team player or a loner. Most departments depend on harmonious teamwork for their success, so describe yourself as a team player. State specifically what you have done that has aided the group process. Are you a motivator? A harmony builder? A task organizer?

39. Do you make your opinions known when you disagree with the views of your supervisor?

If you can, state that you come from an environment in which input is encouraged when it helps the team's ability to get the job done efficiently. "If opinions are sought in a meeting, I will give mine, although I am careful to be aware of others' feelings. I will never criticize a coworker or a superior in open forum. Besides, it is quite possible to disagree without being disagreeable. However, my past manager made it clear that she valued my opinion by asking for it. So, after a while, if there was something I felt strongly about, I would make an appointment to discuss it one-on-one."

40. How would you handle an unfair or difficult supervisor?

If you need to elaborate, try, "I would make an appointment to see the supervisor and diplomatically explain that I felt uncomfortable and that I felt he or she was not treating me as a professional and, therefore, that I might not be performing up to standard. I would ask for his or her input as to what I must do to create a better relationship. I would enter into the discussion in the frame of mind that we were equally responsible for whatever communication problems existed and that this wasn't just the manager's problem."

41. Do you consider yourself to be a natural leader or a born follower?

Assuming you are up for (and want) a leadership position, you might try something like this, "I would be reluctant to regard anyone as a natural leader. Hiring, motivation and disciplining other adults, while at the same time molding them into a cohesive team, involves a number of skills that no honest person can say they possessed from birth. Leadership is a lifetime learning process. Anyone who reckons they have it all under control and have nothing more to learn isn't doing the employer any favors. To me, leadership and followership are about flexibility."

42. When do you expect a promotion?

Tread warily, show that you believe in yourself and have both feet firmly planted on the ground. "That depends on a few criteria. Of course, I cannot expect promotions without the performance that marks me as deserving of promotion. I also need to join a company that has the growth necessary to provide opportunity. I hope that my manager believes in promoting from within and will help me grow so that I will have the skills necessary to be considered for promotion when the opportunity comes along."

43. You have been given a project that requires you to interact with different levels within the company. How do you do this? With what levels are you most comfortable?

This is a two-part question that probes communication and self-confidence skills. The first part asks how you interact with superiors and motivate those working with and for you. The second part of the question is saying, "Tell me whom you regard as your peer group?"

To cover both bases, you will want to include the essence of this response: "There are basically two types of people I would interact with on a project of this nature. First, there are those I report to, who bear the ultimate responsibility for its success. With them, I determine deadlines and how they will evaluate the success of the project. I would outline my approach, breaking the project down into component parts, getting approval on both the approach and the costs. I would keep my supervisors up to date on a regular basis, and seek input whenever needed. My supervisors could expect three things from me—the facts, an analysis of potential problems, and confidence as I tackle the project." Then follow with, "The other people are those who work with and for me. With those people, I would outline the project and explain how a successful outcome will benefit the company. I would assign the component parts to those best suited to each and arrange follow-up times to assure completion by deadline. My role here would be to facilitate, motivate and bring the different personalities together to form a team. As for comfort level, I find this type of approach enables me to interact well with all levels and types of people."

44. Tell me about an event that really challenged you. How did you meet the challenge? In what way was your approach different from others?

This is a straightforward two-part question. The first probes your problem-solving abilities. The second asks you to set yourself apart from the herd. First, outline the problem. The more serious you make the situation sound, the better. Having done that, go ahead and explain your solution, its value to your employer, and how it was different from other approaches.

45. How would you go about making a decision when no procedure exists?

This question probes your analytical skills, integrity, and dedication. Most of all, the interviewer is testing your manageability and adherence to procedures. You need to cover that with, "I would act without my manager's direction only if the situation was urgent and my manager were not available. Then, I would take command of the situation, make a decision based upon the facts and implement it. I would update my boss at the earliest opportunity."

46. That is an excellent answer. Now give me a balanced view, can you give me an example that didn't work out so well?

Here, you are required to give an example of an inadequacy. The trick is to pull something from the past and to finish with what you learned from the experience.

47. What kinds of decisions are most difficult for you?

You are human. Admit it but be careful what you admit. If you have ever had to fire someone, you are in luck because no one likes to do that. Emphasize that having reached a logical conclusion, you act.

48. What area of your skills/professional development do you want to improve at this time?

Another "tell-me-all-your-weaknesses" question. You should try to avoid damaging your candidacy by tossing around careless admissions. However, if there is specialized training you think would help you do the job better, mention it.

49. Your application shows you have been with one company a long time without any appreciable increase in rank or salary. Tell me about this.

You should analyze why you have been at the same level before the interview in anticipation of this question. Answer as positively as you can, possibly indicating that you loved the company and your coworkers, but eventually know it was time for new challenges and growth. Also, avoid putting your salary history on application forms. No one is going to deny you an interview for lack of a salary history if your skills match what the job requires.

50. See this pen I'm holding? Sell it to me.

In today's business world, everyone is required to sell, sometimes products, but more often ideas, approaches and concepts. As such, you are being tested to see whether you understand the basic concepts of features-and-benefits selling, how quickly you think on your feet and how effective your verbal communication is. It's okay to take up to five seconds to think of the best features of the pen, then begin.

Say with enthusiasm, "Let me tell you about the special features of this product. First, it's a highlighter that will emphasize important points in reports or articles and that will save you time. Also, the casing is wide enough to enable you to use it comfortably at your desk or on a flip chart. It has a flat base, so it stands on its own. At one dollar, it is disposable and affordable enough for you to have a handful for your desk, briefcase, car and home, and the bright yellow color means you'll never lose it." Then close with a smile and a question, like, "How many gross shall we deliver?"

51. Why should I hire an outsider when I could fill the job with someone inside the company?

The question isn't as stupid as it sounds. Obviously, the interviewer has examined existing employees with an eye toward their promotion or reassignment. Just as obviously, the job cannot be filled from within the company. If it could be, it would be and for two very good reasons. First, promoting from within is cheaper and, second, it is good for employee morale.

Your answer should include two steps. The first is a simple recitation of your skills and personality profile strengths tailored to the specific requirements of the job. For the second step, realize first that whenever a manager is filling a position, he or she is looking not only for someone who can do the job, but also for someone who can benefit the department in a larger sense. No department is as good as it could be, and a new member can bring fresh ideas. Therefore, in the second part of your answer, include a question of your own, such as, "Those are my general attributes. However, if no one is promotable from inside the company, that means you are looking to add strength to your team in a special way. In what ways do you hope the final candidate will be able to benefit your department?" The answer to this is your cue to sell your applicable qualities.

52. Why were you out of work for so long?

You must have a sound explanation for gaps in your employment history. If not, you are unlikely to receive a job offer. Emphasize that you were not just looking for another paycheck. You were looking for a company with which to settle and to which to make a long-term contribution. If your answer has to do with a layoff due to COVID, say so.

53. Why have you changed jobs so frequently?

If you have jumped around, blame it on youth (even the interviewer was young once). Now you realize what a mistake your job-hopping was and, with your added domestic responsibilities, you are now much more settled. You may wish to impress on the interviewer that your job-hopping was never as a result of poor performance and that you grew professionally as a result of each job change.

54. What was there about your last company that you didn't particularly like or agree with?

You are being checked out as a potential "fly in the ointment." If you have to answer, it might be about how some employees disregarded the bottom line by consciously misunderstanding directives. You could also say, "I didn't like the way some people gave lip service to 'the customer comes first' and really didn't go out of their way to keep the customer satisfied. I don't think it was a fault of management, just a general malaise that seemed to affect a lot of people."

55. What are some things you find difficult to do? Why do you feel that way?

This is a variation on a couple of earlier questions. Remember, anything that goes against the best interests of your employer is difficult to do. If you are pressed for a job function you find difficult, answer in the past tense. That way, you show that you recognize difficulty but that you obviously handle it well.

56. What were some of the minuses on your last job?

This is a variation on the question, "What interests you least about this job?" which was handled earlier. Use the same type of answer. For example, "Like any salesperson I enjoy selling, not doing the paperwork. I grin and bear it." If you are not in sales, use the sales force as a scapegoat. "In accounts receivable, it's my job to get the money in to make payroll. Half the time, the goods get shipped before I get the paperwork because sales says, 'It's a rush order.' That's a real minus to me. My last company tried a new approach. We met with sales and explained our problem. The result was that incremental commissions were based on cash in, not on bill date. They saw the connection and things are much better now."

EXERCISE 10.1 POST-INTERVIEW WORKSHEET

Complete immediately following the interview.

Company name: **Interview date:**

1. What questions were asked?

2. What were your answers?

3. What were your strengths and weaknesses?

4. If you were the interviewer, how would you rate yourself using the form below?

INTERVIEW EVALUATION FORM

What was the applicant's	Poor	Fair	Good	Very Good	Excel- lent
1. Interest in the position					
2. knowledge of company					
3. education or training					
4. experience					
5. maturity					
6. adaptability					
7. assertiveness					
8. ability to communicate					
9. appearance					

10. What are the applicant's major strengths?

11. What are the applicant's major weaknesses?

12. How does this applicant compare to other applicants for this position?

	Favorable			Unfavorable	
Overall Rating					

EXERCISE 10.2 ILLEGAL INTERVIEW QUESTIONS

Questions about age, disability, ethnicity, religion, citizenship or birthplace, gender/sexual identity, and marital/family status are **illegal** in most cases and only appropriate if these have direct bearing on the job. For example, if you are a pastor, it is okay for your interviewer to ask about your beliefs on religious topics.

If you are asked an illegal question, Yale University's Office of Career Strategy suggests that you can either answer it, politely sidestep it, or ask what it has to do with the position.

Rehearse your response to the following illegal questions:

1.   Do you have citizenship in the U.S.?

2.   What country were you born in?

3.   I'm trying to pinpoint your background. What's your heritage?

4.   Are you a man or a woman?

5.   Do you have a family? Are you planning to have children?

6.   Do you have childcare covered? Do you have to look after your parents?

7.   How old are you? What year were your born?

8.   Do you have any medical problems?

9.   Are you on any legal or illegal medication? Have you ever been addicted? Do you drink?

10.   Have you ever been arrested?

11.   Have you ever received psychological counseling?

12.   Do you go to church, synagogue or mosque?

CHAPTER 11
ACING YOUR INTERVIEW PART 3: USING NONVERBAL AND VERBAL EXPRESSION TO WIN

Pretend for a moment you are a hiring manager. You have spent a month, maybe two, searching for the right person to fill a position. You have received several stellar resumes and now have two candidates to interview. Equally qualified on paper, you're hoping to use the interview to ferret out which will be the best fit for your team.

Your first interviewee, Dan, answers all of your questions perfectly, but there is just something about him. He *says* he is enthusiastic about the job but doesn't *seem* enthusiastic. His face never changes expression, and he hides his hands under the table. He punctuates his sentences with "um" and "like" and seems to be searching for answers. Overall, you have the impression he is unprepared.

Next, you interview Susan. Susan has a few deficiencies in her training and experience but, because of her animation, energy, and warmth, you know she is the right one for the job. She is concise and clear in her responses and speaks confidently without hesitation. Your team will love her.

It's not surprising that you hired Susan. Communication scholars have found again and again that over 90% of the message we receive when talking to others comes through our read of their nonverbal communication.

You can be the best person on paper but, if you can't communicate it through your body language and articulation of your ideas, you won't get the job. The problem, however, is that facial expressions and gestures are the first thing to go when you are under the stress of an interview. Poor diction, grammar and clarity are all too common, as well.

How you say what you say is just as important as what you say.

This chapter includes critical tips for managing your verbal and nonverbal behavior in an interview. The key types of communication to control in an interview are as follows:

- Posture
- Eye contact
- Gestures
- Head/neck movement
- Facial expressions

- Appropriate volume
- Pace and pausing
- Avoidance of filler words
- Proper grammar
- Crisp enunciation

In addition to presenting these, I'll show you an excellent technique for using words to move your job search along.

Make no mistake. Your body language is being evaluated by hiring managers. Here are the top interviewee mistakes employers in a 2016 CareerBuilder[35] survey reported:

- Failure to make eye contact [listed as problematic by] 67 percent [by survey participants]
- Failure to smile—39 percent
- Bad posture—31 percent
- Fidgeting too much in one's seat—32 percent

---

35   CareerBuilder (2017). *CareerBuilder releases annual list of strangest interview and body language mistakes.* Retrieved September 12, 2020 from http://press.career-builder.com/2017-01-12-CareerBuilder-Releases-Annual-List-of-Strangest-Interview-and-Body-Language-Mistakes/

- Playing with something on the table—34 percent
- Handshake that is too weak—22 percent
- Crossing one's arms over one's chest—32 percent
- Playing with one's hair or touching one's face—28 percent

"As a professor of communication, I teach students to be highly expressive under duress," Conne says. "Imagine a line of desks with soon-to-be job seekers on either side asking each other interview questions. I walk around them, encouraging them to sit up straight, smile, move their facial features and use their hands to express their ideas. They hate it, but it works. Within 20 minutes I have a room full of excited, persuasive, enthusiastic-looking young professionals who can provide clear, articulate answers without hesitation."

An interviewer will know you may be stressed but it's your job to convey that you are, in spite of your nerves, able to talk under pressure. You're there because you want the job. Let them know it through your body language and verbal expression. Beware of having an "It's just the way I talk" mentality. This isn't about you. It's about how *they* need to see you in order to want to hire you. The good news is that communication difficulties can be fixed. The difficult part is admitting that you need to change.

NONVERBAL COMMUNICATION

Also known as "body language," your nonverbal communication includes thousands of overt and subtle behaviors that your interviewer may correctly or incorrectly interpret. Most of us think we are good at reading body language, but we are not. That doesn't matter in an interview, however, because your interviewer will *believe* he or she knows how you feel based on your nonverbals. Therefore, it is critical for you to present yourself confidently through your posture, gestures and other actions.

POSTURE

In the 80s, college students were taught to sit stiffly in the chair in an interview with their hands folded in their laps, feet uncrossed and placed firmly on the ground. I'm glad the 80s are over. This posture would send the wrong message today, but it has one merit: you still need to sit up straight.

The most common posture problem I see with interviewees is slouching. Turns out your mother was right when she said, "Sit up straight." You may be the hardest worker in the world, but slouching makes you look lazy. Good posture makes you look alert and attentive. No matter how you are sitting—leaning back with knees crossed or pulled up to a desk or table—your back should be straight, and your shoulders should be relaxed. Avoid bouncing your feet or sudden movements that make you look nervous. Remember, it's just a conversation.

EYE CONTACT

I had a client who was superior on paper, had a great personality, was verbally correct and otherwise presented a polished and professional image. He was also a really nice guy. Unfortunately, if you were interviewing him, and were to try to look where his eyes are moving, you would go dizzy and then crazy. I don't know who he was constantly looking at on my office ceiling, but they must have been having a great conversation.

It is a real shame that some people don't understand this vital aspect of body language. The old expression, "The eyes are the window to the soul," is true. How many times do you pass judgment on someone because of his or her eye contact? Look straight at the interviewer and don't take your eyes off him/her for a moment during any question they ask you or during your responses. No exceptions. They won't take it as a stare down, believe me.

GESTURES

Somewhere along the line, someone has probably told you that gestures distract others. Not true. People who gesture normally come across as warmer and more sincere. Use your hands to enhance your message. By all means, keep them IN VIEW, even when video conferencing. When you are listening, rest them on the table or on the arms of the chair.

Gestures aren't only about your hands. You should lift your arms a little such that there are a few inches of space between your elbows and ribcage. Reach out a little, especially when discussing the interviewer or organization (e.g., when you are saying "your").

HEAD AND NECK MOVEMENT

We seldom think of our heads as being expressive, but the tilt and swivel of your head on your neck is highly effective in punctuating your words. A slow nod when you are trying to persuade goes a long way in convincing your listener that what you're saying is true. Don't believe me? Find a partner. Without moving your head say, "I know I'm the right person for the job." Now, repeat the phrase nodding your head slightly. Your partner will say you were more convincing the second time.

FACIAL EXPRESSIONS

Your facial expressions are your superpower in an interview. The human face is a highly complex, 42-muscle mechanism for conveying even the slightest nuance of meaning and it can work along with your head and neck to be powerfully convincing. A flat look will convey a lack of interest, though you may not be feeling disinterested at all. What should your face be saying in an interview? "I'm the best person for the job because I'm passionate about the work and my enthusiasm will be contagious."

You may be surprised to know that two of the most expressive parts of your face are your *eyebrows* and *cheeks*. Actors are taught to create expressions using their eyebrows—a furrow to convey concern or raising to show surprise or pleasure. Find your partner again. Without moving your face, repeat again "I know I'm the right person for the job." Then, say the phrase again, raising your eyebrows a little when saying "I *know*..." Your partner will again be more convinced by your second effort.

Your cheeks control your best friend in an interview: your smile. You have read a hundred times that you should smile in an interview when appropriate (by the way it's appropriate most of the time), but actually doing it is very difficult. Conne tells me, "I had a few jobs in my teens and after the second time I heard, 'You're a really hard worker, Conne, but you need to smile,' I started thinking. I was happy, but I didn't come from a family of smilers. I had to teach herself to smile!" You might have to do so, too. I'm not suggesting that you spend the whole interview looking goofy but **keep your cheeks tight, so you appear to be about ready to break into a smile**. Then, when the time is just right, let them see your Chicklets. Especially smile when you are talking about your previous successes. Bring your smile all the way to your eyes. Exude friendliness.

Posture, gestures, head and neck movement, and facial expressions work together. Just like you wouldn't practice the piano incorrectly, you shouldn't practice answering interview questions without the right expression. Don't count on your ability to come through during the interview. Dedicate the time now to these four elements of body language and enjoy the benefits—and the paycheck—later.

APPROPRIATE VOLUME

No one wants to have to strain to hear you. On the other hand, no one wants to run out for earplugs. I remember a fellow I once knew who literally shouted everything he said and was a real embarrassment in public situations.

In an interview, especially a video interview, you need to speak up. First, you never know when someone is hard of hearing. Second, low volume speech makes you appear under-confident. When you are nervous, your vocal cords will tighten. Forcing extra air through them will help with this phenomenon and make you sound better. Breathing deeply while waiting for your interview to begin will help considerably as well.

VERBAL EXPRESSION

Your verbal expression is just as important as your nonverbal expression. Verbal expression is your ability to articulate—express clearly and without distracting habits—your ideas. Four speech skills including pace and pausing, avoidance of filler words, proper grammar and crisp enunciation contribute to good verbal expression.

PACE AND PAUSING

The National Center for Voice and Speech reports that most Americans speak at a rate of about 150 words per minute in conversation.[36] There is no need to speak any more quickly or slowly in an interview. In fact, if you speak too fast, your interviewer may not be able to absorb what you're saying or may think you are nervous. Speak too slowly and you risk becoming boring.

Analyzing your speaking rate is easy. Simply record yourself answering an interview question, count your words and adjust accordingly.

---

36   National Center for Voice and Speech (n.d.). *Voice qualities.* Retrieved September 30, 2020 from http://www.ncvs.org/ncvs/tutorials/voiceprod/tutorial/quality.html/

Pausing is another speaking tool that can help an interviewer understand you better. One second pauses will give him or her a chance to mentally catch up. Be strategic with your pauses, though. Use them to emphasize important points.

AVOIDANCE OF FILLER WORDS

Um, like, ah, uh, and, well…these are just a few of the many words known as "fillers." We use them when we are not sure what to say next, or sometimes just out of habit. Admit it, you have probably played Count the Ums when listening to a speaker so you know how distracting these fillers can be. Eliminate them from your speech now.

One method of reducing filler words is to ask those around you to raise their hands whenever they hear you use the word you want to eliminate. Every time you say "like" and see hands go up, for example, stop, pause, and return to the beginning of your sentence. It will be frustrating at first, but worth it. Keep at it. You'll see a difference in a few weeks.

PROPER GRAMMAR

This is one of the silent prejudicial barriers that will hold you back. Many people I interview today don't seem to be well spoken. The unfortunate truth is that if you talk like you are stupid, people will think you are stupid (even though you aren't). Almost without exception, if your grammar is poor, you might as well forget about climbing a long-term career ladder. Oh, you might get a job and decent pay but at the point you decide you want to advance and fill a senior manager role, you are dead in the water.

Imagine you are interviewing someone for an $80,000+ marketing director job. You ask what the candidate would like to change first if hired. He/she says, "I done a analysis of your advertising campaign and it don't seem over creative. I wanna make some change to it." Screeeech—you are out!

Since marketing directors often act as liaisons between different levels of personnel within an organization, you need someone who can express ideas well. I have often heard people laugh and pass off bad grammar as simply a reflection of where they are from. It's true that you pick up your speaking habits from those around you, but you have to clean these up if you expect to impress anyone on an interview. At work, you need to "codeswitch," or change your way of speaking to be more correct.

I've also had clients who graduated from well-known schools verbally murder sentence structure. To those of us who are in hiring roles or screening roles, it is like a grenade going off. The solution is again to make a recording of yourself answering interview questions and analyze how you can say what you want to say more correctly. Then PRACTICE, PRACTICE, PRACTICE.

CRISP ENUNCIATION

In the old days, *elocution* was taught in public schools. Elocution is the skill of pronouncing words clearly and crisply. Pay attention to how you say phrases like "the American," "build community" or "this probably." If you're saying "thamerican," "comuny" or "this prolly" you need to change your habits. In the example in the last section, a potential marketing representative with poor enunciation may sound like this, "I done a analis of yer avertising campay and it don't seem over crea'ive. I wanna make some chain to ih." Don't laugh. I have heard it!

It's too bad elocution is no longer taught because its importance is great. A 2020 study by Kraus, Torrez and Park revealed tremendous bias regarding enunciation.[37] They summarized the results as follows:

> *"...we enlisted 274 people with prior hiring experience and had them listen to a 25-second sample of speech from applicants for a lab manager position. As in our other experiments, participants accurately perceived the socioeconomic status of those speaking, and, alarmingly, judged those of lower status to be less competent, a worse fit for the job, and deserving of a lower starting salary and signing bonus than their higher status counterparts. Critically, participants made these judgments without any information about the applicants' qualifications."*

While seemingly unfair, the way you speak DOES have a major impact on your ability to get a job. The importance of your articulation increases tenfold with video interviewing since equipment will degrade the sound of your voice. The good news is that speech enunciation and patterns are skills that you have learned and, as we know, you can change learned behavior with practice. Record yourself. Analyze. Take a public speaking class. Hire a coach.

---

37   Kraus, M., Torrez, B., Park, J. & Ghayebi, F. (2019). Evidence for the reproduction of social class in brief speech. *PNAS Proceedings of the National Academy of Sciences of the United States of America, Vol 116(46)*, Nov 12, 2019. pp. 22998-23003.

Employers will also likely connect your ability to speak correctly with your ability to write well. Since excellent communication skills are sought by most employers, it will pay to improve your speaking *and* writing.

This is a lot to remember when you are experiencing the stress of an interview. The key, of course, is **PRACTICE, PRACTICE, PRACTICE.** Conduct *recorded* mock interviews with your partner and analyze them, substituting good practices for bad. In time you will be able to handle even the toughest interview situations.

THE POWER OF WORDS IN INTERVIEWING AND NETWORKING

Words are important. A simple shift in wording can make an enormous difference in influencing an interviewer. In the process of landing a job, words have the power to make or break you. Therefore, using the right words becomes critical to your success. You must use them correctly and descriptively.

In the sections that follow, we are going to explore how to pick the right words, how to use the right words to motivate and encourage others to assist you in your job search, and how to use some other communication tools that can improve your interviewing and networking outcomes.

I have already revealed that over 90% of the message we receive when talking to others comes through our interpretation of their nonverbal communication. This comes as a big shock to people who work hard on crafting their words! Take heart. The words you use in your interview are also important. Each person perceives words differently, however.

People speaking about technical (concrete) subjects have an advantage because they often use words that are clearly defined. An ohm is an ohm; a volt is a volt; bits and bytes are bits and bytes. Words in scientific, technical, or other highly specific context areas carry great value in communication because of their degree of specificity. They cannot be perceived in numerous ways.

You will undoubtedly be using numerous technical (concrete) words in your interview, but also using words that appeal to feelings will boost your persuasiveness considerably. Words can have tremendous impact when they are part of a story because they stimulate the emotions necessary to motivate us to make decisions. Advertisers make use of this abstract type of communication better than anyone and use our emotions to get us to buy their products. Themes like the underdog winning the day, coming home after a long absence and patriotic pride appear frequently in marketing. When we see these themes, we relate to the characters—and product—on a personal level.

Words stimulate responses: sensory (sight, sound, smell, taste, touch) recall from our individual memories, emotional, empathetic or sympathetic responses, fight or flight impulses, "gut feelings," and so on and cause us to take action. This is exactly what you want in an interview.

Use your words to paint an emotional picture. If I tell you about the fast-food restaurant my family visited under an inspiring sunset one balmy summer, and about the double cheeseburgers, fries and shakes that we enjoyed, aren't you already picturing the scene in your mind? Yet the restaurant you're picturing is not the one I am picturing, nor the food, nor the family, nor the sunset. You are picturing experiences you have had. Through my description, though, I have established a subconscious bond with you.

Conne interviewed a man once who was in a terrible accident while he was in law school. "I was incredibly impressed," she said, "with his story about how he continued through school and into a career while confined to a wheelchair. He described his battle to gain enough strength to learn to walk again and become a volunteer firefighter while pursuing a career in law. What tenacity!"

How can you make words work for you? Let's say I tell you I work in Information Technology (IT). Someone might have the impression I can only fix hard drives or correct software bugs. What happens if I tell you that as an IT leader, I "…integrate technology into business solutions?" Changes your impression of what I do a great deal, doesn't it? I sound like someone who understands the application of technology to a business environment. Your first impression was that I should have $75k job, but your second impression could be that you should pay me $100k+. Quite a shift, based on the use of a few words to describe what I do. Here are some word changes that might make the difference between $100k and $150k+ in your pocket:

Project Management vs. Complex Program Implementation

Training and Development vs. Global Team Development/Deployment

Budgeting and Forecasting vs. Financial Performance Maximization

I'm not suggesting that you create a "glorified" title for your job. Just ask yourself what you really do. What is the positive *result* of your work effort?

One of the best ways to make the best use of words when searching for a job is to read job descriptions for the types of positions you want. Use the phrases that most resonate in your written and oral communication. Then, use a combination of abstract and concrete language related to the job when answering interview questions. How they respond to your words, and how they feel about you, may be the key to whether you get hired.

The words you use will have a major impact on your networking outcomes as well. Here is how most networking conversations start, if not word for word, by intention:

> *Hi, Bob. How are you doing? Hey, you probably know that I'm looking for a job and I wondered if you know anyone that might have an opening for an IT guy? No? Okay. Well, if you hear of anything, let me know, Okay? Thanks, Bob!*

The chance that Bob might know of a position at that moment is virtually 0%. The odds that he might run across an opening are probably only slightly better. If you were Bob, and you knew that I was coming to you with a question like that, would you be thrilled to see me?

By nature, we like to help people if we have the time, the resources, and the inclination. Rarely have I met people that would not want to help a person in a job search if they could, but the odds are stacked against receiving that help because of the way the request was presented—because of the *words* used. We all like to feel important. When someone seeks out our advice, we feel valued and appreciated.

One of the most effective communication models built on that premise is the **Advice, Information, Referral technique—A.I.R.**© While the context here is in job search, you will find this concept applicable to any communication through which you are trying to get buy in from others. **A.I.R.** is also an excellent networking technique.

We all like to give advice. Most of us, however, don't like to ask for advice. Yet asking for it generates some amazing transformations. People feel important when they are asked to share advice. By asking for advice, you have placed yourself at the bottom of the hill and your mentor on the top.

Let's say I come to Bob, and this is my new approach:

Hi, Bob! How are you doing? I need your advice on something. As you know, I'm a senior-level IT executive with a focus on technology integration, and performance improvement. I put together a target list of companies* chosen because they are in fast- changing business environments and my experience in consolidations, mergers and reorganizations is likely to be of value to them at some point. I'm trying to generate conversations with people who either work for the industries or companies, or who might know someone who does. I don't want to chase after these targets if I am not going to be a good fit there.

I'm not asking you to find me a job. I can do that myself, but you come across people with whom I should connect because of their experience in these industries, or because they are well connected. I do not expect them to know of any openings, but their advice might be very valuable in getting me in front of people who do have needs that are not being met. In the event you think of anyone that I should talk to, would you keep me in mind, and I'll stay in touch with you?

What is the chance Bob will say, "Yes" to this request? Probably close to 100%. Bob cannot NOT keep me in mind, as I have provided him with what I call a "baseline" (what I am, where I'm going, and WHY it makes sense).

Second, notice that I did not ask Bob to do anything other than keep me in mind. I asked him if I could stay in touch with him. Why would he say no to that? From that moment on, Bob has added me to his human antenna, his subconscious acting like a little digital recorder, ready to recall me when stimulated by an outside event.

The net result is that by changing the words I used, I made Bob a participant in my search process without his having to do anything other than be himself. When you allow someone to take that role in the conversation, he/she will feel less threatened, and will often give you what you want—**information**.

* Target list is a 1-page word document on your letterhead that has 3-5 industry groups, a number of companies listed under each group with not more than a total of 35-50 companies.

Your job is to know as much as you can about target companies, positions, and people with whom you might be interviewing. Once Bob has identified someone you should contact, pick his brain about the organization and hiring situation. From this information, you will identify SHARE© stories that support your ability to meet the needs of the company and your first contact with them will go more smoothly, increasing your chance of a meeting.

Every conversation with Bob should lead to an outcome, even if that outcome is only to remind him that you are still thinking of making a career move. This is called **referral**. As you chat with Bob periodically, subtly mention your qualifications again and ask if he has thought of anyone with whom you should make contact.

My next step is to make talking to Bob a regular part of my communication. I touch base with Bob periodically NOT to ask if he has done anything for me, but to inquire about him, or to let him know how a conversation turned out that he might be interested in, or about a mutual friend I bumped into. Whatever the reasons, it is a "passive" communication in that I am not expecting anything. My short email shows up in Bob's email and "bingo!" he remembers a connection he wanted to tell me about. Follow up is critical. Not every day; perhaps not every week, but if you do not initiate the contact, you will miss critical information that could shorten your search dramatically.

SUCCESS STORY: NO NONSENSE NONVERBALS

CONTRIBUTED BY CONNE REECE, CO-AUTHOR AND EDITOR

Dylan was a college senior looking to apply to the state police. The process of application is arduous and includes physical and psychological testing, and an in-person interview. Only a small percentage of applicants are accepted annually.

I had Dylan in several communication classes, and he was well-prepared for his interview. We had focused on clarity of responses and how to overcome the lack of animation that often occurs when one is nervous. Additionally, we practiced coming alive and showing personality while remaining confident.

After his interview, Dylan said, "...1670 people took the oral exam and I did better than 1639 of them, which ranked me at 31 overall. My communication classes really helped me in preparing for the interview."

Dylan's success came in part from mastering control of his nonverbal skills *before* the interview.

ADDITIONAL RESOURCES

- Quest, L. (2016, November 7). *7 nonverbal mistakes to avoid making during a job interview.* Forbes.com. https://www.forbes.com/sites/lisaquast/2016/11/07/7-nonverbal-mistakes-to-avoid-making-during-job-interviews/?sh=2e7260d9b4d5/
- Hansen, K. (n.d.). *The unspoken secrets of job interviewing: How your nonverbal presentation and behaviors impact the impression you make.* LiveCareer.com. https://www.livecareer.com/resources/interviews/prep/interviewing-unspoken-secrets/

CHAPTER 12
EVALUATING AND ACCEPTING THE OFFER

Congratulations! You have an offer. Before you accept the position, you need to evaluate one more time whether the position and pay are right for you. This chapter includes information on:

- Analyzing an offer
- Making a counteroffer

There is really no way to predict when a job offer will be forthcoming. Sometimes it takes months. When one does come, however, there are certain protocols that should be followed. No matter what the offer (even if it is the pits), graciously thank the person for thinking enough of you and your skills to want you to join their team.

If you think you can work with the offer, ask for it in writing. Almost all large companies do this as standard operating procedure. Small companies may not. If the company does not, you should offer to jot down the points of the offer just to make sure everyone is on the same page. Read your notes to the hiring authority and ask if there is anything you might have overlooked from your discussions.

Provide your notes to the company and get their agreement on all points before proceeding. This means writing a formal letter thanking them and recapping your notes from the meeting. Ask for a written response that concurs with your notes. If they are not willing to do this then either they are poor managers or crooks, or you are not the candidate of choice and they will likely blow you off anyway.

ANALYZING THE OFFER

Here's a word to the wise. If you are offered an inexplicably high package by any company, look hard at their source of funding and their BURN RATE. It is not how much money they have; it is the speed at which they are spending it! If you ask and they won't tell you, run away as fast as you can. Compensation is also determined by the economic climate of the timeframe in which you are searching.

Make sure you understand each point of the offer. Ask questions about items such as how the commission, bonus or stock options are to be determined. Don't ask these initially. They come later in the interview process. An excellent way of testing your understanding of the offer is to explain each point to another person. If you can't do it, you don't understand it.

There is also more to a meaningful job than just money. The exercises at the end of the chapter will guide you through your decision. After completing them you will know if the company is right for you and have a clearer picture of how to further negotiate your contract.

In addition to the chapter exercises, review the preferences you have selected using the exercises throughout this book. Only you can determine whether an offer is right for you. Use Exercises 12.1, *Analyzing the Job Offer* and 12.2, *Job Advantages and Disadvantages*, to make the best decision. As a quick point of reference, some of the most common criteria for making a choice about accepting an offer are listed below.

THE 6 BENEFITS THAT ATTRACT TOP TALENT[38]

1. Medical and dental. Employees need medical and dental insurance, and 66% of recruiters say it's the most important perk.

2. 401(k) plan

3. Ability to work from home

38   Driver, S. (2018). *The 6 benefits that attract top talent*. Business News Daily. Retrieved March 13, 2021 from https://www.businessnewsdaily.com/11204-top-benefits-attract-top-talent.html/

4.   Being able to wear casual attire

5.   Continuing education reimbursement

6.   Signing bonus

Once you have the offer in writing and have a mutual agreement that all the pertinent points are included, ask for a few days to review. There is really no rule of thumb about how long you should consider an offer. Unless there are extenuating circumstances, such as other pending offers, keep it under a week.

NEGOTIATING THE SALARY AND PACKAGE

Employers want to pay what they want to pay and not a penny more. You want them to pay you what you think you are worth and not a penny less. How you address this variance determines how successful you will be in negotiating a deal that works for you. You don't want to turn them off with ridiculously high demands, but don't assume their offer represents everything they can offer. Do the latter and you will make a serious mistake. A win-win scenario is achieved by developing a close match that is agreeable to both of you.

A consultant I once employed used to tell clients that "...negotiating a salary is much like playing high stakes poker. There are good hands and bad hands, just as there are good offers and bad offers. The expert poker player knows how to handle both." This is very true, isn't it?

As you went through the interview process, you collected information of all kinds. Now you should organize this information so you can form a negotiation strategy. *Before* you begin to negotiate, go through the list and prioritize what you want for yourself. If you have a search partner, they too must go through the list and prioritize what they feel is important. The two lists combined are the backbone of your strategic position.

Explain your salary history if asked but make your salary discussion a friendly experience. Assume amiability when discussing salary, not conflict or controversy. You should make the employer feel that you are on the same side and working together to find a compensation package that will satisfy everyone's needs. Remain calm and poised. Once the offer has been made, if it appears too low, remain quiet as though you were pondering the offer. This will imply your dissatisfaction with the offer, and the uncomfortable silence may prompt the interviewer to improve the offer on his/her own.

Be prepared with salary options. Come up with three salary figures for yourself: the low-ball (not on your life) offer, an offer that would make you smile, and one that would make you jump up and down and call all your friends. Shoot for a salary between your middle figure and your high figure. Know your absolute bottom line, though. Although it is not advisable to bring this up in the interview, you will need to know what you need to maintain your lifestyle.

Remember that the employer has a budget. Understand that most employers have a range in mind and will start at the low end to give themselves some negotiating room. This does not mean they will always try to low-ball the position and pay less than they think the position is worth as it is not in their best interest if they are looking for qualified candidates. Employers like negotiating. In fact, potential employers often look at negotiating for salary favorably. It reinforces the idea that they've made the right decision in offering you the position and lets them feel confident that, because you can keep your best interests in mind, you can probably look after the best interests of the company.

At some point, someone has to put a dollar amount on the table. If they ask what you want, ask *them* if the company has a salary range in mind. If they tell you, great! The sad truth is that even if you do what I've told you in the preceding chapters, there is a better than 50% chance you still might have to be the first to mention a number.

If you are forced into this position, keep these important points in mind. The hiring company really doesn't care what *you* need. Do not say, "I need $90,000" or whatever your target salary might be. Rather, answer that, with what you currently know about the job and its responsibilities, you believe that the salary range for the position should be $90,000 to $120,000. Follow up by asking if this is the salary range that the company has in mind.

Let's assume that the salary range that you have selected is too high. The company has a $80,000 to 95,000 salary range in mind. Because you have attached the salary range only to the *position*, you can get yourself out of trouble. Start by saying that you want to make sure that you have understood the responsibilities of the job. Repeat those responsibilities back to the hiring authority. Your hope is that, by hearing the responsibilities repeated, the hiring authority would realize that the salary he/she has placed on the position is too low and will meet your salary range.

On very rare occasions, the salary range that you have selected is too low. A quick way out of this fix is to say that the dollar figure you gave was base salary, not total compensation.

The higher the position, the longer the interviewing process and salary negotiations will take. Be patient. The rewards are there for those individuals savvy enough to continually add value to themselves in each interview, and for those who strategically plan each interview. Remember that your salary should go up throughout your life and accepting a lower offer now will have a negative effect on your retirement later.

MAKING A COUNTEROFFER

Should you negotiate just for the sake of negotiation? Probably not, except if you believe that the company expects you to make a counteroffer. Play your counteroffer off the personality of the hiring authority and the aggressiveness of the company or business sector.

Think back over the information you gathered when you were diligently researching the company and the people you met during the interviewing process. Is the company known for being aggressive? Does the company have status within its industry? Are the people you met with competitive? If the answer is "yes," you should prepare a counteroffer. In this instance, don't be afraid of losing the deal. Pick some of your expendable "bargaining chips" for use in your counteroffer. For instance, perhaps you are happy with their offer of three weeks of paid time off. Ask for an additional week of vacation anyway. Your potential employer may think the extra week will make or break your desire to work for them. Bargaining with items you can live without makes you appear to be negotiating.

Some companies don't want much, if any, negotiation. **Do not pull the company out of its comfort zone.** They may just decide that you are too much of a firebrand. Save your aggressiveness for the job at hand. Use your salary, package and job criteria to make a yes or no decision. Also understand that some organizations have pay scales that are fixed and they won't be able to negotiate much.

Sometimes people in career transition have to face the reality of accepting or rejecting a less than ideal offer. Rather than slipping into a deep depression, go back to the job analysis form and review your "no" answers. Make a list of them in ascending order of importance. Beside each item, write what you ideally want as well as your "walk-away position." Decide how many you'd like to "win" in order to accept the position.

Be creative. If the company just can't afford a higher salary, try asking for other benefits: a company car or allowances, 3-6-month performance raises, stock options, profit sharing, vacation days, or temporary housing. Consider other options and perks. Sometimes companies offer one-time cash bonuses, or hiring bonuses, to help entice undecided candidates. Don't expect to receive one if you are unemployed because you have less value than if they need to entice you away from a competitor. Draft these options into a letter.

Congratulations! You have your counteroffer.

DELIVERING THE COUNTEROFFER

The ideal way to deliver a counteroffer is face-to-face, if possible. Start out by telling the hiring authority, not the HR clerk, that you are pleased she/he wants you to join the team. Follow-up by saying that you and the organization have a deal but there are a couple of points that need to be discussed. Begin with your least-important item.

You will now see how your new "potential" boss reacts to negotiating with an employee, and you will learn how comfortable you are negotiating with your new boss. If they dig in their heels over a minor issue, *and cannot offer a valid reason for holding firm*, this is probably not a good fit for either of you. On the other hand, it could mean that you have not done a great job of presenting and having them understand and buy into your value-add proposition.

Don't walk away simply because your new boss hangs tough on the first issue. Try the second counter-offer item on your list, using the same strategy. You might say, "We might want to come back to this point later, but let's move on to another matter of importance."

This one might go your way. A good rule of thumb is that, if you have failed to renegotiate three items in a row, you have probably reached the limit of how far the job offer can be negotiated. When you reach this limit, you have a choice to make regarding accepting the position. Remember that, even if you can't increase the salary (because of a fixed company cap), the employer will feel reinforced from your negotiation—as though he got a good deal. This will play better for you when raises are considered in the future.

You can always walk away from the negotiating table if you just aren't getting into your minimum range.

Earlier, you learned the difference between total compensation and base salary. To figure your total compensation, complete Exercise 12.3, *Total Compensation*.

Often economics are the driving force behind accepting a job offer. If this is the case, don't despair. Take the position with the intent of continuing your job search or picking it up again after a pre-established period of time. You never know what opportunities may come your way in the meantime.

SUCCESS STORY: NEGOTIATION VICTORY

CONTRIBUTED BY BILL TEMPLE, EXECUTIVE COACH, STEWART, COOPER & COON

Terry entered negotiations with a transport company that had been in bankruptcy and needed an operations expert to turn things around. He was familiar with their issues and, based on my recommendation, suggested a 3-month probationary contract followed by a permanent placement.

The organization's success seemed like a long shot filled with potential risk. Terry knew he needed complete authority to carry out the necessary changes, even in his 3-month position.

Despite some management changes at the organization during the negotiation, Terry was able to secure a 3-month consultancy followed by a permanent position with the following package:

- $4,500 per week for consulting
- Temporary housing
- 100% reimbursement on transportation expenses

At full time, Terry received:

- $245,000 base salary
- Major medical
- 401K
- Dental and eye insurance
- 3 weeks PTO

The biggest benefit Terry was able to negotiate for, however, was total control over the changes he wanted to implement in various branch operations within the organization. Our strategy had paid off.

ADDITIONAL RESOURCES

- Chapman, J. (2008). *Negotiating your salary: How to make $1000 a minute.* Mt. Vernon Press.
- Coon, F. (n.d.). *Career resources.* StewartCooperCoon.com. https://www.stewart-coopercoon.com/career-resources/

EXERCISE 12.1 ANALYZING THE JOB OFFER

There is more to a meaningful job than just money. To make sure you make a logical decision, take the time to answer the following questions about the new position. After doing this, not only will you know if the company is right for you, but you will also have a clearer picture of how strongly to further negotiate your contract.

The Job	Yes	No
1. Will I get along well with my boss?		
2. Will I have more than one boss?		
3. Do I clearly understand the nature of the work?		
4. Do I know specifically what I will be doing?		
5. Are my responsibilities reflected in my job title?		
6. Is the position interesting and challenging?		
7. Can I make final decisions affecting my work?		
8. Will I get along with coworkers?		
9. Will I need more training?		
10. Will the company pay for it?		
11. Will overtime be necessary?		
12. Will travel create problems?		
13. Will I need to relocate?		
14. Will the company pay for relocation?		
15. Is there reasonable job security?		
16. Will I be proud to tell my friends what I do?		
Positioning		
17. Could this job result in a significant promotion?		

18. Will this job broaden / increase my background?		
19. Can this job be a springboard to something better?		
20. Does this job expose me to other opportunities?		
21. Will I be visible to decision-makers?		
22. How frequent are my performance reviews?		
The Company		
23. Is the organization too large / rigid for my personality?		
24. Is the organization too small to offer room for advancement or impressive credentials for a future resume?		
25. Is a written personnel handbook available?		
26. Is the company growing faster than its competitors?		
27. Is the company's financial position healthy?		
28. Is there a high turnover of personnel?		
29. Is the company's location convenient?		
30. Is the commuting time acceptable?		
31. Is the physical setting acceptable?		
32. If I relocate, will I like the lifestyle of the new location?		
33. Does the firm have a reputation for treating its employees fairly?		
34. Is the organization in a growth industry?		
Financial Rewards		
35. Is the salary competitive?		
36. If not, is it possible to get an early review and increase?		
37. Do I clearly understand the method of payment?		
38. Are raises based on merit, length of service, exams?		

39. Is there health insurance?		
40. Dental insurance?		
41. Vision insurance?		
42. Life insurance?		
43. Retirement plan?		
44. Paid membership dues?		
45. Bonus?		
46. Profit sharing?		
47. Car allowance?		
48. Are there an adequate number of vacation days?		
49. Are there an adequate number of paid holidays?		
50. Are there an adequate number of sick days?		
51. Maternity leave?		
52. Company car?		
53. Clothing allowance?		
54. Expense account?		
55. Employer paid tuition?		
56. Travel to conferences, conventions?		
57. Subscriptions to professional and trade journals?		
58. Stock purchase plan?		

EXERCISE 12.2 JOB ADVANTAGES AND DISADVANTAGES

Aspect of Job	Advantage	Disadvantage
Salary		
Profit sharing plan		
Benefits		
Medical plan		
Travel required		
Location		
Continuing education		
Work environment		
Job satisfaction		
Work hours		
Vacation		
Moving expenses		
Stock options		
Vehicle allowance		
Pension plan		
Life insurance		
Tax assistance		
Child care		
Severance pay		
Athletic club membership		
Other		

EXERCISE 12.3 TOTAL COMPENSATION WORKSHEET

Compensation	Yearly Amount
Base Salary	
Benefits	
Commissions	
Signing Bonus	
Stock Options	
Bonuses	
Potential Raises Within 12 Months	
Memberships	
Car or Transportation Allowances	
Other	
TOTAL COMPENSATION	

CHAPTER 13
THE OVER 45 JOB SEARCH

The Bureau of Labor and Statistics reports that 12.9% of the US workforce is between 45 and 54.[39] Many economic and social forces are contributing to the need for Baby Boomers to work well into their 60s or even 70s. In addition, as we live healthier, longer lives many continue to work for the pleasure of it. Nowadays, most people under 50 will change jobs every three or four years, while the older group is more inclined to remain with a single organization for their whole working career. In this chapter I will:

- Explain a few scenarios that might sound familiar
- Tell you how you can leverage your experience and remain valuable

The following scenarios are a few I have worked through with my clients as a career coach and recruiter. There are too many different situations to list them all, but most people in or approaching their 50's have fallen into one of the scenarios listed below. There is no one solution or answer to solve problems inherent in each situation. There is no magic wand to wave to re-direct circumstance or correct bad judgment or poor decision-making that might have led to these situations. All you can do is plan better in the future and do the best you can to push ahead.

Scenario #1: You are 45+, your credentials are a little out of date, and your salary is a little too high for comparable positions in the same market because you've been at your

---

39   Bureau of Labor Statistics (2020). *Employment projections 2019-2029*. Retrieved October 1, 2020 from https://www.bls.gov/news.release/pdf/ecopro.pdf/

company a long time. Now, for the first time in a long time, you find yourself either unemployed or about to be.

Scenario #2: You are 45+, have been with a company for a number of years, are rocking along fat, dumb and happy, and someone upstairs makes a decision to move the plant and not move you.

Scenario #3: You are 45+, you've been with the organization forever and the scuttlebutt is that they are in financial trouble. There is talk of closing and maybe a filing for bankruptcy.

Scenario #4: At age 40-something, you decided to take a career risk and were lured by the prospect of self-employment or another venture situation. You learn the cash burn-rate is too high and people around you are being laid off. Your time might be any day. You are afraid this serious error in judgement will reflect poorly.

Scenario #5: You are somewhere in your mid-life crisis wondering what to do with the rest of your life, frustrated by your apparent lack of career progress, unhappy about choices you've made and want a change. Either way, you want to make a major move and change career all together.

Scenario #6: You are making excellent money, have good benefits, are respected in the company, but somewhere in the back of your mind you have this feeling that you want to do something else.

Scenario #7: You jumped corporate ship and decided to be a consultant. Now, your market has dried up and you find yourself not meeting your own income or career expectations.

In my role as a certified career coach and retained executive recruiter, I have worked with people in each of these scenarios. I have seen the variety of responses that occur when job tragedy strikes, especially later in one's career, and I want to share some advice about how to handle the common reactions you may experience.

First, losing your job can be a shock. Take some time to adjust, but don't spend too much time feeling sorry for yourself. Anger and feelings of having been treated unfairly are normal but they won't get your job back. Seek professional counseling if you need it. Be careful of venting to your professional connections. Their sympathy will obscure reality and subsequently delay your implementation of a plan to move on. Also, people talk and you don't want to burn bridges.

Second, don't make the mistake of thinking you will get a job more quickly than you might. You may think you are okay financially, but you don't know what lies ahead. Conne has seen this happen as well. "I had a friend who was a highly paid drug sales rep. When his position was eliminated, he waited far too long to start searching for a job believing that, when he was ready, someone would hire him quickly. He ended up losing his house and declaring bankruptcy," she said.

I can't tell you the number of times my executive clients have looked me proudly in the eye and said that they have taken the last 2-6 months off to clear their heads and now they are refreshed and ready to go back to work. My follow-up question is always, "How long can you hold out before you run out of savings and available cash resources?" They usually tell me 3-6 months.

If you have just left a position sporting a salary of $75,000, and we use the U.S. Department of Labor Statistics on job search timing, you will be in a financial hole 45 days before becoming employed again. It could be 60 days before you see any money from your first paycheck.

The good news is that, as an older worker, you have much going for you that younger workers don't. Assuming you have stayed up to date in your field and on technology, you have years of experience that the Millennials and Digitals just don't have. You have value and, if you manage your career moves right, you can capitalize on your strengths and continue to move ahead in your career.

Don't assume that no one will hire you because of your age. First, there are laws against that. Second, organizations these days know that most workers will only stay a few years, so there is little advantage to hiring a younger worker thinking he or she will stay longer than you. Sure, some will think that but, don't worry, your career ain't over yet. Companies are more often recognizing the increasing retirement age segment of the population and the older workers who are returning to the marketplace.

I had a client once who was 68 years old and wanted to work because he felt he had many years of valuable service left in him to give to a company. However, he was told he was too old. Before you get up in arms, no one told him directly he was too old, but he came away from interviews feeling this way. It took him three months to land a job, and he is now happily employed at the student services department of a major university, going to work every day, and giving it 110%.

You may have already retired and are financially stable, but you want to work because you are bored and miss making a contribution. You are in an enviable position, so consider offering your services as a volunteer. Perhaps your local symphony, museum of art, national gallery, or opera house would love to have you as head of charitable fund raising.

Maybe there is a skill you've always wished to acquire, such as computer programming. Consider going back to school. Increasing your aptitude makes you even more valuable. The longer we live the more dependent we are going to become on technology, so having a strong grasp of the fundamentals is a self-benefiting bonus. There is no age limit on furthering your education and it is a fantastic option for the early retiree looking to re-enter the workforce.

Make a list of what you really enjoy and a list of things you would prefer not to do again. If you only want to work for another two or three years you can probably cope with being dissatisfied, but if you're looking at another decade or two, you're going to need something that will sustain your interest, so don't be hasty. If you have decided you are ready to reenter the job market, you may be certain that your years of experience will be an asset. Relying on this factor may also draw attention to your age and stage in life so make as little reference to your age as possible by decreasing the length of your resume.

Decreasing the length of your resume, especially removing items that are irrelevant, can make you more attractive than if you have a long resume polluted with information that has nothing to do with the job for which you are applying. Listing every position you have ever had is not necessary. Additionally, highlight your technological fluency by including your LinkedIn profile URL or mentioning information you gleaned about the organization company through their Facebook or Twitter feed.

Another option you may want to explore is consulting. This is frequently a wonderful choice for established workers who are well-versed in their fields and looking for a significant change of pace in later years. Providing training or applicable insight to others can also prove quite lucrative. While you may feel as though you need to beat the odds as an older member of the job-hunting world, you also possess contacts, networking abilities and skills that the younger generation simply hasn't had the chance to acquire. This alone should give any 45+ job seeker the confidence that change is possible at this stage in their lives.

Here are a few tactics you may wish to employ to deal with the issues of being middle-aged and looking for work.

1. If you have been recently unemployed, or are about to be, cut your expenses immediately! The search will take longer because of your age. Work at the search job a

minimum of 8 and no more than 10 hours each day. It will be a long haul, so don't burn out halfway through and wind up looking bad at your interviews.

2. Don't put more than 15 years of experience on your resume. The objective is to get in front of someone, then sell yourself. If you don't get there, no matter how good you are, you won't be afforded that opportunity.

3. Prepare several versions of your resume. Customize for each position. Review the information in this book about matching key words for applicant tracking systems.

4. Engage in heavy-duty company research and determine their corporate makeup in your targeted area. If the workforce is in their 20s, you probably won't have success there. On the other hand, if the workforce at that company is approaching 40, you are in good shape.

5. Remember at 50+ you are seen as older and less flexible, so improve your appearance to seem like you are "timeless." Update your personal style and wardrobe. Remember, you never get a second chance to make a first impression.

6. Exude energy. Don't complain about your aches and pains or your difficulty mastering new technology. Show everyone—including yourself—that you can keep up. Show them that you are ready to take on new challenges.

7. Go back to school and enroll in a program of your choice. You will be seen as flexible and not locked into older ways of doing things. Some universities will allow you to audit (sit in on) classes at little or no charge. Professors may welcome the input of an experienced worker and, in an interview, you can discuss your up-to-date knowledge of your field and desire to keep learning.

Those over 45 face added discrimination barriers, but they are not insurmountable. You *are* employable. Finding a new job may just take longer, that's all. Therefore, you should accept the challenge, implement the *Ready, Aim, Hired* system and go to work getting work.

SUCCESS STORY: EXPERIENCE = VALUE

CONTRIBUTED BY JO ANN MOSER, SENIOR CAMPAIGN DIRECTOR, STEWART, COOPER & COON

John was retired from 20+ years in the military and was interested in using his considerable skills and experience in the private sector. He was initially reluctant, however, because he was worried that his best years were behind him and that he would have trouble "de-militarizing" himself. He thought no one would recognize his value.

John was wrong. He is now working as Senior Director for Business Development at his organization with the following salary and benefits:

- $180,000 base salary
- $50,000 relocation expenses
- S25,000 sign on bonus
- $4,300 housing subsidy
- Expense-paid house hunting trips for spouse
- Paid closing and realtor fees for home sale
- Medical, dental, vision, life, 401K and more

"I will be making more money than I ever dreamed possible upon leaving the military," said John. Many organizations need workers with military, business and life experience to drive them into the future and are willing to pay the right person well.

ADDITIONAL RESOURCES

- Carosa, C. (2020, January 17). *How to find a full-time job when you're over 50*. Forbes.com. https://www.forbes.com/sites/chriscarosa/2020/01/17/how-to-find-a-full-time-job-when-youre-over-50/?sh=447a0432629f/
- Clark, B. (n.d.). *How to get a good job after age 50*. CareerSidekick.com. https://careersidekick.com/find-job-after-50/
- https://theusatwork.com/—Podcasts—A Truth For 50+ Job Seekers—Fred Coon interviews Chris Gardner, CEO, Artemis Consultants, a well-known executive recruiting firm.

CHAPTER 14
ENTRY-LEVEL JOB SEARCHING

Perhaps you are about to graduate from high school, trade school or college and you are ready to begin your career. Someone (probably your parents) gave you this book. Here you are at the end of school, and you're thinking, "This book is fine for someone on the executive track who has years of experience, but what about me? I just graduated. I have no idea what I'm doing!"

First, take a deep breath. Only a small percent of people know exactly what they want to do while they are still in school or have recently graduated. This book *is* for you. Conne has used it as a textbook for ready-to-graduate college students for years. Simply tailor the concepts to suit your needs, put one foot forward, and begin your search. In this chapter I'll cover:

- A few extra job search concepts you should understand
- Some tips for overcoming the hurdles of getting your first post-graduate job

You already know that COVID has changed the work patterns and modes of employment forever. The economic rippling effect of the pandemic will continue for years even after the disease is well-managed. At the very least, *types* of jobs available will change.

Amanda Stansell, a writer for Glassdoor.com indicates that many new graduates are entering fields that are hiring either because of or despite COVID-19. Urban areas such as New York City and Los Angeles are attracting the most applicants.

Many Millennials and Digitals are reluctant to move away from family, however. The exercises you completed in Chapter 3 should have helped you determine whether you are willing to relocate. If you are not, and you live in a rural area, it may take you longer to find the "ideal job." Consider a move to a city that is close enough to home for you to visit regularly if need be.

The next thing that will interfere with your ability to get a job quickly is your consumption of media. While you want to build your network through appropriate use of LinkedIn, Facebook, etc., overindulgence in phone use for pleasure is getting in your way of doing it right. The average college-age person spends 8-10 hours a day using a cell phone. We feel naked without our phones, but they use up time that could be spent developing job search materials. The good news is that the fix for this problem is easy. Cut down your use by an hour a day and devote that time to your job search. Write extra SHARE© Stories. Start a blog. Volunteer. Do an unpaid internship.

Finally, you might be saying to yourself, "Most employers want to hire someone with experience, but how am I supposed to have experience? I *just* graduated." My response would be, "You graduated. *Why* don't you have experience already?" **If you don't have it, GET IT!**

Almost all high schools, trade schools and colleges offer clubs and activities designed to boost your real-world experiences. Of how many did you take advantage? What have you been doing for the past 4 years? Employers don't care whether you have been paid to work or not so, if you did an internship or were in a club, sorority, or fraternity, you have learned some transferable skills at the very least. You have had academic experiences and volunteer work that could be transferable, as well. For example, have you ever accomplished anything in a team or group? Did you ever write a research paper? You might have to focus on those types of successes until you get your first post-graduate job.

If you are still in school, do an internship. Internships lead to jobs. Conne has seen many marginal students attain success through completing internships. "I had a student who wanted to be a reporter. Unfortunately, she was a poor writer who didn't take school seriously until the second semester of her senior year. Despite having some deficiencies, she applied for an internship with the local newspaper. When she completed the internship with flying colors, they offered her a full-time position."

There are paid and unpaid internships. Interestingly, doing a paid internship will increase your chance of getting a job offer. Robin Porter, a writer for CollegeRecruiter.com, indicates that "...according to [a] NACE study, being paid during an internship makes a difference in employability. The study showed that 66.4 percent of 2019 graduates who had a paid internship received a job offer. On the other hand, just 43.7 percent of unpaid interns were offered a job."[40]

Job shadowing, which requires less commitment than an internship, is another way to impress a potential boss. Simply contact someone who has a job similar to one you'd want. Tell him or her you are about to graduate and would simply like to meet to ask for advice. Ask if you can spend a few hours there to find out what goes on at the organization. In this way, you will build your network. Most people are happy to have anyone show an interest in what they do. Conne requires a job shadow assignment of her students. They abhor the idea at first but are surprised and delighted with the experiences—and job offers—they get through the experience. You can certainly do a job shadow at any point in your career.

If circumstances of your life prevented you from gaining experience before graduating, do so NOW. If no one will hire you, ask to *work for free* just for the experience. **Working a few unpaid hours for an organization gives them a free sample of your work and shows that you are eager to learn as much as you can about your field. This activity will dramatically increase your chance of getting hired.** Working part time for a company for free is the same as working for pay in the eyes of a potential employer. They are interested in what you can do for them, not whether you were paid, so build your resume with these experiences. Think you don't have time? Cut down an hour a day out of your social media use and dedicate it to a job. Lots of jobs can be done via the web.

Another thing you can do to build your value is self-educate. For the past 18 or so years, you have thought of yourself as a vessel that your teachers, coaches and other mentors have been filling. Those days are over. If you graduated with any critical skills that are substandard, it's now YOUR job to fix them. Don't have A+ writing skills? Sign up for an online course. Look for free webinars or online games that will boost your vocabulary, syntax, punctuation, etc. Can't run basic computer programs such as Word and Excel? Find a

---

40 Porter, R. (2019 September 30). How internships impact employability and salary. CollegeRecruiter.com. https://www.collegerecruiter.com/blog/2019/09/30/how-internships-impact-employability-and-salary/

free program that will teach you. Don't complain that your school or teachers didn't cover it in class. Be sure to list webinars and programs you have completed on your resume but, remember, a 5-minute video isn't the same as a 5-hour course. Don't mislead.

I covered it earlier, but it bears repeating: join professional associations. If you aren't sure which ones are appropriate, ask one of your teachers or professors, or someone you know in your field. If that fails, simply do a search for "professional associations related to [your field]."

If you are in the Digital generation, there is an excellent chance you would like to own your own business. One of the reasons this goal is so common among people in your age group is because of the single-case success stories that populate the internet. There are only so many Mark Zuckerbergs, though. Starting your own business takes a tremendous amount of capital and many fail in the first few years. I'm not saying you have to abandon your dreams but, for now, focus on building your experiences such that when the time is right you will have what it takes to run a business that will succeed.

Many students graduate with the goal of entering their career in a director-level position and why not? Popular shows portray young geniuses in high-powered positions. That's not reality, though. The reality is that, like most of us, you will have to start at the bottom, work you're a** off, and gradually move up. You'll have to live without things you want, like expensive cars and vacations. It's okay, though, because it won't last forever and, along the way, you'll be gaining the knowledge and experience you need to move into the next position. Your parents are telling the truth: poverty *is* a character builder.

Finally, understand that you won't love everyone you work with, you won't always be treated fairly, not all aspects of your job will be fun or interesting and that's okay. Don't jump ship right away because you think your boss hates you. I promise he or she does not have time to hate you. **GROW THICK SKIN**. Don't take criticism personally. Act like an adult and present *solutions* to problems, not just complaints. Be direct and honest. Tell your boss what you need to do your job better and, if you don't get it, do the best job you can anyway. You won't be on the bottom of the totem pole very long if you adopt this attitude. You never know what opportunity will come your way, so it pays to be vigilant!

SUCCESS STORY: BEST STORY OF HOPE

CONTRIBUTED BY CONNE REECE, CO-AUTHOR AND EDITOR

Kristy was a talented communication major at Lock Haven University interested in a career in military-related social media. She took a senior-level course in which I use an earlier version of *Ready, Aim, Hired.*

Kristy was reluctant when I gave her class a job shadowing assignment, but she worked with the manager of a local veterans' organization and rolled the experience into an internship. After graduation, Kristy accepted an entry-level position with Hope for the Warriors. HOPE has a 4-star rating from Charity Navigator.

Throughout the years she has worked for HOPE, Kristy's responsibilities have increased. She is now managing their military spouse and caregiver program, designing self-care packages for recipients. "I include the Ready, Aim, Hired book in the HOPE care packages because I loved the book so much during Capstone [class]. I still reference the online resources often," Kristy wrote.

Entry-level positions are just that – *entry* level. People who prove their worth move up quickly.

ADDITIONAL RESOURCES

- The National Association of Colleges and Employers website www.NACE.org/.
- Polner, E. (2021, February 26). *Best entry-level job sites for college graduates and new alumni: Find your first job and start your career strong.* TheBalanceCareers. com. https://www.thebalancecareers.com/best-entry-level-job-sites-2058517/

CHAPTER 15
RULES FOR A SUCCESSFUL WORK LIFE

You are finally ready to begin your new job. You are excited to get to work. It's very tempting to heave a big sigh of relief and charge right in but putting this book on the bookshelf is one of the greatest mistakes you will ever make. This chapter provides some strategies you must employ to ensure that you will love your new job and the company will love you.

Ensure your long-range relationships with your new company and those who helped you in your search by doing the following:

1. **Write thank you and update letters to everyone with whom you came into contact during your search before you begin your new job.** This is easy to say and boring to do, but it is essential to maintain your future referral base. Saying thank you is also a sign of class and professionalism. Every three or four months, take 25% of your referral and contact list, and write them an update of your progress in the job they helped or encouraged you to find. Maintaining your network is one of the critical things you must do to make your next move easier.

2. **Update your resume and the status of your social media.** No later than your first month in your new job, update your resume. You may not be able to fill out the quantifiable accomplishments section right away, but constantly update your resume as you climb each step of your career mountain. Make a note on your calendar to do

it quarterly. Be sure to update your status on LinkedIn, Facebook, etc. If appropriate, ask your company if you can put an announcement about your hiring in the local paper (don't forget to use your professional head shot).

3. **Review your interview notes.** Before you report to your new job, take time to review your interview notes and the expectations of the organization. Look at your new boss's answers to your questions about the job, the company, the people and any other relevant information.

4. **Schedule a meeting with your new manager.** Meet with him or her as soon as possible. Things shift in the hiring process, and you need to know where you stand and what might have changed. One of my clients reported to work his first day only to find that his manager had been assigned to manage another department. Luckily the new manager was nice, but it could have been a disaster. In your meeting with your new boss, confirm all performance goals, expectations, and time schedules. These change, too. What are your immediate assignments? What is the priority and timeline for these duties? "Work with your manager to have a 90-day plan," says Lianne Zhang of Wanderlust Coaching. "Some companies expect you to jump right in while others give you a 90 day to 6-month ramp-up time. Understand expectations so you can set the right goals."[41]

5. **Get on the distribution list**. Zhang goes on to advise that it is important to be on any relevant distribution list. That's anything that has a direct impact on you. Likewise, it doesn't hurt to be in the know so ask to be on lists for information about the company, goals, vision, changes, and anything else that will impact your current and future employment with this company.

6. **Understand expected key performance indicators (KPI).** What are you expected to achieve? What does your boss expect from you in terms of actual quantifiable and measurable results? What training will you require to EXCEED those expectations?

7. **Utilize a schedule and planning system to properly manage your time**. Learning a new job is disorienting for a while but, the faster you appear to catch on, the faster you'll be seen as worth the money...and maybe more!

---

41   Personal communication with L. Zhang (n.d.).

8. **Ask for help only after you have tried to solve a problem on your own.** It's okay to ask for help, but not before you try to find out the answer to your question on your own. Your boss is busy and does not want to answer the same question again and again. Write down what you are told and become self-sufficient.

9. **Stay organized.** Lay out your priorities from the previous day. Don't lose sight of them by getting bogged down in day-to-day minutia. Take notes on what your goals are for tomorrow so when you arrive you can begin working efficiently.

10. **Figure out who the movers and shakers are and get to know them.** It is amazing what you can find out about your boss and others in the company by listening instead of talking about yourself. Make friends with administrative assistants. They know everything.

11. **Don't gossip and spread rumors.** Beware of people who are in conflict with others and may be trying to get you on their side quickly because you don't know any better.

12. **Figure out the logistics of how the company operates.** If possible, schedule brief meetings with those working in other departments and ask them how things work and what their priorities are in terms of your job. Understand the chain of command.

13. **Solicit feedback on your performance.** Your organization will likely have a formal annual or semi-annual performance evaluation system, but it's okay to ask how you are doing occasionally as long as you don't seem insecure. Millennial and Digital workers have higher needs for performance feedback. Be aware that your boss is likely working on his/her own projects and might not have time to give you feedback as often as you wish.

14. **Understand the culture.** Many organizations pride themselves on a strong culture, but that can mean something different everywhere explains Charles Edge, Chief Technical Officer at Bootstrappers.mn.[42] Some places thrive on competition, others focus on harmony.

15. **Don't get sloppy and forget to dress well every day.** Conne told me, "My nephew got a job as a computer customer service rep. None of the customers could see him, but he went to work every day in khakis and a nice shirt. One of his colleagues did not

---

42   Personal communication with C. Edge (n.d.).

take his job as seriously and came to work in a bathing suit...twice. My nephew is now being groomed for a vice presidency. I doubt the bathing suit character is."

16. **Always stay positive**. One thing in life is consistent: negative, pessimistic people seldom rise to the top. They drag everyone down. Optimism and enthusiasm are contagious. Your boss will notice which you are almost instantly and, yes, he/she will let you go if your attitude is bringing down the team.

17. **Volunteer only for projects you know you can tackle with success and ONLY AFTER MANAGING SEVERAL ASSIGNED TASKS TO SUCCESSFUL COMPLETION**. You may be tempted to cull your boss's favor by volunteering for anything but, if you fail, your plan could backfire. Temper your desire to learn new things with building your reputation for doing your job well. Earn their trust.

18. **Keep a *quantifiable* record of your successes**. Each task you do is part of a countable pattern of success. You want to be able to track what you do so you can generate numerical expressions of your progress and value. For example, how many customers did you handle during your busiest times? How were your sales? How much money did you save or make for your company? Every job can be quantified. Keep the ad for your job and keep track of your success doing what they asked. This will help you when you update your resume and also in your performance evaluation. Imagine saying to your boss, "I increased efficiency by 9% since last year." How can he or she deny you the raise you deserve? The worst thing you can do is bumble along from day to day not paying attention to your own success.

19. **Keep *qualitative* proof of your success**. Qualitative proof is the proof that is not necessarily numerical in nature. Save all correspondence in which someone thanks you or pats you on the back for a job well done. Note who sent it and what you did that generated the kind words. Seek permission to use these sentiments as testimonials later. Save all of your performance reviews.

20. **Keep working on an action plan for your career**. Intentional, strategic career planning is essential. Don't let the fact that you just got a new job stop you from looking toward your future. Make a plan for 1-year, 3-years and 5-years out and review it annually, perhaps on the anniversary of your hiring. What do you need to do to meet

your goals? Need more training or education? Experience? Don't forget to discuss your goals with your search partner.

21. **Listen more than you speak.** Good listening skills are highly prized in the business world. Those who listen well are seen as more competent and professional.

22. **Know people's names and how to pronounce them.** Learn the proper spelling and pronunciation of names. Don't evaluate or judge people by their names or make comments about ethnicity.

23. **Maintain good physical, mental and spiritual health**. Your energy level and health have an impact on how you handle your job.

24. **Keep working on your emotional intelligence**. Take stock of pros and cons before making decisions. Think about how your decision will affect others. People's feelings count, but so do results. You are measured on your interpersonal savvy AND the bottom line.

25. **Study the successful people in the company**. Figure out what they did to get where they are. Emulate their behavior and get even better results than they did. Unexpected opportunities are often given to people who master this skill.

26. **Credit others and not yourself.** I promise you that the more you practice this, the more credit you will receive. Humility is a prized and highly respected characteristic in all cultures.

27. **Demonstrate that you are a person of your word**. Keeping your word means you are reliable, and people place a premium on reliability both personally and professionally.

28. **Become an expert on something**. Be *the* company resource. Offer your help to those in need and others will seek out your advice. Advice giving is tantamount to influence and influence is power.

29. **Whenever possible, take the initiative**. This is one of the best ways to distinguish yourself and your capabilities. Only do so with your manager's approval, though.

30. **Do what you can to lessen others' loads**. Think you will have an extra hour today? Ask your boss and coworkers if there is anything you can do for them. If your boss seems stressed, offer to take over a small project. Never quit a project. See all projects through to conclusion.

31. **Go back to school and continue to receive re-training, certification and any other form of continuing education that will enhance your credibility and usefulness to the company.** Don't make the mistake of putting this off until you wind up at age 45 with no MBA, or other advanced degree, and find yourself competing with much younger people who can educationally out-gun you and who will work for less.

32. **Keep your temper to yourself.** People will not like or trust you if you are volatile. Temper tantrums are not acceptable for children, much less the workplace. One bad episode can ruin your career. Learn to handle stress gracefully.

33. **Build up your coworkers.** No one likes a brown-noser, but sincerely complimenting others on their work is a sign of manners and respect. Look for seemingly insignificant situations in which you can make others feel like they do their jobs well.

34. **Never put down a fellow employee in front of others.** Find a private place and gently tell him/her what you would like to see change. Otherwise, you will end up looking like a jerk and the problem will get worse. Praise in public, criticize in private.

35. **Build your own integrity.** No one else will do it for you. Your boss, coworkers and subordinates are watching your more closely than you realize. Don't rip off the company or back-stab others.

36. **Don't neglect communicating.** One of the biggest complaints of employees is being kept in the dark. Conne tells me of a former student working at a large zoo. The COVID situation resulted in major cutbacks, leaving inexperienced, incompetent managers in charge. The stress of the situation resulted in tremendous problems because the inexperienced managers neglected to pass along critical information that enabled the other workers to properly care for the animals and manage visitors' needs.

37. **Be honest and direct.** Many communication problems are caused by the speaker thinking he or she has to beat around the bush to save feelings. This tactic, however, only creates hardship when the recipient does not understand the message. You don't have to be an ogre, but use direct, concrete words to express your ideas. For example, an employee asks you about a sensitive topic. Instead of saying "I don't know," say, "I'm not allowed to discuss that yet. I hope you understand that I'm not trying to be evasive, and I'll let you know what's going on as soon as I can."

I assure you that if you incorporate these suggestions into your daily routine, you *will* succeed. Don't get lazy and forget them, though, or your full career potential will never be realized, and you will look back when you are my age saying I shoulda, coulda, woulda, hadda, oughta, instead of, I did!

SUCCESS STORY: $250,000 CHECKOUT CLERK

CONTRIBUTED BY CONNE REECE, CO-AUTHOR AND EDITOR

The final success story in Ready, Aim, Hired is based on an incident that happened to me recently. Chapter 15 is about how to succeed once you have a job and this is one of the best examples I have ever seen of someone who will go far.

I have some back problems that make taking groceries out of the cart at checkout difficult, but I manage with a little strategy. I mentioned this to Riley, the roughly 18-year-old checkout clerk, as she was getting ready to scan a big bag of dogfood.

Riley then did something I have never seen. Without being asked, she came out from behind the register and cheerfully loaded my groceries on to the belt. I was astonished and sputtered "Thank you!" about a dozen times.

A lot of people my age (let's not mention it exactly) say negative things about the "younger generation," but sometimes I find that they have learned the skills in Chapter 15 better than older workers. Riley isn't making $250,000 like some of the folks featured in this book, but she will...some day.

CONCLUSION

Every day, you make decisions that guide your destiny. Your decision to read *Ready Aim Hired* has put you in control of your job search. You now understand your career needs and brand, and how to market what you have to offer through an accomplishment-focused resume, well-written cover letter and web profile (Career WebFolio). You know how to leverage social media and network. You know how to manage even the toughest interview questions with confidence and negotiate the best salary and benefits. You KNOW how to get a job!

May the very best of luck follow you throughout your journey. I am happy to speak with you about your job search. Contact me at StewartCooperCoon.com.

GOOD LUCK!

ADDITIONAL RESOURCES

- Coon, F. (n.d.). Balancing new standards in job culture. StewartCooperCoon.com.
- https://www.stewartcoopercoon.com/balancing-new-standards-in-job-culture/
- Mindtools (n.d.). *Professionalism: Meeting the standards that matter*. Mindtools. com.
- https://www.mindtools.com/pages/article/professionalism.htm

"THE JOB REAL SEARCH PUZZLE"

INDEX